**Second Edition**

# Longman
# PREPARATION COURSE
## FOR THE TOEFL® TEST

## Volume B
# PRACTICE
# TESTS

## Deborah Phillips

Longman

TOEFL test directions, test format, and answer sheets are reprinted by permission of Educational Testing Service, the copyright owner. However, the test questions and any other testing information are provided in their entirety by Addison-Wesley Publishing Company. No endorsement of this publication by Educational Testing Service should be inferred.

**Longman Preparation Course for the TOEFL® Test, Volume B—Practice Tests, Second Edition**
formerly published as **Longman Practice Tests for the TOEFL**

**Longman, 10 Bank Street, White Plains, N. Y. 10606**

Editorial Director: Joanne Dresner
Acquisition Editor: Allen Ascher
Development Editors: Françoise Leffler, Suzanne Shetler
Senior Production Editor: Carolyn Viola-John
Cassettes Production Editor: Christine Cervoni
Text Design Adaptation: Curt Belshe
Cover Design Adaptation: Michelle Szabo

**Library of Congress Cataloging-in-Publication Data**

Phillips, Deborah, 1952–
 Longman preparation course for the TOEFL test/Deborah Phillips.
 —2nd ed.
   p. cm.
 Contents: v. A. Skills and strategies—v. B. Practice tests.
 ISBN 0-201-84676-4 (v. A.)—ISBN 0-201-84961-5 (v. B.)
 1. Test of English, as a foreign language—Study guides.
2. English language—Textbooks for foreign speakers.   I. Title.
PE1128.P46   1995
428.2'4—dc20                                        95-31469
                                                    CIP

ISBN 0-201-84961-5

10 —CRS— 00

# CONTENTS

## TAPESCRIPTS

## ANSWER KEYS

## SCORING INFORMATION

# INTRODUCTION

## ABOUT THIS BOOK

### PURPOSE OF THE BOOK

This book is intended to prepare students for the TOEFL (Test of English as a Foreign Language) test. It is based on the most up-to-date information available on the format and style of the *new* TOEFL test, introduced in July 1995.

*Longman Preparation Course for the TOEFL® Test: Volume B—Practice Tests, Second Edition* can be used in a variety of ways, depending on the needs of the reader:

1. It can be used in conjunction with *Longman Preparation Course for the TOEFL® Test: Volume A—Skills and Strategies, Second Edition* as the primary classroom text in a course emphasizing TOEFL test preparation.
2. It can be used as a supplementary text to provide TOEFL practice in a more general ESL course.
3. It can be used as a tool for individualized study by students preparing for the TOEFL test outside of the ESL classroom.

### WHAT'S IN THE BOOK

This book contains materials for the practice of test-taking strategies on TOEFL-format tests. The following are included:

1. **TOEFL Strategies** for each of the sections of the TOEFL test, including the Test of Written English (TWE), provide students with clearly defined steps to improve performance on the TOEFL test.
2. **Five TOEFL-format Tests** allow students to practice the suggested strategies.
3. **A Listening Comprehension Tapescript** gives a transcription of the Listening Comprehension section of each Practice Test.
4. **Answer Keys** include answers to all questions on the five Practice Tests.
5. **The Scoring Information** allows students to determine their approximate TOEFL scores on the Practice Tests.
6. **A Chart** allows students to record their progress from Test One through Test Five.
7. **TOEFL Answer Sheets** allow practice in using the test forms correctly; both horizontal and vertical ovals are used on the test and in this book.

## WHAT'S NEW IN THE SECOND EDITION

The Practice Tests in this text have been updated to the new format of the TOEFL test, introduced in July 1995.

1.  **The new Listening Comprehension Part A** consists of *thirty short conversations* between two people. (These questions are similar to the questions previously found in Listening Part B of the old TOEFL test.)
2.  **The new Listening Comprehension Part B** consists of *two long conversations*, each followed by a number of questions. (These conversations are similar to the conversations previously found in Listening Part C of the old TOEFL test.)
3.  **The new Listening Comprehension Part C** consists of *three talks*, each followed by a number of questions. The total number of questions in Listening Part B and Listening Part C together is *twenty*.
4.  **The new Reading Comprehension** consists of *five reading passages* with a total of *fifty* questions. Both reading and vocabulary questions are included with the reading passages. (The vocabulary questions are no longer separate from the reading passages, as they were on the old TOEFL test.)

## OTHER AVAILABLE MATERIALS

Additional materials are available to supplement the materials included in the text.

1.  ***Longman Preparation Course for the TOEFL® Test: Volume B—Cassettes, Second Edition*** contains recordings of the Listening Comprehension sections of the Practice Tests.
2.  ***Longman Preparation Course for the TOEFL® Test: Volume A—Skills and Strategies, Second Edition*** thoroughly prepares students for the TOEFL test. Students learn specific strategies and develop skills for successfully answering each type of TOEFL question. TOEFL-format diagnostic Pre-Tests and Post-Tests are included, as well as one complete Practice Test.
3.  ***Longman Preparation Course for the TOEFL® Test: Volume A—Cassettes, Second Edition*** contains recordings of the Listening Comprehension Diagnostic Pre-Test, Listening Exercises, Listening Comprehension Post-Test, and Listening Comprehension Practice Test.
4.  ***Longman Preparation Course for the TOEFL® Test: User's Guide for Volume A, Second Edition*** includes *Teaching Tips* for each of the sections of the TOEFL test, a *Tapescript* with a transcription of all listening comprehension exercises included on the cassette tapes accompanying the text, and an *Answer Key* with answers to all questions in the Pre-Tests, Exercises, Post-Tests and Complete Practice Test, and Appendixes.

# ABOUT THE TOEFL TEST

## DESCRIPTION OF THE TOEFL TEST

The Test of English as a Foreign Language is a test to measure the level of English proficiency of nonnative speakers of English. It is required primarily by English-language colleges and universities. Additionally, institutions such as government agencies or scholarship programs may require the test.

The test currently has the following sections:

1. **Listening Comprehension** (multiple choice): To demonstrate their ability to understand spoken English, examinees must listen to a tape and respond to various types of questions.
2. **Structure and Written Expression** (multiple choice): To demonstrate their ability to recognize grammatically correct English, examinees must choose the correct way to complete sentences and must find errors in sentences.
3. **Reading Comprehension** (multiple choice): To demonstrate their ability to understand written English, examinees must answer questions about the meanings of words and ideas in reading passages.
4. **Test of Written English (TWE)** (written): Examinees must write an essay on a given topic in thirty minutes to demonstrate their ability to produce correct and meaningful English. The Test of Written English (TWE) is not given with every administration of the TOEFL test. You should check the *Bulletin of Information for TOEFL, TWE, and TSE* for upcoming dates for this test.

The following chart outlines the probable format of a TOEFL test. (It should be noted that on certain occasions a longer version of the TOEFL test is given.)

|  | TOEFL | TIME |
|---|---|---|
| Listening Comprehension | 50 questions | 35 minutes |
| Structure and Written Expression | 40 questions | 25 minutes |
| Reading Comprehension | 50 questions | 55 minutes |
| Test of Written English (TWE) | 1 essay topic | 30 minutes |

When the Test of Written English (TWE) is given, it is generally before the Listening Comprehension section.

## WHAT YOUR TOEFL SCORE MEANS

The TOEFL test is scored on a scale of 217 to 677 points. There is no passing score on the TOEFL test, but various institutions have their own TOEFL score requirements. You must find out from each institution what TOEFL score is required.

When you take the TOEFL Practice Tests in this book, it is possible for you to estimate your TOEFL score. A description of how to estimate your TOEFL score has been provided at the back of this book on pages 176–177.

The score of the Test of Written English (TWE) is not included in your overall TOEFL score. It is a separate score on a scale of 1 to 6.

## WHERE TO GET ADDITIONAL INFORMATION

Additional information is available in the *Bulletin of Information for TOEFL, TWE, and TSE*. This bulletin can be obtained free of charge by sending a request to the following address:

> Test of English as a Foreign Language
> CN 6151
> Princeton, NJ 08541-6151 USA

# TO THE STUDENT _____

## HOW TO PREPARE FOR THE TOEFL TEST

The TOEFL is a *test of English*. To do well on this test, you should therefore work in two areas to improve your score:

1. You must work on improving your knowledge of the English language.
2. You must work on the skills and strategies specific to the TOEFL test.

When preparing for the TOEFL test, it is important to work on TOEFL materials. However, work on TOEFL materials alone will not make you successful; a good basic knowledge of the English language is also necessary. Therefore, do not forget the general study of the English language as you work to prepare for the TOEFL test.

## HOW TO USE THIS BOOK

1. When taking the Practice Tests, try to reproduce the conditions and time pressure of a real TOEFL test.

   - Take each section of the test without interruption.
   - Work on only one section at a time.
   - Use the answer sheets from the back of the book.
   - Use a pencil to *completely* fill in the answer oval that corresponds to the answer you choose. (TOEFL answer sheets may include either horizontal or vertical ovals.)

     **Example:**   Ⓐ ⬤ Ⓒ Ⓓ

   - Erase *completely* any changes that you make on the answer sheet. If answers are not completely erased on an actual TOEFL answer sheet, they will be marked wrong.
   - Time yourself for each test section. You need to experience the time pressure that exists on actual TOEFL tests.
   - Play the listening cassette one time only during the test. (You may play it more times when you are reviewing the test.)
   - Mark only your answer sheet. You cannot write in a TOEFL test book.

2. Check your answers only at the end of each section or test. Do not check your answers after each question.
3. When you have completed a section or test and have checked your answers, compute your score (pages 176–177) and record the results on the chart (page 178). This chart will be a record of your progress as you work through the book.

4. After you compute your score, it is essential to review the answers carefully. The same types of questions appear again and again on the TOEFL test. If you understand a mistake the first time you make it, you will probably get that same type of question correct on the following tests. This is how your TOEFL score will improve.

5. If you consistently miss certain types of questions, you should refer to specific exercises on those types of questions in the *Longman Preparation Course for the TOEFL® Test: Volume A—Skills and Strategies, Second Edition.*

# TO THE TEACHER

## HOW TO PREPARE FOR THE PRACTICE TESTS

Before assigning the Practice Tests, you should be sure that the students have a clear idea of what sections and types of questions to expect on the TOEFL test and of what strategies can be most effective in each of the sections. It can be most helpful to the students to discuss thoroughly the information in the introduction to this text, particularly the sections describing the TOEFL test and the strategies for each section, before undertaking the Practice Tests.

## HOW TO GIVE THE PRACTICE TESTS

It is essential that the Practice Tests be taken under conditions as similar as possible to actual TOEFL test conditions. Make sure that the Listening Comprehension tapes are ready to be played. Show students how to fill out the answer sheets; there is one complete set for each Practice Test at the back of the book. Point out the Test of Written English (TWE), an additional thirty-minute segment of some TOEFL tests.

## HOW TO REVIEW THE PRACTICE TESTS

Students can benefit tremendously from a thorough review of the Practice Tests. The following suggestions can help to make the Practice Test review sessions as effective as possible:

1. As you review the Practice Tests, be sure to discuss each answer—the incorrect answers as well as the correct answers. Discuss how students can determine that an answer is correct or incorrect.

2. As you review the Practice Tests, you should also reinforce how TOEFL test strategies could have been used to determine correct and incorrect answers.

3. Two different methods are possible for reviewing the listening exercises. One way to review these exercises is to play back the tape, stopping after each question to discuss the skills and strategies involved in determining correct and incorrect answers. Another method is to have the students refer to the tapescript at the back to discuss each question.

# TOEFL STRATEGIES

# TOEFL STRATEGIES LISTENING COMPREHENSION

The first section of the TOEFL test is the Listening Comprehension section. This section consists of fifty questions (some tests may be longer). You will listen to recorded materials and respond to questions about the material. You must listen carefully, because you will hear the tape one time only, and the material on the tape is not written in your test booklet.

There are three parts in the Listening Comprehension section of the TOEFL test:

1. **Part A** consists of thirty short conversations, each followed by a question. You must choose the best answer to each question from the four choices in your test book.
2. **Part B** consists of two long conversations, each followed by a number of questions. You must choose the best answer to each question from the four choices in your test book.
3. **Part C** consists of three talks, each followed by a number of questions. You must choose the best answer to each question from the four choices in your test book.

---

### GENERAL STRATEGIES

1. **Be familiar with the directions.** The directions on every TOEFL test are the same, so it is not necessary to listen carefully to them each time. You should be completely familiar with the directions before the day of the test.

2. **Listen carefully to the conversations and talks.** You should concentrate fully on what the speakers are saying on the tape because you will hear the tape one time only.

3. **Know where the easier and more difficult questions are generally found.** Within each part of the Listening Comprehension section, the questions generally progress from easy to difficult.

4. **Never leave any answers blank on your answer sheet.** Even if you are unsure of the correct response, you should answer each question. There is no penalty for guessing.

5. **Use any remaining time to look ahead at the answers to the questions that follow.** When you finish with one question, you may have time to look ahead at the answers to the next question.

---

# THE LISTENING PART A QUESTIONS

For each of the thirty questions in Part A of the Listening Comprehension section of the TOEFL test, you will hear a short conversation between two speakers followed by a question. After you listen to the conversation and question, you must choose the best answer to the question from your test book.

---

*Example*

On the recording, you hear:

(man)    *I've always wanted to visit Hawaii with you.*
(woman)    *Why not next month?*
(narrator)    *What does the woman mean?*

In your test book, you read:

(A)    Next month isn't a good time for the trip.
(B)    She doesn't want to go to Hawaii.
(C)    She suggests taking the trip next month.
(D)    She's curious about why he doesn't want to go.

---

Answer (C) is the best answer to the question. *Why not next month?* is a suggestion that they take the trip next month.

---

### STRATEGIES FOR THE LISTENING PART A QUESTIONS

1.  **As you listen to each short conversation, focus on the second line of the conversation.**    The answer to the question is generally found in the second line.

2.  **Keep in mind that the correct answer is probably a restatement of a key word or idea in the second line of the conversation.**    Think of possible restatements of the second line of the conversation.

3.  **Keep in mind that certain structures and expressions are tested regularly in Listening Part A.**    Listen for these structures and expressions:

    • structures (*passives, negatives, wishes, conditions*)
    • functional expressions (*agreement, uncertainty, suggestion, surprise*)
    • idiomatic expressions (*two-part verbs, three-part verbs, idioms*)

4.  **Keep in mind that these questions generally progress from easy to difficult.**    This means that questions 1 through 5 will be the easiest questions and questions 26 through 30 will be the hardest questions.

5.  **Read the answers and choose the best answer to each question.**    Remember to answer each question even if you are not sure of the correct response. Never leave any answers blank.

6.  **Even if you do not understand the complete conversation, you can find the correct answer.**

    • If you only understood a few words or ideas in the second line, choose the answer that contains a restatement of those words or ideas.
    • If you did not understand anything at all in the second line of the conversation, choose the answer that sounds the most different from what you heard.
    • Never choose an answer because it *sounds like* what you heard in the conversation.

---

# THE LISTENING PART B QUESTIONS

Part B of the Listening Comprehension section of the TOEFL test consists of two long conversations, each followed by a number of questions. You will hear the conversations and the questions on a tape; they are not written in your test booklet. You must choose the best answer to each question from the four choices that are written in your test booklet.

The conversations are often about some aspect of school life (how difficult a class is, how to write a research paper, how to register for a course). The conversations can also be about topics currently in the news in the United States (desalination of the water supply, recycling of used products, damage from a storm or some other type of natural phenomenon).

---

***Example***

On the recording, you hear:

(narrator)  ***Questions 1 through 4.*** *Listen to a conversation between a professor and a student.*

(man)  *Hello, Professor Denton. Are you free for a moment? Could I have a word with you?*

(woman)  *Come on in, Michael. Of course I have some time. These are my office hours, and this is the right time for you to come and ask questions. Now, how can I help you?*

(man)  *Well, I have a quick question for you about the homework assignment for tomorrow. I thought the assignment was to answer the first three questions at the top of page 67 in the text, but when I looked, there weren't any questions there. I'm confused.*

(woman)  *The assignment was to answer the first three questions at the top of page 76, not 67.*

(man)  *Oh, now I understand. I'm glad I came in to check. Thanks for your help.*

(woman)  *No problem. See you tomorrow.*

Questions:

1. On the recording, you hear:

   (narrator)  *Who is the man?*

   In your test book, you read:
   (A)  A professor.
   (B)  An office worker.
   (C)  Professor Denton's assistant.
   (D)  A student.

2. On the recording, you hear:

   (narrator)  *When does the man come to see Professor Denton?*

   In your test book, you read:
   (A)  During regular class hours.
   (B)  Just before class time.
   (C)  As soon as class is finished.
   (D)  During office hours.

*(continued on next page)*

---

3. On the recording, you hear:

    (narrator)    *Why does the man come to see Professor Denton?*

In your test book, you read:    (A)  To turn in an assignment.
                      (B)  To ask a question.
                      (C)  To pick up a completed assignment.
                      (D)  To explain why he did not attend class.

4. On the recording, you hear:

    (narrator)    *What incorrect information did the man have?*

In your test book, you read:    (A)  The date the assignment was due.
                      (B)  The page number of the assignment.
                      (C)  The length of the assignment.
                      (D)  The numbers of the assignment questions.

---

The first question asks you to determine who the man is. Since the man opens the conversation with *Professor Denton* and he asks about the page number of an assignment for tomorrow, he is probably a student. The best answer to this question is therefore answer (D). The second question asks when the man comes to see the professor. The professor says that *these are my office hours,* so the best answer to this question is answer (D). The third question asks why the man comes to see the professor. Since the man says *I have a quick question for you,* the best answer to this question is answer (B). The last question asks what incorrect information the man had. The man thought that the assignment was on page 67 and not on page 76, so he was mistaken about the page of the assignment. The best answer to this question is answer (B).

---

### STRATEGIES FOR THE LISTENING PART B QUESTIONS

1. **If you have time, preview the answers to the Listening Part B questions.** While you are looking at the answers, you should try to do the following:
   - Anticipate the **topics** of the conversations you will hear.
   - Anticipate the **questions** for each of the groups of answers.

2. **Listen carefully to the first line of the conversation.** The first line of the conversation often contains the main idea, subject, or topic of the conversation, and you will often be asked to answer such questions.

3. **As you listen to the conversation, draw conclusions about the situation of the conversation: who is talking, where the conversation takes place, or when the conversation takes place.** You will often be asked to make such inferences about the conversation.

4. **As you listen to the conversation, follow along with the answers in your test booklet and try to determine the correct answers.** Detail questions are generally answered in order in the conversation, and the answers often sound the same as what is said on the tape.

5. **You should guess even if you are not sure.** Never leave any answers blank.

6. **Use any remaining time to look ahead at the answers to the questions that follow.**

# THE LISTENING PART C QUESTIONS

Part C of the Listening Comprehension section of the TOEFL test consists of three talks, each followed by a number of questions. You will hear the talks and the questions on a tape; they are not written in your test booklet. You must choose the best answer to each question from the four choices that are written in your test booklet. Like the conversations in Listening Part B, the talks are often about some aspect of school life or topics currently in the news. It is also very common for the talks to be shortened versions of lectures from courses taught in American colleges and universities.

---

*Example*

On the recording, you hear:

(narrator) **Questions 1 through 4.** *Listen to a talk about the settlement of America.*

(woman) *The settling of the vast farmlands in central North America was delayed at least partly because of an error by one man. In the early nineteenth century, Lieutenant Zebulon Pike of the U.S. Army was sent out to explore and chart the huge expanses of land in the center of the continent. When he returned from his explorations, he wrote a report in which he erroneously stated that the vast plains in the central part of the continent were desertlike, comparable to the Sahara in Africa. In reality, however, these vast plains contained some of the most fertile farmland in the world. Because of Pike's mistake, the maps of the day depicted the central part of what is today the United States as a vast desert rather than the excellent and available farmland that it was. This mistaken belief about the nature of those lands caused settlers to avoid the central plains for years.*

Questions:

1. On the recording, you hear:

   (narrator) *What is the topic of this talk?*

   In your test book, you read:
   (A) Zebulon Pike's career.
   (B) A mistake that influenced the settlement of America.
   (C) A report for the army.
   (D) The farmlands.

2. On the recording, you hear:

   (narrator) *How did Pike describe the area that he explored?*

   In your test book, you read:
   (A) As a desert.
   (B) As usable for army purposes.
   (C) As located in the Sahara.
   (D) As available for farmland.

*(continued on next page)*

> 3. On the recording, you hear:
>
>     (narrator)    *What was this area really like?*
>
> In your test book, you read:    (A)  It was a vast desert.
>     (B)  It was covered with farms.
>     (C)  It was excellent farmland.
>     (D)  It was similar to the Sahara.
>
> 4. On the recording, you hear:
>
>     (narrator)    *This talk would probably be given in which of the following courses?*
>
> In your test book, you read:    (A)  Agricultural Science.
>     (B)  American History.
>     (C)  Geology of the United States.
>     (D)  Military Science.

The first question asks about the topic of the talk. The topic of the talk is found in the first sentence of the talk: *The settling of the vast farmlands in central North America was delayed at least partly because of an error by one man.* Therefore, the best answer to the question is (B). The second question is a detail question that asks how Pike described this area. It is stated in the talk that Pike *wrote a report in which he erroneously stated that the vast plains in the central part of the continent were desertlike. . . .* Therefore, the best answer to this question is (A). The third question is an additional detail question that asks what the area was really like. Because the talk indicates that *in reality . . . these vast plains contained some of the most fertile farmland in the world,* the best answer to this question is (C). The fourth question is an inference question. It asks in which course this lecture would probably be given. The word *probably* indicates to you that the question is not answered directly in the talk. You must draw a conclusion from the information in the talk to answer this question. Because this talk refers to *the early nineteenth century* and discusses the *settling of the vast farmlands in central North America,* it would probably be given in an American History course. The best answer to this question is (B).

---

### STRATEGIES FOR THE LISTENING PART C QUESTIONS

1. **If you have time, preview the answers to the Listening Part C questions.**   While you are looking at the answers, you should try to do the following:

   - Anticipate the **topics** of the talks you will hear.
   - Anticipate the **questions** for each of the groups of answers.

2. **Listen carefully to the first line of the talk.**   The first line of the talk often contains the main idea, subject, or topic of the talk, and you will often be asked this type of question.

3. **As you listen to the talk, draw conclusions about the situation of the talk: who is talking, where or when the talk takes place, which course this lecture might be given in.**   You will often be asked to make such inferences about the talk.

4. **As you listen to the talk, follow along with the answers in your test booklet and try to determine the correct answers.**   Detail questions are generally answered in order in the talk, and the answers often sound the same as what is said on the tape.

5. **You should guess even if you are not sure.**   Never leave any answers blank.

6. **Use any remaining time to look ahead at the answers to the questions that follow.**

# TOEFL STRATEGIES STRUCTURE AND WRITTEN EXPRESSION

The second section of the TOEFL test is the Structure and Written Expression section. This section consists of forty questions (some tests may be longer). You have twenty-five minutes to complete the forty questions in this section.

There are two types of questions in the Structure and Written Expression section of the TOEFL test:

1. **Structure** (questions 1–15) consists of fifteen sentences in which part of the sentence has been replaced with a blank. Each sentence is followed by four answer choices. You must choose the answer that completes the sentence in a grammatically correct way.
2. **Written Expression** (questions 16–40) consists of twenty-five sentences in which four words or groups of words have been underlined. You must choose the underlined word or group of words that is *not* correct.

---

### GENERAL STRATEGIES

1. **Be familiar with the directions.** The directions on every TOEFL test are the same, so it is not necessary to spend time reading the directions carefully when you take the test. You should be completely familiar with the directions before the day of the test.

2. **Begin with questions 1 through 15.** Anticipate that questions 1 through 5 will be the easiest. Anticipate that questions 11 through 15 will be the most difficult. Do not spend too much time on questions 11 through 15. There will be easier questions that come later.

3. **Continue with questions 16 through 40.** Anticipate that questions 16 through 20 will be the easiest. Anticipate that questions 36 through 40 will be the most difficult. Do not spend too much time on questions 36 through 40.

4. **If you have time, return to questions 11 through 15.** You should spend extra time on questions 11 through 15 only after you spend all the time that you want on the easier questions.

5. **Never leave any answers blank on your answer sheet.** Even if you are not sure of the correct response, you should answer each question. There is no penalty for guessing.

# THE STRUCTURE QUESTIONS

Questions 1 through 15 in the Structure and Written Expression section of the TOEFL test examine your knowledge of the correct structure of English sentences. The questions in this section are multiple-choice questions in which you must choose the letter of the answer that best completes the sentence.

---

***Example***

_____ is taking a trip to New York.

    (A)   They
    (B)   When
    (C)   The woman
    (D)   Her

---

In this example, you should notice immediately that the sentence has a verb (*is taking*), and that the verb needs a subject. Answers (B) and (D) are incorrect because *when* and *her* are not subjects. In answer (A), *they* is a subject, but *they* is plural and the verb *is taking* is singular. The correct answer is answer (C); *the woman* is a singular subject. You should therefore choose answer (C).

---

### STRATEGIES FOR THE STRUCTURE QUESTIONS

1.  **First study the sentence.**    Your purpose is to determine what is needed to complete the sentence correctly.

2.  **Then study each answer based on how well it completes the sentence.**    Eliminate answers that do not complete the sentence correctly.

3.  **Do not try to eliminate incorrect answers by looking only at the answers.**    The incorrect answers are generally correct by themselves. The incorrect answers are generally incorrect only when used to complete the sentence.

4.  **Never leave any answers blank.**    Be sure to answer each question even if you are unsure of the correct response.

5.  **Do not spend too much time on the Structure questions.**    Be sure to leave adequate time for the Written Expression questions.

# THE WRITTEN EXPRESSION QUESTIONS

Questions 16 through 40 in the Structure and Written Expression section of the TOEFL test examine your knowledge of the correct way to express yourself in English writing. Each question in this section consists of one sentence in which four words or groups of words have been underlined. You must choose the letter of the word or group of words that is *not* correct.

---

***Example I***

The <u>final</u> delivery of <u>the day</u> <u>is</u> the <u>importantest</u>.
    A              B   C       D

---

If you look at the underlined words in this example, you should notice immediately that *importantest* is not correct. The correct superlative form of *important* is *the most important*. Therefore, you should choose answer (D) because (D) is not correct.

---

***Example II***

The books <u>that</u> I <u>read</u> <u>was</u> <u>interesting</u>.
          A     B   C    D

---

If you look at the underlined words in this example, each word by itself appears to be correct. However, the singular verb *was* is incorrect because it does not agree with the plural subject *books;* the verb should be *were* instead. Therefore, you should choose answer (C) because (C) is not correct.

---

### STRATEGIES FOR THE WRITTEN EXPRESSION QUESTIONS

1. **First look at the underlined word or groups of words.** You want to see if you can spot which of the four answer choices is *not* correct.

2. **If you have been unable to find the error by looking only at the four underlined expressions, then read the complete sentence.** Often an underlined expression is incorrect because of something in another part of the sentence.

3. **Never leave any answers blank.** Be sure to answer each question even if you are unsure of the correct response.

# TOEFL STRATEGIES
# READING
# COMPREHENSION

The third section of the TOEFL test is the Reading Comprehension section. This section consists of fifty questions (some tests may be longer). You have fifty-five minutes to complete the fifty questions in this section.

In this part of the test you will be given reading passages, and you will be asked two types of questions about the reading passages:

1.  **Reading Comprehension** questions ask you to answer questions about the information given in the reading passages. There will be a variety of questions about each reading passage, including main idea questions, directly answered detail questions, and implied detail questions.

2.  **Vocabulary** questions ask you to identify the meanings of vocabulary words in the reading passages. To answer these questions, you may have to know the meanings of the words. You can also identify the meanings of some of the words by understanding the context surrounding the words, by using structural clues to identify the meanings of the words, or by breaking down the unknown words into known word parts in order to identify them.

---

### GENERAL STRATEGIES

1.  **Be familiar with the directions.** The directions on every TOEFL test are the same, so it is not necessary to spend time reading the directions carefully when you take the test. You should be completely familiar with the directions before the day of the test.

2.  **Do not spend too much time reading the passages!** You do not have time to read each reading passage in depth, and it is quite possible to answer the questions correctly without first reading the passages in depth. Some students prefer to spend a minute or two on each passage reading for the main idea before starting on the questions. Other students prefer to move directly to the questions without reading the passages first.

3.  **Do not worry if a reading passage is on a topic that you are unfamiliar with.** All of the information that you need to answer the questions is included in the passages. You do not need any background knowledge to answer the questions.

4.  **Never leave any answers blank on your answer sheet.** Even if you are unsure of the correct response, you should answer each question. There is no penalty for guessing.

---

# THE READING COMPREHENSION QUESTIONS

The Reading Comprehension section of the TOEFL test consists of five reading passages, each followed by a number of reading comprehension and vocabulary questions. Topics of the reading passages are varied, but they are often informational subjects that might be studied in an American university: American history, literature, art, architecture, geology, geography, and astronomy, for example.

Time is definitely a factor in the Reading Comprehension section. Many students who take the TOEFL test note that they are unable to finish all the questions in this section. Therefore, you need to make the most efficient use of your time in this section to get the highest score. The following method is the best way of attacking a reading passage to get the most questions correct in a limited amount of time.

---

### STRATEGIES FOR THE READING COMPREHENSION QUESTIONS

1. **Skim the reading passage to determine the main idea and the overall organization of ideas in the passage.** You do not need to understand every detail in each passage to answer the questions correctly. It is therefore a waste of time to read the passage with the intent of understanding every single detail before you try to answer the questions.

2. **Look ahead at the questions to determine what types of questions you must answer.** Each type of question is answered in a different way.

3. **Find the section of the passage that deals with each question.** The question-type tells you exactly where to look in the passage to find correct answers.

   - For *main idea questions,* look at the first line of each paragraph.
   - For *directly* and *indirectly answered detail questions,* choose a key word in the question, and skim for that key word (or a related idea) in order in the passage.
   - For *vocabulary questions,* the question will tell you where the word is located in the passage.
   - For *overall review questions,* the answers are found anywhere in the passage.

4. **Carefully read the part of the passage that contains the answer.** The answer will probably be in the same sentence (or one sentence before or after) the key word or idea.

5. **Choose the best answer to each question from the four answer choices listed in your test booklet.** You can choose the best answer according to what is given in the appropriate section of the passage, eliminate definitely wrong answers, and mark your best guess on the answer sheet.

# *TOEFL STRATEGIES*
# THE TEST OF WRITTEN ENGLISH (TWE)

The Test of Written English (TWE) is a writing section that appears on the TOEFL test several times a year. You should check the *Bulletin of Information for TOEFL, TWE, and TSE* for the dates that the TWE will be administered. If you are required to take the TWE, be sure to sign up for the TOEFL test in one of the months that the TWE is given.

On the TWE you will be given a specific topic and you will be asked to write an essay on that topic in thirty minutes. The TWE will be given at the beginning of the TOEFL test, before the Listening Comprehension, Structure and Written Expression, and Reading Comprehension sections.

Because you must write a complete essay in such a short period of time, it is best for you to aim to write a basic, clear, concise, and well-organized essay. The following strategies should help you to write this type of essay.

---

### STRATEGIES FOR THE TEST OF WRITTEN ENGLISH (TWE)

1. **Read the topic carefully and write about it exactly as it is presented.** Take several minutes at the beginning of the test to be sure that you understand the topic and to outline a response.

2. **Organize your response very clearly.** You should think of having an introduction, body paragraphs that develop the introduction, and a conclusion to end your essay. Use transitions to help the reader understand the organization of ideas.

3. **Whenever you make any general statement, be sure to support that statement.** You can use examples, reasons, facts, or similar details to support any general statement.

4. **Stick to vocabulary and sentence structures that you know.** This is not the time to try out new words or structures.

5. **Finish writing your essay a few minutes early so that you have time to proof what you wrote.** You should spend the last three to five minutes checking your essay for errors.

---

# PRACTICE TESTS

# 1 □ 1 □ 1 □ 1 □ 1 □ 1 □ 1 □ 1

# PRACTICE TEST ONE

## SECTION 1
## LISTENING COMPREHENSION
### Time—approximately 35 minutes
### (including the reading of the directions for each part)

In this section of the test, you will have an opportunity to demonstrate your ability to understand conversations and talks in English. There are three parts to this section. Answer all the questions on the basis of what is <u>stated</u> or <u>implied</u> by the speakers you hear. Do <u>not</u> take notes or write in your test book at any time. Do not turn the pages until you are told to do so.

## Part A

**Directions:** In Part A you will hear short conversations between two people. After each conversation, you will hear a question about the conversation. The conversations and questions will not be repeated. After you hear a question, read the four possible answers in your test book and choose the best answer. Then, on your answer sheet, find the number of the question and fill in the space that corresponds to the letter of the answer you have chosen.

Listen to an example.                                **Sample Answer**

On the recording, you hear:                          Ⓐ Ⓑ Ⓒ ●

    (man)     *That exam was just awful.*
  (woman)    *Oh, it could have been worse.*
(narrator)    *What does the woman mean?*

In your test book, you read:    (A)   The exam was really awful.
                                 (B)   It was the worst exam she had ever seen.
                                 (C)   It couldn't have been more difficult.
                                 (D)   It wasn't that hard.

You learn from the conversation that the man thought the exam was very difficult and that the woman disagreed with the man. The best answer to the question, "What does the woman mean?" is (D), "It wasn't that hard." Therefore, the correct choice is (D).

1. (A) He doesn't know how to type.
   (B) He doesn't want to type anymore.
   (C) He hasn't typed the paper.
   (D) He believes they're out of paper.

2. (A) She was not allowed to fight.
   (B) Something scared her.
   (C) She made a loud noise that frightened some people.
   (D) Some loud neighbors had a fight.

3. (A) At a bus stop.
   (B) At a school.
   (C) In a dentist's office.
   (D) At a cleaning supply store.

4. (A) She'd rather work alone.
   (B) Group work is her preference.
   (C) She's working on a project about group preferences.
   (D) She projected that the group wouldn't work.

5. (A) He's in his last week of work.
   (B) He doesn't expect the work to last.
   (C) The work isn't really hard.
   (D) He's only been working for a week.

6. (A) Amy always studied at the same time as Mel.
   (B) Mel studied for the exam before Amy.
   (C) Both Amy and Mel studied hard.
   (D) Amy thought that Mel would study for the exam.

7. (A) He always watches television from 1:00 to 2:00.
   (B) He'll watch in an hour or two.
   (C) He just got a television this week.
   (D) He doesn't see many programs.

8. (A) See the personnel manager immediately.
   (B) Wait for the personnel manager to arrive.
   (C) Arrange to meet with the personnel manager the next day.
   (D) Break her appointment with the personnel manager.

9. (A) A mathematician.
   (B) A reporter.
   (C) An accountant.
   (D) An arithmetic teacher.

10. (A) She paid more than the man.
    (B) She had good fortune when she bought the television.
    (C) Fifty dollars is a fortune to her.
    (D) Fifty dollars is too much to pay for a television.

11. (A) He believes that the administration building is near the bookstore.
    (B) He wonders if the bookstore is in the administration building.
    (C) The administrators went next door to the bookstore.
    (D) The administrators have decided to build a new bookstore.

12. (A) Listen to the symphony concert alone.
    (B) Stand on a long line.
    (C) Discuss a good idea of hers with the man.
    (D) Go to a concert tomorrow night.

13. (A) Greg was quite early.
    (B) Greg was barely on time.
    (C) Greg arrived a minute after they called him.
    (D) Greg arrived soon after the man.

14. (A) Sally was mad about the end of the assignment.
    (B) Sally never finished the math assignment.
    (C) Sally was forced to complete the assignment.
    (D) He finished the assignment for Sally.

15. (A) She refuses to help the man.
    (B) She's afraid she can't be of much assistance.
    (C) The man doesn't know enough for her to help him.
    (D) The man should try to do it on his own.

**GO ON TO THE NEXT PAGE**

16. (A) He didn't accomplish much because of the weather.
    (B) It couldn't be too hot to work.
    (C) He completed a lot of work in spite of the weather.
    (D) Unless it's very hot, he doesn't get much work done.

17. (A) She wants to be a school playground leader.
    (B) Her new role is to lead the school.
    (C) She's seen some students rolling on the ground.
    (D) She's acting in a school theater production.

18. (A) She looked in the ditch under the bridge.
    (B) When she looked up, she saw the dictionary.
    (C) She found the meaning of the word.
    (D) She defined what she was looking for.

19. (A) He prefers to watch sports.
    (B) He'll watch the movie if he has time.
    (C) He never watches movies on television.
    (D) He had the idea at the same time that the woman did.

20. (A) Pat's minding the laundry with Jim.
    (B) Neither Pat nor Jim likes doing the laundry.
    (C) Both Pat and Jim will wash clothes without complaining.
    (D) Pat doesn't mind when Jim does the laundry.

21. (A) There's been nothing but snow for quite some time.
    (B) He's bored with the changing weather.
    (C) He believes that it'll snow in two weeks.
    (D) His friends think that he's boring when he talks about the weather.

22. (A) The man should order a history book immediately.
    (B) The man can't get a text from the bookstore in time for the exam.
    (C) There are no more history texts on order at the bookstore.
    (D) The man's friend is using the history text during the exam.

23. (A) The film wasn't very funny.
    (B) It was a rather boring movie.
    (C) He couldn't move any further.
    (D) The movie was extremely amusing.

24. (A) He doesn't believe in signing leases.
    (B) He thought his signature was unnecessary.
    (C) His taste in apartments is different from theirs.
    (D) He doesn't always say what he means.

25. (A) It is necessary for her to go.
    (B) She doesn't have to go, but she'll go anyway.
    (C) She is not going this afternoon.
    (D) She wishes she could go.

26. (A) It was lucky that Tom wasn't injured in the accident.
    (B) Tom was a nervous wreck after the accident.
    (C) It was just an accident that Tom got a new car.
    (D) Tom wasn't very lucky.

27. (A) She'll be very careful this month.
    (B) She'll take care of the children.
    (C) She'll pay the rent.
    (D) She'll be cautious with the money.

GO ON TO THE NEXT PAGE ➡

28. (A) The man would remember to bring
        her the book.
    (B) The man had forgotten that she
        wanted the book.
    (C) The man would lend her the book
        any time.
    (D) The man wanted to borrow the book
        from her.

29. (A) They don't have any lights.
    (B) He didn't pay the bill on time.
    (C) The lights they have are not electric.
    (D) He already paid the bill.

30. (A) He was late for a boat trip.
    (B) He thought that the professor had left
        on a boat trip.
    (C) He did not hear when the professor
        canceled the exam.
    (D) He heard the professor's
        announcement about a trip.

**GO ON TO THE NEXT PAGE**

## Part B

**Directions:** In this part of the test, you will hear longer conversations. After each conversation, you will hear several questions. The conversations and questions will not be repeated.

After you hear a question, read the four possible answers in your test book and choose the best answer. Then, on your answer sheet, find the number of the question and fill in the space that corresponds to the letter of the answer you have chosen.

Remember, you are <u>not</u> allowed to take notes or write in your test book.

31. (A) Motivation.
    (B) Research for a management class.
    (C) Finding journal articles in the library.
    (D) The management professor.

32. (A) He can't decide on a topic.
    (B) He doesn't have too much time to complete the research.
    (C) He doesn't know where the library is.
    (D) He is uncertain how to find references.

33. (A) Both books and journals.
    (B) Just references on motivation from the card catalogue.
    (C) Only management and business books.
    (D) Journal articles only.

34. (A) Begin his research.
    (B) Go to management class.
    (C) Write a journal.
    (D) Look for a greeting card.

35. (A) Immediately.
    (B) A week from now.
    (C) In June.
    (D) During the ski season.

36. (A) Winter.
    (B) Spring.
    (C) Summer.
    (D) Fall.

37. (A) By car.
    (B) On a mountain bike.
    (C) On foot.
    (D) On horseback.

38. (A) Snowy.
    (B) Overly hot.
    (C) Cold and wet.
    (D) Mild.

GO ON TO THE NEXT PAGE

## Part C

**Directions:** In this part of the test, you will hear several talks. After each talk, you will hear some questions. The talks and questions will not be repeated.

After you hear a question, read the four possible answers in your test book and choose the best answer. Then, on your answer sheet, find the number of the question and fill in the space that corresponds to the letter of the answer you have chosen.

Here is an example.

On the recording, you hear:

(narrator)     *Listen to an instructor talk to his class about painting.*

(man)     *Artist Grant Wood was a guiding force in the school of painting known as American regionalist, a style reflecting the distinctive characteristics of art from rural areas of the United States. Wood began drawing animals on the family farm at the age of three, and when he was thirty-eight one of his paintings received a remarkable amount of public notice and acclaim. This painting, called* American Gothic, *is a starkly simple depiction of a serious couple staring directly out at the viewer.*

Now listen to a sample question.                    **Sample Answer**

(narrator)     *What style of painting is known as American regionalist?*     Ⓐ Ⓑ Ⓒ ⬤

In your test book, you read:     (A)   Art from America's inner cities.
                                  (B)   Art from the central region of the U.S.
                                  (C)   Art from various urban areas in the U.S.
                                  (D)   Art from rural sections of America.

The best answer to the question, "What style of painting is known as American regionalist?" is (D), "Art from rural sections of America." Therefore, the correct choice is (D).

Now listen to another sample question.                    **Sample Answer**

(narrator)     *What is the name of Wood's most successful painting?*     Ⓐ Ⓑ ⬤ Ⓓ

In your test book, you read:     (A)   "American Regionalist."
                                  (B)   "The Family Farm in Iowa."
                                  (C)   "American Gothic."
                                  (D)   "A Serious Couple."

The best answer to the question, "What is the name of Wood's most successful painting?" is (C), "American Gothic." Therefore, the correct choice is (C).

Remember, you are <u>not</u> allowed to take notes or write in your test book.

Wait

39. (A) The standard grading system.
    (B) The difference between required and elective courses.
    (C) A special grading system.
    (D) The types of courses that must be taken during the graduate program.

40. (A) This student is using the standard grading system.
    (B) This student has passed the course.
    (C) This student is taking a required course.
    (D) This student has not done acceptable work.

41. (A) One.
    (B) Two.
    (C) Three.
    (D) Four.

42. (A) All required courses.
    (B) Some required courses.
    (C) All elective courses.
    (D) Some elective courses.

43. (A) A spoken language.
    (B) A written language.
    (C) A language based on road signs.
    (D) A language based on hand movements.

44. (A) The Native American tribes didn't have spoken languages.
    (B) The Native American tribes spoke many different languages.
    (C) The Native Americans were unable to use their mouths.
    (D) Sign language is much more advanced than spoken language.

45. (A) Frequently.
    (B) Occasionally.
    (C) Seldom.
    (D) Never.

46. (A) As a highly developed language.
    (B) As more sophisticated than spoken language.
    (C) As a basic means of communication.
    (D) As an impossible way to communicate.

47. (A) Edgar Allan Poe.
    (B) American poets.
    (C) The novel.
    (D) Short story writers.

48. (A) Short.
    (B) Symbolic.
    (C) Tragic.
    (D) Fulfilled.

49. (A) Symbolism.
    (B) Impressionism.
    (C) Eerie tone.
    (D) Humor.

50. (A) Read about Poe's life.
    (B) Prepare for a discussion of a short story.
    (C) Study the American novelist.
    (D) Write an analysis of one of the stories.

**This is the end of Section 1.**
**Stop work on Section 1.**

**Turn off your cassette player.**

**Read the directions for Section 2 and begin work.**
**Do NOT read or work on any other section**
**of the test during the next 25 minutes.**

**No test material on this page.**

## SECTION 2
## STRUCTURE AND WRITTEN EXPRESSION
**Time—25 minutes**
**(including the reading of the directions)**
**Now set your clock for 25 minutes.**

This section is designed to measure your ability to recognize language that is appropriate for standard written English. There are two types of questions in this section, with special directions for each type.

## Structure

**Directions:** Questions 1–15 are incomplete sentences. Beneath each sentence you will see four words or phrases, marked (A), (B), (C), and (D). Choose the <u>one</u> word or phrase that best completes the sentence. Then, on your answer sheet, find the number of the question and fill in the space that corresponds to the letter of the answer you have chosen. Fill in the space so that the letter inside the oval cannot be seen.

Look at the following examples.

*Example I*

The president _____ the election by a landslide.

(A)   won
(B)   he won
(C)   yesterday
(D)   fortunately

**Sample Answer**

● Ⓑ Ⓒ Ⓓ

The sentence should read, "The president won the election by a landslide." Therefore, you should choose (A).

*Example II*

When _____ the conference?

(A)   the doctor attended
(B)   did the doctor attend
(C)   the doctor will attend
(D)   the doctor's attendance

**Sample Answer**

Ⓐ ● Ⓒ Ⓓ

The sentence should read, "When did the doctor attend the conference?" Therefore, you should choose (B).

Now begin work on the questions.

GO ON TO THE NEXT PAGE ➤

1. The sport of hang gliding _____ by the Federal Aviation Administration (FAA).

   (A) regulated it
   (B) is regulated
   (C) that was regulated
   (D) that it was regulated

2. The adder is a venomous snake _____ bite may prove fatal to humans.

   (A) its
   (B) whom its
   (C) that
   (D) whose

3. The javelin used in competition must be between 260 and 270 centimeters _____ .

   (A) in length
   (B) it is long
   (C) its length
   (D) lengthily

4. In an internal combustion engine, _____ and air are heated inside a cylinder.

   (A) and gasoline vapor
   (B) both gasoline vapor
   (C) gasoline vaporizes
   (D) besides gasoline vapor

5. In November of 1863, the city of Atlanta _____ during Sherman's famous "March to the Sea."

   (A) was completely burned
   (B) completely burning
   (C) it was burned completely
   (D) completely burned it

6. The Kentucky Derby _____ every May at Churchill Downs in Louisville, Kentucky.

   (A) to be run
   (B) run
   (C) it may be run
   (D) is run

7. _____ have captured the spirit of the conquest of America as well as James Fenimore Cooper.

   (A) Few writers
   (B) The few writers
   (C) The writers are few
   (D) Few are the writers

8. Prospectors rushed to Nevada in 1859 _____ was discovered there.

   (A) after gold soon
   (B) soon after gold
   (C) gold soon after
   (D) soon gold after

9. _____ heat from the Sun is trapped near the Earth's surface, the greenhouse effect occurs.

   (A) No
   (B) When
   (C) That
   (D) What

10. _____, the outer layer of the skin, contains pigments, pores, and ducts.

    (A) That the epidermis
    (B) The epidermis is
    (C) The epidermis
    (D) The epidermis which

11. Keynes argued that to avoid an economic depression the government _____ spending and lower interest rates.

    (A) is
    (B) higher
    (C) increase
    (D) should increase

12. _____ a bee colony gets, the more the queen's egg-laying capability diminishes.

    (A) It is more overcrowded
    (B) The more overcrowded
    (C) More overcrowded than
    (D) More than overcrowded

**GO ON TO THE NEXT PAGE**

13. Unlike the Earth, which rotates once every twenty-four hours, _____ once every ten hours.

    (A)   the rotation of Jupiter
    (B)   the occurrence of Jupiter's rotation
    (C)   Jupiter rotates
    (D)   Jupiter's rotating

14. _____ peaches are classified as freestone or clingstone depends on how difficult it is to remove the pit.

    (A)   The
    (B)   About
    (C)   Whether
    (D)   Scientifically

15. Out of John Kenneth Galbraith's *The Affluent Society* _____ for an increase in public goods, potentially at the expense of private goods.

    (A)   came the argument
    (B)   his argument
    (C)   argued
    (D)   the economist is arguing

GO ON TO THE NEXT PAGE →

## Written Expression

**Directions:** In questions 16–40, each sentence has four underlined words or phrases. The four underlined parts of the sentence are marked (A), (B), (C), and (D). Identify the <u>one</u> underlined word or phrase that must be changed in order for the sentence to be correct. Then, on your answer sheet, find the number of the question and fill in the space that corresponds to the letter of the answer you have chosen.

Look at the following examples.

*Example I*                                                    **Sample Answer**

The four string on a violin are tuned
  A    B               C  D

in fifths.

Ⓐ ● Ⓒ Ⓓ

The sentence should read, "The four strings on a violin are tuned in fifths." Therefore, you should choose (B).

*Example II*                                                   **Sample Answer**

The research for the book *Roots* taking
    A      B               C

Alex Haley twelve years.
           D

Ⓐ Ⓑ ● Ⓓ

The sentence should read, "The research for the book *Roots* took Alex Haley twelve years." Therefore, you should choose (C).

Now begin work on the questions.

**GO ON TO THE NEXT PAGE** ➤

16. Soon after the United States' entrance into the war, the major hotels in Atlantic City was
        A                                    B                                C                        D

    transformed into military barracks.

17. Major advertising companies have traditionally volunteered its time to public service accounts.
            A                              B                        C              D

18. The value of precious gems is determined by their hardness, color, and brilliant.
                    A        B                          C                                D

19. Find in 1933, *The New York Sun* was the first successful penny newspaper.
        A                              B    C                                    D

20. The 3,500-foot George Washington Bridge spans the Hudson River to link New York City
                                              A    B                          C

    also New Jersey.
        D

21. Some researchers believe that an unfair attitude toward the poor will contributed to the
            A                            B                            C          D

    problem of poverty.

22. Gene therapy it is the latest advance in a revolutionary branch of medicine called
                    A        B                    C                                    D

    molecular genetics.

23. Astronomers do not know how many galaxies there are, but is it thought that there are
                                A                  B            C

    millions or perhaps billions.
                D

24. The amino acids serve as the building block of proteins.
        A            B    C                D

25. The most popular breed of dog in the United States are cocker spaniel, poodle, and retriever.
        A                B        C                                                        D

26. A water molecule consists two hydrogen atoms and one oxygen atom.
        A                B                        C        D

27. Once the scientist had figured out the precise path of the comet, he is finding that he was able
        A                                                                    B

    to predict its next appearance.
        C        D

28. The intent of the Historical Society is to restore old buildings and increasing interest in the
        A                                    B                                    C

    history of the area.
                D

29. The amount of copper sulfate used in the experiment depends from the intensity of the heat.
        A                                                    B    C                    D

GO ON TO THE NEXT PAGE →

30. After the yolk is <u>separated</u> <u>from</u> the white, it must be <u>boil</u> <u>immediately</u>.
                           A        B                           C     D

31. <u>Through</u> the years, scientists <u>have developed</u> smaller but <u>increasingly</u> more powerful batteries
    A                            B                  C

    for the growing number of portable electrical <u>device</u>.
                                           D

32. <u>More than</u> 80 percent of the <u>labors</u> at the construction site <u>are</u> <u>temporary</u> workers.
    A                     B                       C   D

33. The development of motor skills in <u>babies begins</u> with <u>the head</u> and <u>progress</u> downward
                                 A            B         C

    through <u>other</u> parts of the body.
               D

34. The *USS Bonhomme Richard* <u>was</u> commanded by John Paul Jones, <u>that</u> won <u>a notable</u> sea
                              A                         B       C

    battle <u>during</u> the Revolution.
            D

35. There <u>exists</u> <u>more than</u> 2,600 different varieties of palm trees, with <u>varying</u> flowers, leaves,
          A      B                                      C

    and <u>fruits</u>.
       D

36. <u>Most</u> American Indian <u>cultures</u> <u>were</u> agricultural <u>societies</u> since 2000 B.C.
    A                    B   C              D

37. <u>An</u> huge winter storm <u>has</u> brought <u>snow</u> to Northern California's mountain <u>counties</u>.
  A                B         C                             D

38. Nutritionists <u>recommend</u> that foods from each of the four basic groups <u>be eaten</u> on a
                  A                                         B

    <u>regularly</u> <u>daily</u> basis.
     C     D

39. Neon <u>is often</u> used in airplane beacons because neon beacons are <u>too</u> visible that <u>they</u> can be
        A                                          B         C

    seen <u>even through</u> dense fog.
          D

40. <u>Her</u> <u>best-known</u> <u>role</u> of Judy Garland was <u>as</u> Dorothy in *The Wizard of Oz*.
    A     B     C                 D

**This is the end of Section 2.**
**If you finish before 25 minutes has ended,**
**check your work on Section 2 only.**

**At the end of 25 minutes, go on to Section 3.**
**Use exactly 55 minutes to work on Section 3.**

## SECTION 3
## READING COMPREHENSION
**Time—55 minutes**
**(including the reading of the directions)**
**Now set your clock for 55 minutes.**

This section is designed to measure your ability to read and understand short passages similar in topic and style to those that students are likely to encounter in North American universities and colleges.

**Directions:** In this section you will read several passages. Each one is followed by a number of questions about it. You are to choose the <u>one</u> best answer, (A), (B), (C), or (D), to each question. Then, on your answer sheet, find the number of the question and fill in the space that corresponds to the letter of the answer you have chosen.

Answer all questions about the information in a passage on the basis of what is <u>stated</u> or <u>implied</u> in that passage.

Read the following passage:

> John Quincy Adams, who served as the sixth president of the United States from 1825 to 1829, is today recognized for his masterful statesmanship and diplomacy. He dedicated his life to public service, both in the presidency and in the various other political offices that he
> *Line* held. Throughout his political career he demonstrated his unswerving belief in freedom of
> (5) speech, the antislavery cause, and the right of Americans to be free from European and Asian domination.

*Example I*                                    **Sample Answer**

To what did John Quincy Adams devote his life?

(A)   Improving his personal life
(B)   Serving the public
(C)   Increasing his fortune
(D)   Working on his private business

According to the passage, John Quincy Adams "dedicated his life to public service." Therefore, you should choose (B).

*Example II*                                    **Sample Answer**

In line 4, the word "unswerving" is closest in meaning to

(A)   moveable
(B)   insignificant
(C)   unchanging
(D)   diplomatic

The passage states that John Quincy Adams demonstrated his unswerving belief "throughout his career." This implies that the belief did not change. Therefore, you should choose (C).

Now begin work on the questions.

**GO ON TO THE NEXT PAGE**

**Questions 1–10**

The White House, the official home of the United States president, was not built in time for George Washington to live in it. It was begun in 1792 and was ready for its first inhabitants, President and Mrs. John Adams, who moved in on November 1, 1800. When the Adamses moved in, the White
*Line* House was not yet complete, and the Adamses suffered many inconveniences; for example, the main
*(5)* staircase was incomplete, which hindered movement from floor to floor, and the future laundry yard was merely a pool of mud, so wet laundry was hung in the unfinished East Room to dry. Thomas Jefferson, the third president, improved the comfort of the White House in many respects and added new architectural features such as the terraces on the east and west ends.

When the British forces burned the White House on August 24, 1814, President Madison was
*(10)* forced to leave. All that remained after the fire was the exterior walls; the interior was completely destroyed. It was not until December of 1817 that the following president, James Monroe, was able to move into a rebuilt residence. Since then, the White House has continued to be modified but has been continuously occupied by each succeeding U.S. president.

1. Which of the following would be the most appropriate title for this passage?

    (A) George Washington's Life in the White House
    (B) The Burning of the White House
    (C) The Early History of the White House
    (D) Presidential Policies of Early U.S. Presidents

2. Why did George Washington NOT live in the White House?

    (A) It had been burned by the British.
    (B) He did not like the architectural features.
    (C) He did not want to suffer the inconveniences that the Adamses had suffered.
    (D) Construction had not yet been completed.

3. The word "inhabitants" in line 2 is closest in meaning to

    (A) modifications
    (B) moves
    (C) residents
    (D) celebrations

4. It can be inferred from the passage that John Adams was

    (A) the first president of the United States
    (B) the second president of the United States
    (C) the third president of the United States
    (D) the fourth president of the United States

5. The author most likely discusses the "staircase" in line 5 in order to

    (A) show the elegance of the new White House
    (B) explain the architectural features added by Jefferson
    (C) demonstrate what had to be rebuilt after the fire
    (D) provide an example of an inconvenience in the White House

6. The word "hindered" in line 5 is closest in meaning to

    (A) obstructed
    (B) reinforced
    (C) returned
    (D) favored

**GO ON TO THE NEXT PAGE** ▶

7. The word "forces" in line 9 could best be replaced by

   (A) power
   (B) effort
   (C) military
   (D) energy

8. According to the passage, which of the following best describes Thomas Jefferson's tenure in the White House?

   (A) He had to flee the White House because of the war with the British.
   (B) He was accepting of the many inconveniences.
   (C) He removed the terraces that had been added by Adams.
   (D) He worked to improve the appearance and convenience of the White House.

9. According to the passage, when James Monroe came to the White House, it had been

   (A) repressed
   (B) reconstructed
   (C) relocated
   (D) reserved

10. The paragraph following the passage most likely discusses

   (A) modifications by presidents who followed
   (B) the details of the destruction of the White House by the British
   (C) James Monroe's policies as president
   (D) other presidents who were unable to occupy the White House

GO ON TO THE NEXT PAGE

## Questions 11–22

Algae is a primitive form of life, a single-celled or simple multiple-celled organism that is able to conduct the process of photosynthesis. It is generally found in water but can also be found elsewhere, growing on such surfaces as rocks or trees. The various types of algae are classified according to
*Line* pigment.
*(5)*    Blue-green algae, or *Cyanophyta*, can grow at very high temperatures and under high-intensity light. This is a microscopic type of algae, and some species consist of only one cell. Blue-green algae is the oldest form of life with photosynthetic capabilities, and fossilized remains of this type of algae more than 3.4 billion years old have been found in parts of Africa.

Green algae, or *Chlorophyta*, is generally found in fresh water. It reproduces on the surfaces of
*(10)* enclosed bodies of water such as ponds or lakes and has the appearance of a fuzzy green coating on the water. In large quantities, this type of algae may reproduce enough to give a green color to an entire lake.

Brown algae, or *Phaeophyta*, grows in shallow, temperate water. This type of algae is the largest in size and is most recognizable as a type of seaweed; kelp is a type of brown algae that has grown to
*(15)* lengths of up to 200 feet. Its long stalks can be enmeshed on the ocean floor, or it can float freely on the ocean's surface.

Red algae, or *Rhodophyta*, is a small, delicate organism found in the deep waters of the subtropics, where it often grows with coral. This type of algae has an essential role in the formation of coral reefs: it secretes lime from the seawater to foster the formation of limestone deposits.

11.  What is the author's main purpose?

(A)  To show what color algae is
(B)  To differentiate the various classifications of algae
(C)  To describe where algae is found
(D)  To clarify the appearance of the different types of algae

12.  Which of the following is NOT true about algae?

(A)  All types have only one cell.
(B)  It can be found out of water.
(C)  It can use photosynthesis.
(D)  It is not a relatively new form of life.

13.  The word "pigment" in line 4 means

(A)  size
(B)  shape
(C)  composition
(D)  color

14.  The word "microscopic" in line 6 is closest in meaning to

(A)  mechanical
(B)  tiny
(C)  visual
(D)  bacterial

15.  Algae remnants found in Africa are

(A)  still flourishing
(B)  photogenic
(C)  extremely old
(D)  red in color

16.  Green algae is generally found

(A)  on the ocean floor
(B)  on top of the water
(C)  throughout ponds and lakes
(D)  surrounding enclosed bodies of water

17.  The word "coating" in line 10 could best be replaced by

(A)  clothing
(B)  covering
(C)  warmth
(D)  sweater

18.  Brown algae would most likely be found

(A)  on trees
(B)  near green algae
(C)  on rocks
(D)  in the ocean

**GO ON TO THE NEXT PAGE**

19. The word "stalks" in line 15 is closest in meaning to

    (A) stems
    (B) leaves
    (C) flowers
    (D) branches

20. According to the passage, red algae is

    (A) sturdy
    (B) huge
    (C) fragile
    (D) found in shallow water

21. It can be inferred from the passage that limestone deposits serve as the basis of

    (A) coral reefs
    (B) red algae
    (C) subtropical seawater
    (D) secret passages

22. This passage would most probably be assigned reading in a course on

    (A) chemistry
    (B) physics
    (C) botany
    (D) zoology

GO ON TO THE NEXT PAGE

**Questions 23–31**

Niagara Falls, one of the most famous North American natural wonders, has long been a popular tourist destination. Tourists today flock to see the two falls that actually constitute Niagara Falls: the 173-foot-high Horseshoe Falls on the Canadian side of the Niagara River in the Canadian province of
Line Ontario and the 182-foot-high American Falls on the U.S. side of the river in the state of New York.
(5) Approximately 85 percent of the water that goes over the falls actually goes over Horseshoe Falls, with the rest going over American Falls.

Most visitors come between April and October, and it is quite a popular activity to take a steamer out onto the river and right up to the base of the falls for a close-up view. It is also possible to get a spectacular view of the falls from the strategic locations along the Niagara River, such as Prospect
(10) Point or Table Rock, or from one of the four observation towers which have heights up to 500 feet.

Tourists have been visiting Niagara Falls in large numbers since the 1800's; annual visitation now averages above 10 million visitors per year. Because of concern that all these tourists would inadvertently destroy the natural beauty of this scenic wonder, the State of New York in 1885 created Niagara Falls Park in order to protect the land surrounding American Falls. A year later Canada
(15) created Queen Victoria Park on the Canadian side of the Niagara, around Horseshoe Falls. With the area surrounding the falls under the jurisdiction of government agencies, appropriate steps could be taken to preserve the pristine beauty of the area.

23. What is the major point that the author is making in this passage?

    (A) Niagara Falls can be viewed from either the American side or the Canadian side.
    (B) A trip to the U.S. isn't complete without a visit to Niagara Falls.
    (C) Niagara Falls has had an interesting history.
    (D) It has been necessary to protect Niagara Falls from the many tourists who go there.

24. The word "flock" in line 2 could best be replaced by

    (A) come by plane
    (B) come in large numbers
    (C) come out of boredom
    (D) come without knowing what they will see

25. According to the passage, which of the following best describes Niagara Falls?

    (A) Niagara Falls consists of two rivers, one Canadian and the other American.
    (B) American Falls is considerably higher than Horseshoe Falls.
    (C) The Niagara River has two falls, one in Canada and one in the U.S.
    (D) Although the Niagara River flows through the U.S. and Canada, the falls are only in the U.S.

26. A "steamer" in line 7 is probably

    (A) a bus
    (B) a boat
    (C) a walkway
    (D) a park

**GO ON TO THE NEXT PAGE** ➤

27. The expression "right up" in line 8 could best be replaced by

    (A) turn to the right
    (B) follow correct procedures
    (C) travel upstream
    (D) all the way up

28. The passage implies that tourists prefer to

    (A) visit Niagara Falls during warmer weather
    (B) see the falls from a great distance
    (C) take a ride over the falls
    (D) come to Niagara Falls for a winter vacation

29. According to the passage, why was Niagara Park created?

    (A) To encourage tourists to visit Niagara Falls
    (B) To show off the natural beauty of Niagara Falls
    (C) To protect the area around Niagara Falls
    (D) To force Canada to open Queen Victoria Park

30. The word "pristine" in line 17 is closest in meaning to

    (A) pure and natural
    (B) highly developed
    (C) well-regulated
    (D) overused

31. The paragraph following the passage most probably discusses

    (A) additional ways to observe the falls
    (B) steps taken by government agencies to protect the falls
    (C) a detailed description of the division of the falls between the U.S. and Canada
    (D) further problems that are destroying the area around the falls

**GO ON TO THE NEXT PAGE**

**Questions 32–41**

Herman Melville, an American author best known today for his novel *Moby Dick*, was actually more popular during his lifetime for some of his other works. He traveled extensively and used the knowledge gained during his travels as the basis for his early novels. In 1837, at the age of eighteen, *Line* Melville signed as a cabin boy on a merchant ship that was to sail from his Massachusetts home to (5) Liverpool, England. His experiences on this trip served as a basis for the novel *Redburn* (1849). In 1841 Melville set out on a whaling ship headed for the South Seas. After jumping ship in Tahiti, he wandered around the islands of Tahiti and Moorea. This South Sea island sojourn was a backdrop to the novel *Omoo* (1847). After three years away from home, Melville joined up with a U.S. naval frigate that was returning to the eastern United States around Cape Horn. The novel *White-Jacket* (1850) describes this (10) lengthy voyage as a navy seaman.

With the publication of these early adventure novels, Melville developed a strong and loyal following among readers eager for his tales of exotic places and situations. However, in 1851, with the publication of *Moby Dick*, Melville's popularity started to diminish. *Moby Dick*, on one level the saga of the hunt for the great white whale, was also a heavily symbolic allegory of the heroic struggle of (15) humanity against the universe. The public was not ready for Melville's literary metamorphosis from romantic adventure to philosophical symbolism. It is ironic that the novel that served to diminish Melville's popularity during his lifetime is the one for which he is best known today.

32. The main subject of the passage is

    (A) Melville's travels
    (B) the popularity of Melville's novels
    (C) Melville's personal background
    (D) *Moby Dick*

33. According to the passage, Melville's early novels were

    (A) published while he was traveling
    (B) completely fictional
    (C) all about his work on whaling ships
    (D) based on his travels

34. In what year did Melville's book about his experiences as a cabin boy appear?

    (A) 1837
    (B) 1841
    (C) 1847
    (D) 1849

35. The word "basis" in line 5 is closest in meaning to

    (A) foundation
    (B) message
    (C) bottom
    (D) theme

36. The passage implies that Melville stayed in Tahiti because

    (A) he had unofficially left his ship
    (B) he was on leave while his ship was in port
    (C) he had finished his term of duty
    (D) he had received permission to take a vacation in Tahiti

37. A "frigate" in line 8 is probably

    (A) an office
    (B) a ship
    (C) a troop
    (D) a train

**GO ON TO THE NEXT PAGE**

38. The expression "a strong and loyal following" in lines 11–12 could best be replaced by

    (A) an ending
    (B) a resolution
    (C) results
    (D) fans

39. How did the publication of *Moby Dick* affect Melville's popularity?

    (A) His popularity increased immediately.
    (B) It had no effect on his popularity.
    (C) It caused his popularity to decrease.
    (D) His popularity remained as strong as ever.

40. According to the passage, *Moby Dick* is

    (A) a romantic adventure
    (B) a single-faceted work
    (C) a short story about a whale
    (D) symbolic of humanity fighting the environment

41. The word "metamorphosis" in line 15 is closest in meaning to

    (A) circle
    (B) change
    (C) mysticism
    (D) descent

**GO ON TO THE NEXT PAGE**

**Questions 42–50**

The Works Progress Administration (WPA) was formed in 1935 during the height of the Great Depression as part of President Franklin Delano Roosevelt's New Deal package to bring the economy around and provide relief for the millions of unemployed throughout the country; the goal of the
*Line* program was to maintain peoples' skills and respect by providing work to as many as possible during
(5) this period of massive unemployment. For the eight years that the WPA was in existence from 1935 to 1943, the WPA was responsible for providing jobs to approximately eight million people at a cost of more than eleven billion dollars.

One of the more controversial programs of the WPA was the Federal Arts Project, a program to employ artists full-time at such tasks as painting murals in libraries, theaters, train stations, and
(10) airports; teaching various techniques of art; and preparing a comprehensive study of American crafts. Criticism of the program centered on what was perceived as the frivolity of supporting the arts at a time when millions were starving, industry was sagging, farms were barren, and all that could flourish were bankruptcy courts and soup kitchens.

42. This passage mainly discusses

(A) the Great Depression
(B) the benefits of Franklin Delano Roosevelt's New Deal
(C) the New Deal and one of its controversies
(D) bankruptcy courts and soup kitchens

43. The word "package" in line 2 could best be replaced by

(A) carton
(B) secret gift
(C) box
(D) bundle of related items

44. According to the passage, the stated purpose of the WPA was to

(A) create new American masterpieces
(B) raise the standard of American art
(C) introduce new art techniques to the American public
(D) improve the economy

45. The word "massive" in line 5 is closest in meaning to

(A) tremendous
(B) rocky
(C) clustered
(D) dangerous

46. The word "controversial" in line 8 is closest in meaning to

(A) disputed
(B) successful
(C) creative
(D) comprehensive

47. All the following probably helped to make the Federal Arts Project controversial EXCEPT that

(A) the Federal Arts Project employed many who would otherwise have been out of work
(B) train stations and airports were decorated with murals
(C) the Federal Arts Project commissioned art works
(D) a tremendous study of American crafts was produced

48. The expression "centered on" in line 11 could best be replaced by

(A) encircled
(B) located on
(C) focused on
(D) surrounded

**GO ON TO THE NEXT PAGE**

49. When the author states that ". . . all that could flourish were bankruptcy courts and soup kitchens," he or she probably means that

(A) banks and restaurants did well during the Depression
(B) the poor could not afford to use banks or eat soup
(C) the only organizations to thrive were those that dealt with the poor
(D) many restaurants declared bankruptcy during the Depression

50. Where in the passage does the author give examples of artistic jobs?

(A) Lines 1–5
(B) Lines 5–7
(C) Lines 8–10
(D) Lines 11–13

**This is the end of Section 3.**

**If you finish in less than 55 minutes, check your work on Section 3 only. Do NOT read or work on any other section of the test.**

GO ON TO THE NEXT PAGE

# TEST OF WRITTEN ENGLISH
## TWE ESSAY TOPIC
### Time—30 minutes

*Some people argue that vast sums of money should be spent to explore space. Others argue that it is better to solve Earth's problems before going out into space. Tell which position you agree with and why.*

Write your answer on the answer sheet for the Test of Written English (TWE), Practice Test One, on pages 181–182.

# 1 □ 1 □ 1 □ 1 □ 1 □ 1 □ 1 □ 1 □ 1 □ 1 □ 1

# PRACTICE TEST TWO

## SECTION 1
## LISTENING COMPREHENSION
### Time—approximately 35 minutes
### (including the reading of the directions for each part)

In this section of the test, you will have an opportunity to demonstrate your ability to understand conversations and talks in English. There are three parts to this section. Answer all the questions on the basis of what is <u>stated</u> or <u>implied</u> by the speakers you hear. Do <u>not</u> take notes or write in your test book at any time. Do not turn the pages until you are told to do so.

### Part A

**<u>Directions:</u>** In Part A you will hear short conversations between two people. After each conversation, you will hear a question about the conversation. The conversations and questions will not be repeated. After you hear a question, read the four possible answers in your test book and choose the best answer. Then, on your answer sheet, find the number of the question and fill in the space that corresponds to the letter of the answer you have chosen.

Listen to an example.

**Sample Answer**

On the recording, you hear:

Ⓐ
Ⓑ
Ⓒ
●

| (man) | *That exam was just awful.* |
| (woman) | *Oh, it could have been worse.* |
| (narrator) | *What does the woman mean?* |

In your test book, you read:
(A) The exam was really awful.
(B) It was the worst exam she had ever seen.
(C) It couldn't have been more difficult.
(D) It wasn't that hard.

You learn from the conversation that the man thought the exam was very difficult and that the woman disagreed with the man. The best answer to the question, "What does the woman mean?" is (D), "It wasn't that hard." Therefore, the correct choice is (D).

**Wait**

1. (A) In a restaurant.
   (B) In a grocery store.
   (C) In an airplane.
   (D) At a movie theater.

2. (A) She usually reads her mail while eating lunch.
   (B) Occasionally the letter carrier arrives after noon.
   (C) She doesn't always check the mail at lunchtime.
   (D) She doesn't always have time for lunch.

3. (A) To drink some coffee in a while.
   (B) To prepare the coffee herself.
   (C) To get the man some coffee later.
   (D) To drink something else.

4. (A) She doesn't want to go to the beach today.
   (B) She doesn't know why the weather is so nice.
   (C) She'd rather be outside today.
   (D) It's not the best time for a walk at the beach.

5. (A) He thought it was fascinating.
   (B) He agreed with the woman.
   (C) He thought it should have been longer.
   (D) He thought it was boring.

6. (A) She can't find her briefcase.
   (B) Her briefcase is smaller than the man's.
   (C) Their briefcases are different sizes.
   (D) The man gave his briefcase to her.

7. (A) Her roommate helped eat some cake.
   (B) She made the cake with some assistance.
   (C) She didn't exactly help her roommate.
   (D) She and her roommate didn't exactly make a cake.

8. (A) He's going to talk to the board.
   (B) He's sorry about what he said.
   (C) He has to decide about the boards.
   (D) He agrees with the woman.

9. (A) She only has to attend one meeting.
   (B) She's already attended the meeting.
   (C) She doesn't want to go.
   (D) She'll only go if she doesn't have plans.

10. (A) The history paper will get done in time.
    (B) She rarely gets her work done when she should.
    (C) She almost never gets to history class on time.
    (D) She doesn't read the paper completely before history class.

11. (A) She moved from the curb into the traffic.
    (B) A nosy neighbor disturbed her.
    (C) The loud sounds from the street bothered her.
    (D) She disrupted the traffic with her noise.

12. (A) She thinks it's a good place to get some shoes.
    (B) She'd like to sell her shoes.
    (C) She's sure there's a sale at the store.
    (D) She wonders if the shoe store is for sale.

13. (A) She refunded the money to the salesclerk.
    (B) The salesclerk refused to give her the money.
    (C) She was mad when the salesclerk refused her money.
    (D) The salesclerk returned her money.

14. (A) The dormitory hours.
    (B) The problem with the rulebook.
    (C) The door number of the dormitory.
    (D) When the dormitory opens.

15. (A) He found the assignment very difficult.
    (B) He finds it hard to believe how much time the woman spent.
    (C) The woman couldn't finish because she had other work to do.
    (D) The assignment was difficult to complete in thirty minutes.

16. (A) He can easily type for fifty minutes.
    (B) This is the easiest of fifty jobs he has applied for.
    (C) He's able to type very quickly.
    (D) This job is easy for anyone to do.

**GO ON TO THE NEXT PAGE** ➤

17. (A) He's tired of running.
    (B) He's finished running.
    (C) He has to run a race tomorrow.
    (D) He doesn't have enough time.

18. (A) He wants to get another refrigerator.
    (B) He thinks they need more drinks.
    (C) They have plenty of drinks.
    (D) He doesn't think there are enough.

19. (A) He believes that Carla didn't take the money.
    (B) It was hard for Carla to insist that she didn't do it.
    (C) In spite of what Carla says, it appears that she stole the money.
    (D) Although Carla insisted, she didn't take the money.

20. (A) He should receive checks for the students on assignment.
    (B) It's impossible to know the names of the students doing the assignment.
    (C) He should indicate who has finished the work.
    (D) He was checking to see that the students were working on the assignment.

21. (A) This class isn't very important to her.
    (B) Nothing at all is important to her.
    (C) This class could be more important to her.
    (D) This class is extremely important to her.

22. (A) She's glad to be going to the game.
    (B) She was already at a football game recently.
    (C) She is unable to go.
    (D) She is really going to try to get there.

23. (A) The prices of microcomputers are increasing.
    (B) Better technology should lead to decreased prices.
    (C) The decreased prices should make the technology better.
    (D) Because the prices of microcomputers are extremely high, they should come down.

24. (A) He's pleased with his results.
    (B) He isn't satisfied with all his work.
    (C) He found that all his work wasn't satisfactory.
    (D) He's satisfied that he has found the right process.

25. (A) Dinner will get cold.
    (B) The cafeteria will close.
    (C) The line will quickly get too long.
    (D) The woman will have dinner somewhere else.

26. (A) The authorities have prohibited security personnel from entering the test site.
    (B) The security guard is prohibited from entering the test site.
    (C) The security guard prohibits anyone from entering the test site.
    (D) They probably won't be allowed in.

27. (A) She doesn't believe that Sally broke the vase.
    (B) Sally told her that she had broken the vase.
    (C) Sally never tells the man anything.
    (D) Sally knows what happened, but she isn't telling anyone.

28. (A) He was just a little upset.
    (B) He was devastated.
    (C) He was a part of the news.
    (D) He felt upset about his hearing.

29. (A) The man should take the advanced course.
    (B) The man should attach the cart to the horse.
    (C) The man is doing things in the wrong order.
    (D) The man would like learning to paint horses.

30. (A) The woman had gotten rid of her bicycle.
    (B) The woman did not want to sell the bicycle.
    (C) It would take the woman longer to get there.
    (D) The woman would never ride a bicycle.

**GO ON TO THE NEXT PAGE**

**Part B**

**Directions:** In this part of the test, you will hear longer conversations. After each conversation, you will hear several questions. The conversations and questions will not be repeated.

After you hear a question, read the four possible answers in your test book and choose the best answer. Then, on your answer sheet, find the number of the question and fill in the space that corresponds to the letter of the answer you have chosen.

Remember, you are <u>not</u> allowed to take notes or write in your test book.

31. (A) Two students.
    (B) Two professors.
    (C) Two sociologists.
    (D) Two lecturers.

32. (A) She wants his opinion of sociologists.
    (B) She wants to hear him lecture.
    (C) She wants to know about a course he took.
    (D) She wants to meet Professor Patterson.

33. (A) A course where the professor lectures.
    (B) A course where the students just listen and take notes.
    (C) A course with Professor Patterson.
    (D) A course where the students take part in discussion.

34. (A) She thinks it'll be boring.
    (B) She doesn't want to take it.
    (C) It sounds good to her.
    (D) She'd prefer a course with more student participation.

35. (A) From a friend.
    (B) From the newspaper.
    (C) From a discussion.
    (D) From the utility company.

36. (A) In a far desert.
    (B) Close by.
    (C) At the utility company's headquarters.
    (D) The man has no idea.

37. (A) It's cheaper in the short run.
    (B) The utility company won't need any extra money.
    (C) The plant's far away.
    (D) It exists in large quantities.

38. (A) She's concerned it'll be too costly.
    (B) She thinks the price is too low.
    (C) She thinks the plant is totally unnecessary.
    (D) She thinks the utility company has a good idea.

GO ON TO THE NEXT PAGE

## Part C

**Directions:** In this part of the test, you will hear several talks. After each talk, you will hear some questions. The talks and questions will not be repeated.

After you hear a question, read the four possible answers in your test book and choose the best answer. Then, on your answer sheet, find the number of the question and fill in the space that corresponds to the letter of the answer you have chosen.

Here is an example.

On the recording, you hear:

(narrator)    *Listen to an instructor talk to his class about painting.*

(man)    *Artist Grant Wood was a guiding force in the school of painting known as American regionalist, a style reflecting the distinctive characteristics of art from rural areas of the United States. Wood began drawing animals on the family farm at the age of three, and when he was thirty-eight one of his paintings received a remarkable amount of public notice and acclaim. This painting, called* American Gothic, *is a starkly simple depiction of a serious couple staring directly out at the viewer.*

Now listen to a sample question.

**Sample Answer**

(narrator)    *What style of painting is known as American regionalist?*

Ⓐ
Ⓑ
Ⓒ
●

In your test book, you read:    (A)  Art from America's inner cities.
(B)  Art from the central region of the U.S.
(C)  Art from various urban areas in the U.S.
(D)  Art from rural sections of America.

The best answer to the question, "What style of painting is known as American regionalist?" is (D), "Art from rural sections of America." Therefore, the correct choice is (D).

Now listen to another sample question.

**Sample Answer**

(narrator)    *What is the name of Wood's most successful painting?*

Ⓐ
Ⓑ
●
Ⓓ

In your test book, you read:    (A)  "American Regionalist."
(B)  "The Family Farm in Iowa."
(C)  "American Gothic."
(D)  "A Serious Couple."

The best answer to the question, "What is the name of Wood's most successful painting?" is (C), "American Gothic." Therefore, the correct choice is (C).

Remember, you are <u>not</u> allowed to take notes or write in your test book.

39. (A) The Employment Office manager.
    (B) The university registrar.
    (C) The bookstore manager.
    (D) A student working in the bookstore.

40. (A) Prepare a schedule.
    (B) Decide which workers to hire.
    (C) Plan student course schedules.
    (D) Train office workers.

41. (A) What the students' majors are.
    (B) When the students are able to work.
    (C) Why the students want to work.
    (D) In which jobs the students have
        experience.

42. (A) Cashier.
    (B) Shelf stocker.
    (C) Business office worker.
    (D) Phone operator.

43. (A) Soft, warm clothing.
    (B) Problems in landfills.
    (C) How fleece is obtained.
    (D) Recycling soda bottles.

44. (A) They were left in landfill areas.
    (B) They were reused.
    (C) They were recycled.
    (D) They were refilled.

45. (A) Dye.
    (B) Warm, soft clothing.
    (C) Computer chips.
    (D) Glass bottles.

46. (A) Buying plastic bottles.
    (B) Solving the problems in landfills.
    (C) Buying these recycled products.
    (D) Becoming aware of the environment.

47. (A) The Central Pacific Group.
    (B) The Transcontinental Railroad
        Company.
    (C) A group from Ogden, Utah.
    (D) Two separate railroad companies.

48. (A) They had to lay tracks across a
        mountain range.
    (B) They had to cross all of Nebraska.
    (C) They had to work for another railroad
        company.
    (D) They had to move westward to
        Sacramento, California.

49. (A) Several days.
    (B) Several weeks.
    (C) Several months.
    (D) Several years.

50. (A) Dynamite was used to blast out
        access.
    (B) A golden spike was hammered into
        the last track.
    (C) The workers labored dangerously and
        exhaustingly.
    (D) The workers traversed the Sierra
        Nevadas.

**This is the end of Section 1.
Stop work on Section 1.**

**Turn off your cassette player.**

**Read the directions for Section 2 and begin work.
Do NOT read or work on any other section
of the test during the next 25 minutes.**

# 2 • 2 • 2 • 2 • 2 • 2 • 2 • 2 • 2

## STRUCTURE AND WRITTEN EXPRESSION
### Time—25 minutes
### (including the reading of the directions)
### Now set your clock for 25 minutes.

This section is designed to measure your ability to recognize language that is appropriate for standard written English. There are two types of questions in this section, with special directions for each type.

### Structure

**Directions:** Questions 1–15 are incomplete sentences. Beneath each sentence you will see four words or phrases, marked (A), (B), (C), and (D). Choose the <u>one</u> word or phrase that best completes the sentence. Then, on your answer sheet, find the number of the question and fill in the space that corresponds to the letter of the answer you have chosen. Fill in the space so that the letter inside the oval cannot be seen.

Look at the following examples.

*Example I*

The president _____ the election by a landslide.

(A)   won
(B)   he won
(C)   yesterday
(D)   fortunately

**Sample Answer**

● B C D

The sentence should read, "The president won the election by a landslide." Therefore, you should choose (A).

*Example II*

When _____ the conference?

(A)   the doctor attended
(B)   did the doctor attend
(C)   the doctor will attend
(D)   the doctor's attendance

**Sample Answer**

A ● C D

The sentence should read, "When did the doctor attend the conference?" Therefore, you should choose (B).

Now begin work on the questions.

GO ON TO THE NEXT PAGE ➔

1. _____ of the Stamp Act in 1765 provoked strong opposition among the American colonists.

   (A) The passage was
   (B) It was the passage
   (C) Before the passage
   (D) The passage

2. In 1905 Juneau replaced Sitka _____ Alaska.

   (A) the capital was
   (B) as the capital of
   (C) was the capital of
   (D) the capital being

3. _____ were first viewed through a telescope by Galileo.

   (A) Jupiter has four moons
   (B) Jupiter's four moons
   (C) Jupiter surrounded by four moons
   (D) Surrounded by four moons, Jupiter

4. _____ the end of the Ice Age around 8000 B.C., mammoths became extinct.

   (A) With
   (B) It was
   (C) That
   (D) In addition

5. There are two basic kinds of air compressors, reciprocating and _____.

   (A) another kind that is rotating
   (B) one that rotates
   (C) a rotating kind
   (D) rotating

6. The human body has four jugular veins, _____ each side of the neck.

   (A) there are two on
   (B) it has two on
   (C) two are on
   (D) two on

7. _____ its proximity to New York, New Jersey is an important link in the nation's transportation system.

   (A) Since
   (B) As a result
   (C) However
   (D) Because of

8. Agronomists work to improve the quality of crops, increase the yield of fields, and _____ of the soil.

   (A) the quality is maintained
   (B) maintain the quality
   (C) the maintenance of the quality
   (D) maintaining the quality

9. From 1898 to 1933, the U.S. Weather Bureau obtained information about the weather from _____ to box kites.

   (A) attached devices
   (B) attached to devices
   (C) devices attached
   (D) devices were attached

10. Projective tests _____ as the Rorschach Test have no right or wrong answers.

    (A) such
    (B) similar
    (C) like
    (D) same

11. One purpose _____ to decide if there is sufficient evidence to try a person for a crime.

    (A) of a grand jury is
    (B) of a grand jury
    (C) for a grand jury
    (D) of a grand jury which is

**GO ON TO THE NEXT PAGE** →

12. _____ in 1937, the Golden Gate Bridge spans the channel at the entrance to San Francisco Bay.

    (A) Completes
    (B) Completed
    (C) Completing
    (D) To complete

13. A slipped disk is a condition _____ the intervertebral disk protrudes and presses on nerves.

    (A) what
    (B) which is
    (C) in which
    (D) that

14. Scientists stress that the overall warming trend of the last decade holds much more significance _____ single year's temperatures.

    (A) any do
    (B) than do any
    (C) than any do
    (D) do than

15. When _____ impulses from many of the neurons in one part of the brain, an epileptic seizure occurs.

    (A) the simultaneous bursts
    (B) simultaneously burst
    (C) there are simultaneous bursts of
    (D) simultaneously bursting

GO ON TO THE NEXT PAGE

## Written Expression

**Directions:** In questions 16–40, each sentence has four underlined words or phrases. The four underlined parts of the sentence are marked (A), (B), (C), and (D). Identify the <u>one</u> underlined word or phrase that must be changed in order for the sentence to be correct. Then, on your answer sheet, find the number of the question and fill in the space that corresponds to the letter of the answer you have chosen.

Look at the following examples.

*Example I*                                                                 **Sample Answer**

The four string on a violin are tuned
‾‾‾‾      ‾‾‾‾‾‾          ‾‾‾   ‾‾‾‾‾
A         B              C     D

in fifths.

Ⓐ
●
Ⓒ
Ⓓ

The sentence should read, "The four strings on a violin are tuned in fifths." Therefore, you should choose (B).

*Example II*                                                               **Sample Answer**

The research for the book *Roots* taking
‾‾‾‾‾‾‾‾   ‾‾‾‾‾‾‾‾‾           ‾‾‾‾‾‾
A          B                   C

Alex Haley twelve years.
‾‾‾‾‾‾‾‾‾‾‾
D

Ⓐ
Ⓑ
●
Ⓓ

The sentence should read, "The research for the book *Roots* took Alex Haley twelve years." Therefore, you should choose (C).

Now begin work on the questions.

**GO ON TO THE NEXT PAGE**

16. Latex rubber is <u>made from</u> a <u>milky</u> <u>substantial</u> in plants and <u>trees</u> of the sapodilla family.
                              A           B      C                        D

17. The state <u>with the</u> <u>most large</u> production of tobacco <u>products</u> <u>is</u> North Carolina.
                  A        B                              C  D

18. Ballads, <u>like</u> folk tales, began <u>thousands</u> of years ago <u>among</u> people who could not read or
             A                  B                C

    <u>writing</u>.
      D

19. <u>The first</u> professional baseball game it took place in 1846 <u>when the</u> New York Nine <u>defeated</u> the
      A                                   B             C                    D

    New York Knickerbockers 23 to 1.

20. <u>More than</u> 300 different <u>kinds</u> of nails is <u>manufactured</u> in the United States.
        A                    B        C      D

21. <u>Among</u> Thomas Jefferson's many <u>accomplishment</u> was <u>his</u> work <u>to establish</u> the University of
      A                                B          C        D

    Virginia.

22. The state of New Mexico <u>is not</u> densely <u>population</u>, <u>with an</u> average of <u>only</u> four people per square
                               A             B        C            D

    kilometer.

23. <u>Alike</u> bases <u>which</u> cause litmus to turn blue, <u>acids</u> <u>cause</u> litmus to turn red.
     A        B                          C   D

24. Plant cuttings <u>who</u> are <u>placed</u> in water will develop roots and can <u>then</u> be planted <u>in soil</u>.
                  A      B                             C        D

25. Lead <u>poisoning</u> can result if <u>to</u> much lead <u>builds up</u> in <u>the body</u>.
        A              B          C     D

26. Many American <u>childrens</u> learned to read <u>from</u> the <u>more than</u> 120 million copies of *McGuffy's*
                 A              B     C  D

    *Reader*.

27. In *A Farewell to Arms (1926)* Hemingway <u>tried</u> to <u>capture</u> the <u>feelings</u> the American people at
                                      A    B        C

    <u>the end of</u> World War I.
      D

28. From 1785 <u>to</u> 1790, <u>the</u> <u>capital</u> of the U.S. <u>is</u> located in New York City.
             A        B  C           D

29. <u>Many</u> Civil War battles <u>were fought</u> in Virginia than in any <u>other</u> <u>state</u>.
     A                 B                         C  D

30. When T. S. Eliot's *The Wasteland* appeared in 1922, <u>critics</u> were divided <u>as</u> to how <u>well</u> it was
                                            A              B      C

    <u>wrote</u>.
      D

**GO ON TO THE NEXT PAGE** ➡

31. The Wagner Act guarantees workers in the U.S. the right to organizing labor unions.
              A      B            C      D

32. According the kinetic theory, all matter consists of constantly moving particles.
        A                  B     C    D

33. The average salt content of seawater is more than 3 percents.
          A    B         C    D

34. The isotopes of one element can have different weighs.
        A     B        C  D

35. It is in the troposphere, the lowest part of the atmosphere, that wind, storms, and another kinds
                      A                  B        C

    of weather take place.
           D

36. The differing curricula at the community colleges in Kent County reflect the fact that the student
        A                                B

    population at each sites is not consistent.
             C      D

37. Of the two Diomede Islands, only one belongs the United States.
     A  B              C     D

38. The novels of Kurt Vonnegut present a desperately comic aware of human nature.
                   A     B      C     D

39. In spite of her physician handicaps, Helen Keller graduated from Radcliffe with honors.
        A      B                  C  D

40. Some toxins are produced by alive bacteria, but others are released only after a bacterium dies.
      A             B        C        D

**This is the end of Section 2.**
**If you finish before 25 minutes has ended,**
**check your work on Section 2 only.**

**At the end of 25 minutes, go on to Section 3.**
**Use exactly 55 minutes to work on Section 3.**

## SECTION 3
## READING COMPREHENSION
**Time—55 minutes**
**(including the reading of the directions)**
**Now set your clock for 55 minutes.**

This section is designed to measure your ability to read and understand short passages similar in topic and style to those that students are likely to encounter in North American universities and colleges.

**Directions:** In this section you will read several passages. Each one is followed by a number of questions about it. You are to choose the <u>one</u> best answer, (A), (B), (C), or (D), to each question. Then, on your answer sheet, find the number of the question and fill in the space that corresponds to the letter of the answer you have chosen.

Answer all questions about the information in a passage on the basis of what is <u>stated</u> or <u>implied</u> in that passage.

Read the following passage:

> John Quincy Adams, who served as the sixth president of the United States from 1825 to 1829, is today recognized for his masterful statesmanship and diplomacy. He dedicated his life to public service, both in the presidency and in the various other political offices that he
> *Line* held. Throughout this political career he demonstrated his unswerving belief in freedom of
> (5) speech, the antislavery cause, and the right of Americans to be free from European and Asian domination.

*Example I*                                                                 **Sample Answer**

To what did John Quincy Adams devote his life?

(A)   Improving his personal life
(B)   Serving the public
(C)   Increasing his fortune
(D)   Working on his private business

According to the passage, John Quincy Adams "dedicated his life to public service." Therefore, you should choose (B).

*Example II*                                                                **Sample Answer**

In line 4, the word "unswerving" is closest in meaning to

(A)   moveable
(B)   insignificant
(C)   unchanging
(D)   diplomatic

The passage states that John Quincy Adams demonstrated his unswerving belief "throughout his career." This implies that the belief did not change. Therefore, you should choose (C).

Now begin work on the questions.

**GO ON TO THE NEXT PAGE**

**Questions 1–9**

Samuel Morse accomplished something that is rarely accomplished: he achieved fame and success in two widely differing areas. Throughout his youth he studied art, and after graduating from Yale University he went on to London in 1811, where his early artistic endeavors met with acclaim. In
*Line* London he was awarded the gold medal of the Adelphi Art Society for a clay figure of Hercules, and his
(5) paintings *The Dying Hercules* and *The Judgement of Jupiter* were selected for exhibit by the Royal Academy. Later in life, after returning to America, Morse became known for his portraits. His portraits of the Marquis de Lafayette are on exhibit in the New York City Hall and the New York Public Library.

In addition to his artistic accomplishments, Morse is also well known for his work developing the telegraph and what is known as Morse Code. He first had the idea of trying to develop the telegraph
(10) in 1832, on board a ship returning to America from Europe. It took eleven long years of ridicule by his associates, disinterest by the public, and a shortage of funds before Congress finally allocated $30,000 to Morse for his project. With these funds, Morse hung a telegraph line from Washington, D.C., to Baltimore, and on May 24, 1844, a message in the dots and dashes of Morse Code was successfully transmitted.

1.  Which of the following is the best topic of this passage?

    (A)  Samuel Morse's artistic talents
    (B)  The use of Morse Code in art
    (C)  The invention of the telegraph
    (D)  Samuel Morse's varied successes

2.  The word "rarely" in line 1 is closest in meaning to which of the following?

    (A)  Never
    (B)  Seldom
    (C)  Usually
    (D)  Sometimes

3.  According to the passage, in his early life, Morse concentrated on preparing for which of the following careers?

    (A)  A career as an inventor
    (B)  A career as an artist
    (C)  A career as a telegraph operator
    (D)  A career developing Morse Code

4.  The word "acclaim" in line 3 is closest in meaning to

    (A)  amusement
    (B)  disinterest
    (C)  praise
    (D)  sorrow

5.  According to the passage, Morse won a prize for which of the following works?

    (A)  A statue of Hercules
    (B)  *The Dying Hercules*
    (C)  *The Judgement of Jupiter*
    (D)  A portrait of Lafayette

6.  The word "accomplishments" in line 8 is closest in meaning to

    (A)  disasters
    (B)  sensitivities
    (C)  desires
    (D)  achievements

**GO ON TO THE NEXT PAGE**

7. Which of the following is NOT mentioned as a problem encountered by Morse in developing the telegraph?

   (A) His coworkers laughed at him.
   (B) The public was not interested in what he was doing.
   (C) He suffered numerous mechanical problems.
   (D) He did not have enough money.

8. The expression "dots and dashes" in line 13 could best be replaced by which of the following?

   (A) Short sounds and long sounds
   (B) Circles and segments
   (C) Points and lines
   (D) Ups and downs

9. It is implied in the passage that the development of the telegraph

   (A) took place instantaneously
   (B) was more difficult for Morse than his artistic achievements
   (C) was a project that Morse often gave up on
   (D) was an idea that was really developed by someone else

GO ON TO THE NEXT PAGE

**Questions 10–20**

Mount Rushmore is a well-known monument in the Black Hills of South Dakota that features the countenances of four U. S. presidents: Washington, Jefferson, Roosevelt, and Lincoln. What is not so well known is that the process of creating this national treasure was not exactly an uneventful
*Line* one.
(5)    Mount Rushmore was the project of the visionary sculptor John Gutzen de la Mothe Borglum, who was born in Idaho but studied sculpture in Paris in his youth and befriended the famous French sculptor Auguste Rodin. In 1927 Borglum was granted a commission by the federal government to create the sculpture on Mount Rushmore. Though he was nearly sixty years old when he started, he was undaunted by the enormity of the project and the obstacles that it engendered. He optimistically
(10)  asserted that the project would be completed within five years, not caring to recognize the potential problems that such a massive project would involve, the problems of dealing with financing, with government bureaucracy, and with Mother Nature herself. An example of what Mother Nature had to throw at the project was the fissure that developed in the granite where Jefferson was being carved. Jefferson had to be moved to the other side of Washington, next to Roosevelt, because of the break in
(15)  the stone. The work that had been started on the first Jefferson had to be dynamited away.

Mount Rushmore was not completed within the five years predicted by Borglum and was in fact not actually completed within Borglum's lifetime, although it was almost finished. Borglum died on March 6, 1941, at the age of seventy-four, after fourteen years of work on the presidents. His son, Lincoln Borglum, who had worked with his father throughout the project, completed the monument
(20)  within eight months of his father's death.

10. Which of the following best expresses the main idea of the passage?

    (A)  Mount Rushmore was a huge project filled with numerous obstacles.
    (B)  Mount Rushmore is a famous American monument.
    (C)  Mount Rushmore has sculptures of four U.S. presidents on it.
    (D)  John Gutzen de la Mothe Borglum created Mount Rushmore.

11. The word "countenances" in line 2 could best be replaced by

    (A)  museums
    (B)  faces
    (C)  graves
    (D)  relatives

12. Which of the following best describes the relationship between Borglum and Rodin in Borglum's early years?

    (A)  Borglum studied about Rodin in Paris.
    (B)  Borglum was far more famous than Rodin as a sculptor.
    (C)  Borglum and Rodin were born and raised in the same place.
    (D)  Borglum and Rodin were friends.

13. The word "nearly" in line 8 could best be replaced by which of the following?

    (A)  Over
    (B)  Closely
    (C)  Almost
    (D)  Barely

**GO ON TO THE NEXT PAGE**

14. Which of the following is NOT true about Borglum?

    (A) He began Mount Rushmore around the age of sixty.
    (B) He predicted that Mount Rushmore would be finished around 1932.
    (C) Mount Rushmore was finished when Borglum predicted it would be.
    (D) Borglum worked on Mount Rushmore for more than a decade.

15. It can be inferred from the passage that Borglum was someone who

    (A) expected the best to happen
    (B) set realistic goals
    (C) never tried anything too challenging
    (D) was always afraid that bad things were going to happen

16. A "fissure" in line 13 is a

    (A) discoloration
    (B) crack
    (C) unevenness
    (D) softness

17. Why does the author mention the fact that the carving of Thomas Jefferson was moved?

    (A) It shows what a perfectionist Borglum was.
    (B) It demonstrates Borglum's artistic style.
    (C) It gives insight into Jefferson's character.
    (D) It is an example of a problem caused by nature.

18. The pronoun "it" in line 17 refers to which of the following?

    (A) The first Jefferson
    (B) Mount Rushmore
    (C) Borglum's lifetime
    (D) Fourteen years of work

19. Which of the following is closest in meaning to the expression "within eight months of his father's death" in line 20?

    (A) More than eight months before his father's death
    (B) Less than eight months before his father's death
    (C) Less than eight months after his father's death
    (D) More than eight months after his father's death

20. Where in the passage does the author mention when the Mount Rushmore project got started?

    (A) Lines 1–4
    (B) Lines 7–8
    (C) Lines 9–12
    (D) Lines 17–18

GO ON TO THE NEXT PAGE

**Questions 21–30**

Carbon dating can be used to estimate the age of any organic natural material; it has been used successfully in archeology to determine the age of ancient artifacts or fossils as well as in a variety of other fields. The principle underlying the use of carbon dating is that carbon is a part of all living
*Line* things on Earth. Since a radioactive substance such as carbon-14 has a known half-life, the amount of
(5) carbon-14 remaining in an object can be used to date that object.

Carbon-14 has a half-life of 5,570 years, which means that after that number of years half of the carbon-14 atoms have decayed into nitrogen-14. It is the ratio of carbon-14 to nitrogen-14 in that substance that indicates the age of the substance. If, for example, in a particular sample the amount of carbon-14 is roughly equivalent to the amount of nitrogen-14, this indicates that roughly half of the
(10) carbon-14 has decayed into nitrogen-14, and the sample is approximately 5,570 years old.

Carbon dating cannot be used effectively in dating objects that are older than 80,000 years. When objects are that old, much of the carbon-14 has already decayed into nitrogen-14, and the minuscule amount that is left does not provide a reliable measurement of age. In the case of older objects, other age-dating methods are available, methods which use radioactive atoms with longer half-lives than
(15) carbon has.

21. This passage is mainly about

    (A) the differences between carbon-14 and nitrogen-14
    (B) one method of dating old objects
    (C) archeology and the study of ancient artifacts
    (D) various uses for carbon

22. The word "estimate" in line 1 is closest in meaning to

    (A) understand
    (B) hide
    (C) rate
    (D) approximate

23. The pronoun "it" in line 1 refers to

    (A) carbon dating
    (B) the age
    (C) any organic natural material
    (D) archeology

24. Which of the following is NOT true about carbon-14?

    (A) It is radioactive.
    (B) Its half-life is more than 5,000 years.
    (C) It and nitrogen always exist in equal amounts in any substance.
    (D) It can decay into nitrogen-14.

25. The word "underlying" in line 3 could best be replaced by

    (A) below
    (B) requiring
    (C) being studied through
    (D) serving as a basis for

26. It can be inferred from the passage that if an item contains more carbon-14 than nitrogen-14, then the item is

    (A) too old to be age-dated with carbon-14
    (B) not as much as 5,570 years old
    (C) too radioactive to be used by archeologists
    (D) more than 5,570 years old

27. The expression "roughly equivalent" in line 9 could best be replaced by

    (A) exactly the same
    (B) similar in all respects
    (C) rather ambivalent
    (D) approximately equal

**GO ON TO THE NEXT PAGE**

28. The expression "is left" in line 13 could best be replaced by

    (A) remains
    (B) has disappeared
    (C) changes
    (D) is gone

29. It is implied in the passage that

    (A) carbon dating could not be used on an item containing nitrogen
    (B) fossils cannot be age-dated using carbon-14
    (C) carbon-14 does not have the longest known half-life
    (D) carbon dating has no known uses outside of archeology

30. The paragraph following the passage most probably discusses

    (A) how carbon-14 decays into nitrogen-1
    (B) various other age-dating methods
    (C) why carbon-14 has such a long half-life
    (D) what substances are part of all living things

GO ON TO THE NEXT PAGE

**Questions 31–39**

In the beginning of the nineteenth century, the American educational system was desperately in need of reform. Private schools existed, but only for the very rich, and there were very few public schools because of the strong sentiment that children who would grow up to be laborers should not
*Line* "waste" their time on education but should instead prepare themselves for their life's work. It was in
*(5)* the face of this public sentiment that educational reformers set about their task. Horace Mann, probably the most famous of the reformers, felt that there was no excuse in a republic for any citizen to be uneducated. As Superintendent of Education in the state of Massachusetts from 1837 to 1848, he initiated various changes, which were soon matched in other school districts around the country. He extended the school year from five to six months and improved the quality of teachers by instituting
*(10)* teacher education and raising teacher salaries. Although these changes did not bring about a sudden improvement in the educational system, they at least increased public awareness as to the need for a further strengthening of the system.

31. Which of the following would be the most appropriate title for the passage?

(A) A Fight for Change
(B) Nineteenth-Century Reform
(C) American Education
(D) The Beginnings of Reform in American Education

32. It is implied in the passage that to go to a private school, a student needed

(A) a high level of intelligence
(B) a strong educational background
(C) good grades
(D) a lot of money

33. The word "sentiment" in line 3 is closest in meaning to

(A) action
(B) opinion
(C) sensation
(D) disagreement

34. Why is the word "waste" in line 4 punctuated in this manner?

(A) The author wants to emphasize how much time was wasted on education.
(B) The author is quoting someone else who said that education was a waste of time.
(C) The author thinks that education is not really a waste of time.
(D) The author does not want students to waste their time on education.

35. What are "reformers" in line 5?

(A) People who try to change things for the better
(B) People who really enjoy teaching
(C) People who believe that education is wasted
(D) People who work for the government

GO ON TO THE NEXT PAGE

36. According to the passage, why did Horace Mann want a better educational system for Americans?

   (A) Education at the time was so cheap.
   (B) In a republic, all citizens should be educated.
   (C) People had nothing else to do except go to school.
   (D) Massachusetts residents needed something to do with their spare time.

37. The word "initiated" in line 8 is closest in meaning to

   (A) regretted
   (B) broadened
   (C) overturned
   (D) started

38. The word "matched" in line 8 could best be replaced by

   (A) observed
   (B) equaled
   (C) fitted
   (D) burnt

39. According to the passage, which of the following is a change that Horace Mann instituted?

   (A) Better teacher training
   (B) Increased pay for students
   (C) The five-month school year
   (D) The matching of other districts' policies

GO ON TO THE NEXT PAGE

**Questions 40–50**

In 1969, the Apollo 11 astronauts made their historic landing on the surface of the Moon. This momentous trip for humanity also provided scientists with an abundance of material for study; from rock and soil samples brought back from the Moon, scientists have been able to determine much about
*Line* the composition of the Moon as well as to draw inferences about the development of the Moon from its
*(5)* composition.

The Moon soil that came back on Apollo 11 contains small bits of rock and glass which were probably ground from larger rocks when meteors impacted with the surface of the Moon. The bits of glass are spherical in shape and constitute approximately half of the Moon soil. Scientists found no trace of animal or plant life in this soil.
*(10)* In addition to the Moon soil, astronauts gathered two basic types of rocks from the surface of the Moon: *basalt* and *breccia*. Basalt is a cooled and hardened volcanic lava common to the Earth. Since basalt is formed under extremely high temperatures, the presence of this type of rock is an indication that the temperature of the Moon was once extremely hot. Breccia, the other kind of rock brought back by the astronauts, was formed during the impact of falling objects on the surface of the Moon. This
*(15)* second type of rock consists of small pieces of rock compressed together by the force of impact. Gases, such as hydrogen and helium, were found in some of the rocks, and scientists believe that these gases were carried to the Moon by the solar wind, the streams of gases that are constantly emitted by the Sun.

40. Which of the following would be the most appropriate title for this passage?

    (A) The Apollo Astronauts
    (B) Soil on the Moon
    (C) What the Moon Is Made Of
    (D) Basalt and Breccia

41. An "abundance" in line 2 is

    (A) a disorderly pile
    (B) a wealthy bunch
    (C) an insignificant proportion
    (D) a large amount

42. According to the passage, what does Moon soil consist of?

    (A) Hydrogen and helium
    (B) Large chunks of volcanic lava
    (C) Tiny pieces of stones and glass
    (D) Streams of gases

43. The word "spherical" in line 8 is closest in meaning to

    (A) earthen
    (B) circular
    (C) angular
    (D) amorphous

44. Which of the following was NOT brought back to the Earth by the astronauts?

    (A) Basalt
    (B) Soil
    (C) Breccia
    (D) Plant life

45. An "indication" in line 12 is

    (A) an exhibition
    (B) a clue
    (C) a denial
    (D) a dictate

**GO ON TO THE NEXT PAGE**

46. According to the passage, breccia was formed

   (A)  when objects struck the Moon
   (B)  from volcanic lava
   (C)  when streams of gases hit the surface of the Moon
   (D)  from the interaction of helium and hydrogen

47. It is implied in the passage that scientists believe that the gases found in the Moon rocks

   (A)  were not originally from the Moon
   (B)  were created inside the rocks
   (C)  traveled from the Moon to the Sun
   (D)  caused the Moon's temperature to rise

48. The word "emitted" in line 17 is closest in meaning to

   (A)  set off
   (B)  vaporized
   (C)  sent out
   (D)  separated

49. The author's purpose in this passage is to

   (A)  describe some rock and soil samples
   (B)  explain some of the things learned from space flights
   (C)  propose a new theory about the creation of the Moon
   (D)  demonstrate the difference between *basalt* and *breccia*

50. It can be inferred from the passage that

   (A)  the only items of importance that astronauts brought back from the Moon were rock and soil samples
   (B)  scientists learned relatively little from the Moon rock and soil samples
   (C)  scientists do not believe that it is necessary to return to the Moon
   (D)  rock and soil samples were only some of a myriad of significant items from the Moon

**This is the end of Section 3.**

**If you finish in less than 55 minutes,
check your work on Section 3 only.
Do NOT read or work on any other section of the test.**

# TEST OF WRITTEN ENGLISH
## TWE ESSAY TOPIC
### Time—30 minutes

Do you agree or disagree with the following statement?

*People should always be polite, no matter what the situation.*

Use specific reasons and details to support your answer. Write your answer on the answer sheet for the Test of Written English, Practice Test Two, on pages 185–186.

# 1 □ 1 □ 1 □ 1 □ 1 □ 1 □ 1 □ 1 □ 1

# PRACTICE TEST THREE

## SECTION 1
## LISTENING COMPREHENSION
### Time—approximately 35 minutes
### (including the reading of the directions for each part)

In this section of the test, you will have the opportunity to demonstrate your ability to understand conversations and talks in English. There are three parts to this section. Answer all the questions on the basis of what is <u>stated</u> or <u>implied</u> by the speakers you hear. Do <u>not</u> take notes or write in your test book at any time. Do not turn the pages until you are told to do so.

### Part A

**Directions:** In Part A you will hear short conversations between two people. After each conversation, you will hear a question about the conversation. The conversations and questions will not be repeated. After you hear a question, read the four possible answers in your test book and choose the best answer. Then, on your answer sheet, find the number of the question and fill in the space that corresponds to the letter of the answer you have chosen.

Listen to an example.

**Sample Answer**

Ⓐ Ⓑ Ⓒ ●

On the recording, you hear:

| (man) | *That exam was just awful.* |
| (woman) | *Oh, it could have been worse.* |
| (narrator) | *What does the woman mean?* |

In your test book, you read:
(A)  The exam was really awful.
(B)  It was the worst exam she had ever seen.
(C)  It couldn't have been more difficult.
(D)  It wasn't that hard.

You learn from the conversation that the man thought the exam was very difficult and that the woman disagreed with the man. The best answer to the question, "What does the woman mean?" is (D), "It wasn't that hard." Therefore, the correct choice is (D).

**Wait**

1. (A) At a sporting event.
   (B) In front of the police station.
   (C) In front of a movie theater.
   (D) At a film developer's.

2. (A) Leave the session.
   (B) Sit down.
   (C) Mind him.
   (D) Conduct the session.

3. (A) The presentation is soon.
   (B) She suggests working on the project at 12:00.
   (C) She'd like to meet the man later today for lunch.
   (D) She'll present her work to the man.

4. (A) The woman is always talking about the test.
   (B) It's all right if the woman keeps talking.
   (C) He would like the woman to repeat what she said.
   (D) He agrees that the exam was terrible.

5. (A) A surveyor.
   (B) An architect.
   (C) A gardener.
   (D) A hairdresser.

6. (A) He's reserved in answering the question.
   (B) It's possible to sit anywhere.
   (C) Some of the seats are being saved for others.
   (D) There's only one section of seats.

7. (A) She doesn't like the idea of bringing a camera.
   (B) Using a camera with sound is a bad idea.
   (C) She doesn't like the sound of the camera.
   (D) She'd like to take some pictures.

8. (A) He's finished with the dishes.
   (B) He worked on his term paper after finishing the dishes.
   (C) He doesn't like doing his term paper.
   (D) The dishes aren't done yet.

9. (A) It's too far to go.
   (B) She would also like to drop a class.
   (C) She believes that it's possible.
   (D) It's possible to drop classes.

10. (A) The size of the electric bill.
    (B) A problem with the lights.
    (C) Turning in the utility bill.
    (D) Keeping the utility bill high.

11. (A) She typed every word of the lecture.
    (B) She needs the tape to listen to the lecture again.
    (C) She didn't understand that the lecture would be taped.
    (D) She's glad that the lecturer didn't understand a word.

12. (A) That she leave New York with Mike.
    (B) That she go to the airport after work.
    (C) That she ask someone else to take her.
    (D) That she leave tomorrow at noon.

13. (A) They haven't finished their work.
    (B) The factory will shut down because it's late.
    (C) They aren't supposed to work at night.
    (D) They should shout about how much they have to do.

14. (A) He doesn't like the Bahamas.
    (B) He can't make time for a trip to the Bahamas.
    (C) He can't afford the trip.
    (D) He wants to spend his money in the Bahamas.

15. (A) It's been partly fixed.
    (B) It's unrepaired.
    (C) It was left exactly as it had been.
    (D) Bob left only part of it.

16. (A) Get drinks.
    (B) Watch the game for now.
    (C) Listen to the anthem.
    (D) Finish the game.

**GO ON TO THE NEXT PAGE** ➤

17. (A) He's seen the announcement.
    (B) He isn't sure what the announcement means.
    (C) He's uncertain where the lobby is.
    (D) He doesn't know what she's referring to.

18. (A) It's rare for her to work during her time off.
    (B) Her office is vacant when she has time off.
    (C) She almost never takes a break from her job.
    (D) Her vacations are rarely full of work.

19. (A) She's doubtful about the lecture.
    (B) She'll go to the lecture without her watch.
    (C) The worth of the lecture is uncertain.
    (D) She believes the talk will be valuable.

20. (A) This is the second largest football crowd ever.
    (B) This is the only time that a large crowd has attended a football game.
    (C) This is only the second football game this year.
    (D) There have never before been so many people at a football game.

21. (A) They should look at some property with an agent.
    (B) They should find out about buying skis.
    (C) They should get some more information.
    (D) They should make a deal with the travel agent.

22. (A) He doesn't like to meet most people.
    (B) He doesn't look like he participates in sports.
    (C) It occurred to him that most people aren't athletes.
    (D) He isn't an athlete.

23. (A) She couldn't have said anything.
    (B) She must have said all that she could.
    (C) She couldn't have said that.
    (D) She must have said more.

24. (A) All of her exams are over, too.
    (B) She's happy for him that his exams are over.
    (C) The man is wrong about what he believes.
    (D) She still has more exams to take.

25. (A) She and the man are in agreement.
    (B) She'd like to go to the Moon.
    (C) She thinks the airplane's flying reasonably high.
    (D) She finds the prices reasonable.

26. (A) The amount that he prepared was unbelievable.
    (B) She was surprised that he wasn't ready.
    (C) It was impossible to prepare for his presentation.
    (D) What he presented was unbelievable.

27. (A) She didn't leave when the report was finished.
    (B) The report never got finished.
    (C) She was unable to leave because it never got done.
    (D) Of course she completed the work.

28. (A) He never gives them any help.
    (B) He enjoys working in the garden.
    (C) He never gives direct answers.
    (D) He always beats them when they play.

29. (A) The man was not interested in the tickets.
    (B) The man wanted to buy the tickets.
    (C) The man really wanted to attend the concert.
    (D) The man was able to afford the tickets.

30. (A) He had something important to show the woman at the meeting.
    (B) He thought the woman was not going to come.
    (C) He waited to try to show the woman up.
    (D) He thought he would have to show the woman where the meeting was.

**GO ON TO THE NEXT PAGE**

## Part B

**Directions:** In this part of the test, you will hear longer conversations. After each conversation, you will hear several questions. The conversations and questions will not be repeated.

After you hear a question, read the four possible answers in your test book and choose the best answer. Then, on your answer sheet, find the number of the question and fill in the space that corresponds to the letter of the answer you have chosen.

Remember, you are <u>not</u> allowed to take notes or write in your test book.

31. (A) To write his paper.
    (B) To help him decide on a topic.
    (C) To teach him about history.
    (D) To discuss history with him.

32. (A) At the beginning of the semester.
    (B) Before the start of the semester.
    (C) Near the end of the semester.
    (D) One week after the semester is finished.

33. (A) The topic's too general.
    (B) He isn't interested in technology.
    (C) He doesn't have enough time.
    (D) Technology has nothing to do with American history.

34. (A) A month.
    (B) The semester.
    (C) Seven days.
    (D) A day or two.

35. (A) Fire damage to some apartments.
    (B) How to prevent fires.
    (C) An apartment fire and what one can learn from it.
    (D) An early morning news story.

36. (A) One was damaged more severely than the others.
    (B) All the apartments were completely destroyed.
    (C) There was one thousand dollars of damage.
    (D) All twenty apartments suffered some damage.

37. (A) They were killed.
    (B) They were taken to the hospital.
    (C) The damage to the apartments was more serious than the harm to the residents.
    (D) They weren't frightened.

38. (A) Call the fire department.
    (B) Rush to the hospital.
    (C) Listen for a smoke alarm.
    (D) Have an alarm and extinguisher in good condition.

**GO ON TO THE NEXT PAGE**

## Part C

**Directions:** In this part of the test, you will hear several talks. After each talk, you will hear some questions. The talks and questions will not be repeated.

After you hear a question, read the four possible answers in your test book and choose the best answer. Then, on your answer sheet, find the number of the question and fill in the space that corresponds to the letter of the answer you have chosen.

Here is an example.

On the recording, you hear:

(narrator) *Listen to an instructor talk to his class about painting.*

(man) *Artist Grant Wood was a guiding force in the school of painting known as American regionalist, a style reflecting the distinctive characteristics of art from rural areas of the United States. Wood began drawing animals on the family farm at the age of three, and when he was thirty-eight one of his paintings received a remarkable amount of public notice and acclaim. This painting, called* American Gothic, *is a starkly simple depiction of a serious couple staring directly out at the viewer.*

Now listen to a sample question.                                **Sample Answer**

(narrator) *What style of painting is known as American regionalist?*

In your test book, you read:     (A)   Art from America's inner cities.
                                 (B)   Art from the central region of the U.S.
                                 (C)   Art from various urban areas in the U.S.
                                 (D)   Art from rural sections of America.

The best answer to the question, "What style of painting is known as American regionalist?" is (D), "Art from rural sections of America." Therefore, the correct choice is (D).

Now listen to another sample question.                          **Sample Answer**

(narrator) *What is the name of Wood's most successful painting?*

In your test book, you read:     (A)   "American Regionalist."
                                 (B)   "The Family Farm in Iowa."
                                 (C)   "American Gothic."
                                 (D)   "A Serious Couple."

The best answer to the question, "What is the name of Wood's most successful painting?" is (C), "American Gothic." Therefore, the correct choice is (C).

Remember, you are <u>not</u> allowed to take notes or write in your test book.

39. (A) A professional dancer.
    (B) A student in the dance department.
    (C) The head of the dance department.
    (D) A choreographer.

40. (A) Which dance degree to take.
    (B) Whether or not to major in dance.
    (C) Whether to be a professional dancer
        or choreographer.
    (D) Whether to specialize in dance
        therapy or dance history.

41. (A) Physical therapy.
    (B) Dance history.
    (C) Choreography.
    (D) Dance administration.

42. (A) They are both intended for
        professional dancers.
    (B) They involve mostly the same
        courses.
    (C) They do not need to be selected until
        later.
    (D) They are both four-year programs.

43. (A) A Cajun.
    (B) A tourist.
    (C) An Acadian.
    (D) A tour guide.

44. (A) They went to Acadia in the eighteenth
        century.
    (B) They came from France in the
        eighteenth century.
    (C) They maintained characteristics of
        their old culture.
    (D) They assimilated completely into the
        new culture.

45. (A) Very spicy.
    (B) Full of sugar.
    (C) Salty.
    (D) Full of tobacco.

46. (A) An Acadian will give a talk.
    (B) The bus ride will continue.
    (C) They will stop in Lafayette.
    (D) They will see the exhibition at
        Acadian Village.

47. (A) The purpose of the FCC.
    (B) The relatively rapid development of
        radio.
    (C) Interference from competing radio
        stations.
    (D) The first U.S. radio station.

48. (A) Introduction to Engineering.
    (B) Popular Radio Programs.
    (C) Ethics in Journalism.
    (D) The History of Communication.

49. (A) The many radio stations were highly
        regulated.
    (B) In 1930 there was only one radio
        station in the U.S.
    (C) The existing radio stations were
        totally uncontrolled.
    (D) The FCC was unable to control the
        radio stations.

50. (A) First Communications Committee.
    (B) First Control Committee.
    (C) Federal Control of Communications.
    (D) Federal Communications
        Commission.

**This is the end of Section 1.
Stop work on Section 1.**

**Turn off your cassette player.**

STOP STOP STOP **STOP** STOP STOP STOP

**Read the directions for Section 2 and begin work.
Do NOT read or work on any other section
of the test during the next 25 minutes.**

## SECTION 2
## STRUCTURE AND WRITTEN EXPRESSION
**Time—25 minutes**
**(including the reading of the directions)**
**Now set your clock for 25 minutes.**

This section is designed to measure your ability to recognize language that is appropriate for standard written English. There are two types of questions in this section, with special directions for each type.

### Structure

**Directions:** Questions 1–15 are incomplete sentences. Beneath each sentence you will see four words or phrases, marked (A), (B), (C), and (D). Choose the <u>one</u> word or phrase that best completes the sentence. Then, on your answer sheet, find the number of the question and fill in the space that corresponds to the letter of the answer you have chosen. Fill in the space so that the letter inside the oval cannot be seen.

Look at the following examples.

*Example I*                                         **Sample Answer**

The president _____ the election by a landslide.        ● Ⓑ Ⓒ Ⓓ

    (A)  won
    (B)  he won
    (C)  yesterday
    (D)  fortunately

The sentence should read, "The president won the election by a landslide." Therefore, you should choose (A).

*Example II*                                        **Sample Answer**

When ___ the conference?                                 Ⓐ ● Ⓒ Ⓓ

    (A)  the doctor attended
    (B)  did the doctor attend
    (C)  the doctor will attend
    (D)  the doctor's attendance

The sentence should read, "When did the doctor attend the conference?" Therefore, you should choose (B).

Now begin work on the questions.

**GO ON TO THE NEXT PAGE**

1. Overexposure to the sun causes _____ health problems.

   (A) various
   (B) among
   (C) but
   (D) of

2. Birds head south to warmer climates when _____.

   (A) is cold weather
   (B) does cold weather come
   (C) cold weather comes
   (D) comes cold weather

3. The city council is empowered not only to enact new laws, _____ select a new mayor between elections should the need arise.

   (A) and to
   (B) but also to
   (C) and
   (D) so that

4. Drying of meats and vegetables is no longer considered one of _____ of preserving food.

   (A) the ways are useful
   (B) useful ways
   (C) the most useful ways
   (D) most are useful ways

5. A giant kind of grass, bamboo may reach a height of 120 feet and _____.

   (A) a diameter of 1 foot
   (B) its diameter is 1 foot
   (C) there is a diameter of 1 foot
   (D) which is a diameter of 1 foot

6. Somerset Maugham, a novelist, _____ about a restless man's quest for inner understanding in *The Razor's Edge*.

   (A) who wrote this
   (B) who wrote
   (C) when he wrote
   (D) wrote

7. Aspirin is used _____ a constriction of the blood vessels.

   (A) the counteraction
   (B) to counteract
   (C) counteract
   (D) counteracting

8. The nuthatch _____ six inches long.

   (A) grows seldom more than
   (B) more than seldom grows
   (C) seldom grows more than
   (D) grows more than seldom

9. Composing more than 40 percent of the diet, fats are _____ by the body for energy.

   (A) using specifically
   (B) used specifically
   (C) specific use
   (D) the specific use

10. The sea mammal *medusa* is popularly called a jellyfish because it _____ jelly.

    (A) looks rather like
    (B) looks like rather
    (C) likes looking rather
    (D) rather likes looking

11. Therapists are currently using mental imagery in the hope that it might prove _____ in the treatment of cancer.

    (A) helpful
    (B) for help
    (C) helpfully
    (D) with the help

**GO ON TO THE NEXT PAGE**

12. By praying outside saloons, throwing rocks in saloon windows, and destroying saloons with her hatchet, _____.

    (A) alcohol was prohibited by Carrie Nation
    (B) Carrie Nation worked to prohibit alcohol
    (C) prohibiting alcohol by Carrie Nation
    (D) Carrie Nation's work for the prohibition of alcohol

13. More drugmakers are changing their target market from physician to patient _____ the patient as the key to increasing market share.

    (A) that they see
    (B) sees them
    (C) they see
    (D) in that they see

14. _____ cockroach is the pest most in need of eradication is generally agreed upon by housing authorities everywhere.

    (A) When the
    (B) It is the
    (C) That the
    (D) The

15. _____, the jaguar used to roam freely in the southwestern United States.

    (A) It is now found only in Central and South America
    (B) Finding in Central and South America
    (C) To be found in Central and South America
    (D) Now found only in Central and South America

GO ON TO THE NEXT PAGE

## Written Expression

**Directions:** In questions 16–40, each sentence has four underlined words or phrases. The four underlined parts of the sentence are marked (A), (B), (C), and (D). Identify the <u>one</u> underlined word or phrase that must be changed in order for the sentence to be correct. Then, on your answer sheet, find the number of the question and fill in the space that corresponds to the letter of the answer you have chosen.

Look at the following examples.

*Example I*                                                  **Sample Answer**

                                                                   (A) ● (C) (D)

    The four <u>string</u> on a violin <u>are</u> <u>tuned</u>
    <u> A </u>     B             C   D

    in fifths.

The sentence should read, "The four strings on a violin are tuned in fifths." Therefore, you should choose (B).

*Example II*                                                  **Sample Answer**

                                                                     (A) (B) ● (D)

    The <u>research</u> <u>for the</u> book *Roots* <u>taking</u>
           A       B                   C

    Alex Haley <u>twelve years.</u>
                   D

The sentence should read, "The research for the book *Roots* took Alex Haley twelve years." Therefore, you should choose (C).

Now begin work on the questions.

**GO ON TO THE NEXT PAGE** ➤

16. The larger of the forty-eight continental states in the United States is Texas.
        A                  B            C              D

17. According to the experts, genetic inheritance is probability the most important factor in
                              A                  B    C

    determining a person's health.
        D

18. The railroad was one of the first methods of transportation to be use extensively in early
                A    B                              C          D

    American history.

19. Often when the weather is extremely hot, people have very thirsty but are not terribly hungry.
      A                                   B         C        D

20. Pioneers on the plains sometimes living in dugouts, sod rooms cut into hillsides.
            A          B     C                  D

21. Balloons have been used in various wars not only to direct artillery fire and report troop
                  A      B

    movements however to carry bombs and protect against low-flying planes.
             C                    D

22. The National Wildflower Research Center which was established in 1982 by Lady Bird Johnson
                                         A                  B

    on sixty acres of land east of Austin.
           C        D

23. The idea that artistic achievements rank in importance with scientific achievements has been
           A                    B

    upheld by painters, writers, and musicals for centuries.
      C                          D

24. To improvement the stability of the building, a concrete foundation two feet thick must be
         A          B                           C

    installed.
      D

25. In 1786 Benjamin Franklin first suggested daylight savings time as a means of cutting down on
                          A                        B   C

    the consumes of candles.
        D

26. An alligator is an animal somewhat like a crocodile, but with a broad, flatten snout.
               A      B             C         D

27. An extremely dangerous forms of cocaine, crack attacks the nervous system, brain, and body in a
                   A               B                        C

    sharper fashion than cocaine.
      D

28. It is the role of the National Bureau of Standards to establish accurate measurements for science,
    A                                    B          C

    industrial, and commerce.
      D

**GO ON TO THE NEXT PAGE** ➤

29. <u>Into among</u> the five Great Lakes, only Lake Michigan <u>is located</u> <u>entirely</u> within the <u>territorial</u>
       A                                       B     C              D
    boundaries of the United States.

30. Teddy Roosevelt <u>demonstrated</u> his <u>competitive</u> spirit and tireless energy in 1905 <u>what</u> he <u>led</u>
                        A           B                             C   D
    the Rough Riders up San Juan Hill.

31. The "Fairness Doctrine" of the FCC <u>requires that</u> radio and television <u>stations</u> give equal time to
                                       A                         B

    <u>opposing sides</u> of <u>issues controversial</u>.
           C             D

32. Mary Harris Jones, <u>known</u> as "Mother Jones," was a <u>prominence</u> figure in the <u>labor movement</u> at
                       A                            B               C
    the <u>turn</u> of the century.
        D

33. <u>Consequently</u> the kit fox is <u>an</u> endangered species, wildlife experts in the California desert are
        A               B
    <u>using</u> various methods to protect <u>it</u>.
      C                      D

34. <u>In addition</u> to <u>serving</u> as <u>members</u> of the president's cabinet, the attorney general is <u>the head</u>
       A        B        C                                     D
    of the Justice Department.

35. The need <u>to improve</u> technique <u>motivates</u> ballerinas <u>exercising</u> and rehearse for hours <u>daily</u>.
             A                 B               C                      D

36. The narwhal can be easily <u>to recognize</u> by the long <u>spiraled</u> tusk <u>attached</u> to the left side of <u>its</u> head.
                             A             B       C                 D

37. The <u>poet</u> Ogden Nash <u>often used</u> a <u>comic</u> style <u>to do</u> a serious point.
        A               B      C     D

38. The water in the Great Salt Lake is <u>a</u> <u>less</u> <u>four times</u> <u>saltier than</u> seawater.
                                     A   B    C   D

39. On February 20, 1962, *Friendship 7* <u>has</u> orbited the Earth in a <u>manned</u> <u>flight</u> that <u>lasted just</u>
                                          A                 B    C        D
    under five hours.

40. It <u>has been</u> suggested that the battleship *Missouri* <u>be</u> brought back to <u>active</u> duty, at <u>cost</u> of
       A                                           B             C    D
    $475 million.

**This is the end of Section 2.**
**If you finish before 25 minutes has ended,**
**check your work on Section 2 only.**

**At the end of 25 minutes, go on to Section 3.**
**Use exactly 55 minutes to work on Section 3.**

## SECTION 3
## READING COMPREHENSION
### Time—55 minutes
### (including the reading of the directions)
### Now set your clock for 55 minutes.

This section is designed to measure your ability to read and understand short passages similar in topic and style to those that students are likely to encounter in North American universities and colleges.

**Directions:** In this section you will read several passages. Each one is followed by a number of questions about it. You are to choose the <u>one</u> best answer, (A), (B), (C), or (D), to each question. Then, on your answer sheet, find the number of the question and fill in the space that corresponds to the letter of the answer you have chosen.

Answer all questions about the information in a passage on the basis of what is <u>stated</u> or <u>implied</u> in that passage.

Read the following passage:

> John Quincy Adams, who served as the sixth president of the United States from 1825 to 1829, is today recognized for his masterful statesmanship and diplomacy. He dedicated his life to public service, both in the presidency and in the various other political offices that he
> *Line* held. Throughout his political career he demonstrated his unswerving belief in freedom of
> (5) speech, the antislavery cause, and the right of Americans to be free from European and Asian domination.

**Sample Answer**

Ⓐ ● Ⓒ Ⓓ

*Example I*

To what did John Quincy Adams devote his life?

(A)   Improving his personal life
(B)   Serving the public
(C)   Increasing his fortune
(D)   Working on his private business

According to the passage, John Quincy Adams "dedicated his life to public service." Therefore, you should choose (B).

**Sample Answer**

Ⓐ Ⓑ ● Ⓓ

*Example II*

In line 4, the word "unswerving" is closest in meaning to

(A)   moveable
(B)   insignificant
(C)   unchanging
(D)   diplomatic

The passage states that John Quincy Adams demonstrated his unswerving belief "throughout his career." This implies that the belief did not change. Therefore, you should choose (C).

Now begin work on the questions.

**GO ON TO THE NEXT PAGE** ➤

**Questions 1–11**

Sharpshooter Annie Oakley is a mainstay in the folklore of the Old West. Born Phoebe Ann Moses in 1860, Annie learned to shoot at a very young age out of necessity: she hunted for birds and small game animals to help feed her family and to make some extra money by supplying the local hotel
*Line* restaurant with her catch. She soon became known for her excellent marksmanship and began taking
*(5)* part in shooting competitions at a very young age. It was rather unusual for a young girl not only to take part in such competitions but to win over older, more experienced male competitors. At the age of fifteen, she defeated Frank Butler, a professional marksman, in a competition. She and Butler were married a year later, and together they took part in shooting exhibitions.

In 1885, they joined probably the most famous of all western shows, Buffalo Bill's Wild West
*(10)* touring show. As part of their act, Annie shot a cigarette out of her husband's mouth; Frank Butler's participation in this part of the act clearly demonstrated his faith in his wife's shooting ability. Annie also accepted volunteers from the audience to take part in her act, and on one occasion, while touring Europe, she even shot a cigarette out of the mouth of Crown Prince Wilhelm of Germany.

1. Which of the following is closest in meaning to "folklore" in line 1?

   (A) Traditional stories
   (B) Western stories
   (C) Children's stories
   (D) Cowboy stories

2. The passage indicates that

   (A) the name Annie Oakley was given to her at birth
   (B) Annie changed her name to Phoebe at a young age
   (C) the name Phoebe Ann Moses was Annie's choice
   (D) Annie did not use her given name

3. The passage indicates that Annie learned to hunt

   (A) for pleasure
   (B) in order to survive
   (C) as part of a competition
   (D) because it was a normal activity for someone her age

4. The word "marksmanship" in line 4 indicates

   (A) competitiveness
   (B) ability to earn money
   (C) ability with a gun
   (D) attitude about work

5. How was the young Annie different from other girls her age?

   (A) She used a boy's name.
   (B) She worked in a local hotel.
   (C) She married at a much younger age than was considered normal.
   (D) She won shooting competitions.

6. According to the passage, what did Annie do one year prior to her marriage?

   (A) She defeated her future husband in a shooting match.
   (B) She learned to shoot.
   (C) She changed her name.
   (D) She joined Buffalo Bill's Wild West touring show.

**GO ON TO THE NEXT PAGE** ▶

7. The pronoun "they" in line 8 refers to

   (A) male competitors
   (B) Annie and Frank
   (C) shooting exhibition
   (D) western shows

8. The word "demonstrated" in line 11 is closest in meaning to

   (A) disproved
   (B) showed
   (C) tested
   (D) demanded

9. The passage suggests that Annie took a shot at Crown Prince Wilhelm because

   (A) Wilhelm wanted her to do it
   (B) Annie disliked him tremendously
   (C) Germany was at war with the U. S.
   (D) Annie disliked smoking

10. Where in the passage does the author describe one of the tricks in Annie's act?

    (A) Lines 1–4
    (B) Lines 4–5
    (C) Lines 9–10
    (D) Lines 10–11

11. The information in the passage

    (A) lists a cause followed by an effect
    (B) moves from general to specific ideas
    (C) is in chronological order
    (D) is in spatial order

**GO ON TO THE NEXT PAGE**

**Questions 12–20**

To understand the forces behind thunder and lightning, one must recall basic information about electricity, that things can become either positively or negatively charged with electricity and that two things with opposite charges will attract each other. As the opposite charges become stronger, the
*Line* attraction becomes greater; eventually the attraction becomes strong enough to result in a discharge
(5) that makes the two things electrically neutral again.

Lightning results when one cloud full of moisture develops an opposite charge in relation to another cloud. The pressure continues to build until there is enough pressure to break down the air separating the two clouds. A discharge occurs to neutralize the opposite charges in the two clouds, and this discharge is what we see as lightning. As this discharge of lightning is occurring, the lightning
(10) follows the "path of least resistance"; it therefore does not follow a straight line but zigzags in order to find the easiest route.

Thunder occurs during the discharge of electricity. As the discharge occurs, the air in the vicinity expands and contracts rapidly; the rushing air currents collide, causing the sound that we hear as thunder. Light travels much faster than sound (the speed of light is 186,284 miles per second, while the
(15) speed of sound is 1,100 feet per second), so we see the light first and then hear the sound later. Of course, the farther away the thunder and lightning are, the greater the lapsed time between the two. In fact the amount of lapsed time between the two can be used to determine how far away the thunder and lightning are.

12. What does the passage mainly discuss?

(A) Basic information about electricity
(B) The causes of thunder and lightning
(C) How lightning occurs
(D) Why thunder and lightning do not seem to occur together

13. Which of the following is NOT true about electric charges?

(A) Something can have either a positive charge or a negative charge.
(B) If one thing is positive and the other is negative, they will attract each other.
(C) If two things have strong negative charges, they will attract each other strongly.
(D) If the attraction between two things gets very strong, a discharge can occur.

14. The word "moisture" in line 6 is closest in meaning to

(A) wetness
(B) electricity
(C) gas
(D) positive charge

15. The passage states that lightning occurs when opposite charges develop in two

(A) drops of moisture
(B) air currents
(C) paths
(D) clouds

16. The "path of least resistance" in line 10 is what type of path?

(A) The easiest
(B) The strongest
(C) The brightest
(D) The most electrically charged

17. The word "zigzags" in line 10 indicates that something

(A) curves
(B) moves directly
(C) proceeds with sharp turns
(D) shines

18. The word "contracts" in line 13 is closest in meaning to

(A) becomes larger
(B) associates
(C) speeds up
(D) reduces

**GO ON TO THE NEXT PAGE**

19. Which of the following is implied in the passage?

   (A) The speed of sound is faster than the speed of light.
   (B) If you see and hear something at the same time, it is far away.
   (C) Humans can travel faster than the speed of light.
   (D) Something that is very close will be seen and heard at roughly the same time.

20. The paragraph following the passage most probably discusses

   (A) why lightning is not straight
   (B) the speed of light versus the speed of sound
   (C) further characteristics of electricity
   (D) figuring out how far away thunder and lightning are

GO ON TO THE NEXT PAGE

**Questions 21–30**

The cliff dwellings of the southwestern United States provide another mystery to intrigue archeologists. Located in the Four Corners area of the U.S., where Colorado, Utah, Arizona, and New Mexico meet, the cliff dwellings were constructed during the Great Pueblo period, from approximately
*Line* 1050 to 1300. The cliff dwellings are whole series of contiguous rooms built in layers into the sides of
(5) cliffs. The sleeping rooms of the cliff dwellings were very tiny, often only one to two meters wide and little more than one meter high, and they were built in complexes of up to several hundred rooms together. The front rooms of the complexes were considerably larger. These larger rooms were apparently the rooms where daily life took place.

When the cliff dwellings were first found by explorers, they had been abandoned. Archeologists
(10) today are uncertain as to when or why they were abandoned and where the inhabitants went. There is some evidence, however, that the inhabitants left the cliff dwellings near the end of the thirteenth century because of a serious drought that is known to have occurred in the area from 1276 to 1299. Archeologists believe that the inhabitants could have left the cliff dwellings to move southwest and southeast. Today the descendants of the cliff dwellers are probably members of the Native American
(15) tribes of that area.

21. The paragraph preceding this passage most probably discussed

   (A) another puzzle for archeologists
   (B) the development of the Four Corners area
   (C) the explorers who found the cliff dwellers
   (D) today's descendants of the cliff dwellers

22. Which of the following best describes the topic of this passage?

   (A) The Great Pueblo period
   (B) A description of cliff dwellings
   (C) What is known and unknown about the cliff dwellings
   (D) The Four Corners area of the United States

23. Why did the Four Corners area receive its name?

   (A) The area is a square with four corners.
   (B) The cliff dwellings in the area each have four corners.
   (C) The Great Pueblos are four-cornered.
   (D) The corners of four states meet there.

24. According to the passage, when were the cliff dwellings built?

   (A) During the Great Pueblo period
   (B) After the drought
   (C) Sometime before 1050
   (D) At the same time that the explorers found them

25. The word "tiny" in line 5 is closest in meaning to which of the following?

   (A) Wide
   (B) Small
   (C) High
   (D) Large

26. The word "abandoned" in line 9 is closest in meaning to which of the following?

   (A) Thriving
   (B) Full of daily life
   (C) Empty
   (D) In a state of drought

27. A "drought" in line 12 is

   (A) a lack of food
   (B) warfare with neighboring tribes
   (C) a desire to find a safer location
   (D) a shortage of water

**GO ON TO THE NEXT PAGE**

28. According to the passage, which of the following are the authorities certain about?

    (A) Why the cliff dwellers abandoned their homes
    (B) That a drought occurred in the Four Corners area from 1276 to 1299
    (C) Where the inhabitants of the cliff dwellings went
    (D) When the cliff dwellers abandoned their homes

29. The word "descendants" in line 14 can best be replaced by

    (A) subordinates
    (B) offspring
    (C) inferiors
    (D) ancestors

30. Which of the following is NOT discussed in the passage?

    (A) The life-style of the cliff dwellers
    (B) The size of the cliff dwellings
    (C) The mystery surrounding the abandonment of the cliff dwellings
    (D) The location of the cliff dwellings

GO ON TO THE NEXT PAGE

**Questions 31–40**

Distillation, the process of separating the elements of a solution, is widely used in industry today. The two most common methods of distillation are fractional distillation, used in the preparation of alcoholic beverages, and flash distillation, used for the conversion of ocean water to fresh water.

*Line*
*(5)* In fractional distillation a mixture is separated into its various component parts by boiling. This method makes use of the fact that different elements boil at varying temperatures. For example, alcohol has a considerably lower boiling temperature than water: the boiling temperature of water is 212 degrees Fahrenheit, and the boiling temperature of alcohol is 172 degrees Fahrenheit. Thus, when a mixture of alcohol and water is heated, the alcohol vaporizes more quickly than the water. The distillate is collected and the process is repeated until the desired purity has been achieved.

*(10)* Flash distillation does not require high temperatures but instead is based on pressure. In this process, a liquid that is to be separated is forced from a compartment kept under high pressure into a compartment kept at a lower pressure. When a liquid moves into the low-pressure chamber, it suddenly vaporizes, and the vapor is then condensed into distillate.

31. The word "fresh" in line 3 could most easily be replaced by

(A) original
(B) modern
(C) inexperienced
(D) nonsaline

32. According to the passage, what makes fractional distillation occur?

(A) Time
(B) Pressure
(C) Heat
(D) Water

33. The word "Thus" in line 7 is closest in meaning to which of the following?

(A) However
(B) Moreover
(C) Furthermore
(D) Therefore

34. According to the passage, what happens when water and alcohol are heated together?

(A) Both the water and the alcohol evaporate at the same rate.
(B) The alcohol cannot evaporate because of the water.
(C) The alcohol evaporates at a temperature of 212 degrees Fahrenheit.
(D) The alcohol evaporates from the mixture first.

35. The word "purity" in line 9 means

(A) goodness
(B) cleanness
(C) righteousness
(D) thoroughness

36. According to the passage, in the flash distillation process, what causes the liquid to vaporize?

(A) The pressure on the liquid is suddenly changed.
(B) The liquid changes compartments.
(C) The addition of seawater to a solution causes a chemical change to occur.
(D) There is a rapid increase in the pressure on the liquid.

37. Which of the following processes would probably involve distillation?

(A) Adding a new substance to a mixture
(B) Dividing a pure element into smaller quantities
(C) Mixing two elements together to form a new solution
(D) Removing impurities from a solution

GO ON TO THE NEXT PAGE

38. The word "vaporizes" in line 13 could best be replaced by

    (A) becomes gaseous
    (B) disappears
    (C) becomes stressed
    (D) solidifies

39. The main purpose of this passage is to

    (A) explain how salt water can be turned into fresh water
    (B) give an example of fractional distillation
    (C) describe a scientific process
    (D) discuss the boiling temperatures of various liquids

40. This passage would most probably be assigned reading in which of the following courses?

    (A) Biology
    (B) Aquatics
    (C) Physiology
    (D) Chemistry

GO ON TO THE NEXT PAGE

**Questions 41–50**

At first glance it might seem that a true artist is a solitary toiler in possession of a unique talent that differentiates her or him from the rest of society. But after further reflection it is quite apparent that the artist is a product of the society in which she or he toils rather than an entity removed from
*Line* society. The genius of an artist is really a measure of the artist's ability to work within the framework
(5) imposed by society, to make use of the resources provided by society, and, most important, to mirror a society's values. It is society that imposes a structure on the artist, and the successful artist must work within this framework. Societies have found various methods to support and train their artists, be it the Renaissance system of royal support of the sculptors and painters of the period or the Japanese tradition of passing artistic knowledge from father to son. The artist is also greatly affected by the
(10) physical resources of her or his society. The medium chosen by the artist is a reflection not only of the artist's perception of aesthetic beauty but of resources that society has to supply. After all, wood carvings come from societies with forests, bronze statues come from societies with available supplies of metal, and woven woolen rugs come from societies of shepherds. Finally, the artist must reflect the values, both aesthetic and moral, of the society in which she or he toils. The idea of beauty changes
(15) from society to society, as seen in the oft cited example of Rubens' rounded women versus today's gaminlike sylphs, and the artist must serve as a mirror of her or his society's measure of perfection. And society's moral values must equally be reflected in art if it is to be universally accepted.

41. What does the passage mainly discuss?

    (A) The effect of the artist on society
    (B) The role of the artist in improving society
    (C) The relation between an artist and society
    (D) The structure of society

42. The word "solitary" in line 1 is closest in meaning to

    (A) sociable
    (B) monogamous
    (C) sensitive
    (D) lone

43. The author thinks that an artist is

    (A) separate from society
    (B) a part of society
    (C) differentiated from society
    (D) an entity removed from society

44. The word "mirror" in line 5 is closest in meaning to

    (A) shine
    (B) return
    (C) reflect
    (D) reject

45. According to the passage, which of the following is NOT a way that society imposes its structure on an artist?

    (A) Society has found ways to train and support its artists.
    (B) Society provides physical resources to an artist.
    (C) Social imposes its values on the artist.
    (D) Society allows the artist to use her or his unique talent to lead a solitary life.

46. The word "medium" in line 10 could best be replaced by

    (A) social milieu
    (B) means of expression
    (C) neutrality of position
    (D) mediocrity of performance

47. Which of the following physical resources of art is NOT mentioned in the passage?

    (A) Stone
    (B) Wood
    (C) Wool
    (D) Metal

**GO ON TO THE NEXT PAGE** →

48. In line with the author's point about resources, an area near an ocean might feature what type of art?

    (A) Shell jewelry
    (B) Water color portraits
    (C) Wood carvings of fish
    (D) Paintings of seascapes

49. A "sylph" in line 16 is probably someone who is

    (A) artistic
    (B) pretty
    (C) curved
    (D) slim

50. The example of Rubens' women is used to show that the artist

    (A) has been supplied by society
    (B) makes use of society's physical resources
    (C) reflects society's aesthetic values
    (D) reflects society's moral values

**This is the end of Section 3.**

STOP STOP STOP STOP STOP STOP STOP

**If you finish in less than 55 minutes,
check your work on Section 3 only.
Do NOT read or work on any other section of the test.**

**GO ON TO THE NEXT PAGE**

# TEST OF WRITTEN ENGLISH
## TWE ESSAY TOPIC
### Time—30 minutes

*Some educators believe that to graduate from a university a student should study courses from a wide variety of subjects. Other educators believe that it is better for a university graduate to have a strong specialization. Discuss the advantages of each position. Then indicate which position you think is better and justify your response.*

Write your answer on the answer sheet for the Test of Written English, Practice Test Three, on pages 189–190.

# PRACTICE TEST FOUR

## SECTION 1
## LISTENING COMPREHENSION
**Time—approximately 35 minutes**
**(including the reading of the directions for each part)**

In this section of the test, you will have an opportunity to demonstrate your ability to understand conversations and talks in English. There are three parts to this section. Answer all the questions on the basis of what is <u>stated</u> or <u>implied</u> by the speakers you hear. Do <u>not</u> take notes or write in your test book at any time. Do not turn the pages until you are told to do so.

### Part A

**Directions:** In Part A you will hear short conversations between two people. After each conversation, you will hear a question about the conversation. The conversations and questions will not be repeated. After you hear a question, read the four possible answers in your test book and choose the best answer. Then, on your answer sheet, find the number of the question and fill in the space that corresponds to the letter of the answer you have chosen.

Listen to an example.

**Sample Answer**

On the recording, you hear:

Ⓐ
Ⓑ
Ⓒ
●

| (man) | *That exam was just awful.* |
| (woman) | *Oh, it could have been worse.* |
| (narrator) | *What does the woman mean?* |

In your test book, you read:

    (A) The exam was really awful.
    (B) It was the worst exam she had ever seen.
    (C) It couldn't have been more difficult.
    (D) It wasn't that hard.

You learn from the conversation that the man thought the exam was very difficult and that the woman disagreed with the man. The best answer to the question, "What does the woman mean?" is (D), "It wasn't that hard." Therefore, the correct choice is (D).

1. (A) In a bus terminal.
   (B) In a tourist agency.
   (C) At an airport ticket counter.
   (D) At a train station.

2. (A) If the car ran out of gas.
   (B) If the car will start.
   (C) Where the gas station is.
   (D) If she should send a check to the service station.

3. (A) The woman should leave in the morning.
   (B) The woman should finish the problems before midnight.
   (C) The woman should work from midnight to morning.
   (D) The woman shouldn't try to finish everything tonight.

4. (A) The traffic is unusually light.
   (B) She shares the man's opinion.
   (C) The cars should stay on the road.
   (D) According to the clock, traffic is getting heavier.

5. (A) The plants need more water today.
   (B) The plants don't need to be watered.
   (C) Yesterday's watering was insufficient.
   (D) He thinks he should water the plants.

6. (A) It is unfortunate that the competition did not take place.
   (B) He hasn't seen the competition results.
   (C) Luckily, he did better than the woman did.
   (D) They both performed poorly.

7. (A) She doesn't know what time it is.
   (B) She thinks it's late.
   (C) She believes they can still go.
   (D) She believes the market will be closed.

8. (A) She fears that someone took her wallet.
   (B) She can't find what she needs in her wallet.
   (C) She is relieved that her wallet was not stolen.
   (D) All the worry has taken its toll.

9. (A) Someone talked out loud.
   (B) No one was allowed to talk.
   (C) The meeting seemed long to everyone.
   (D) A lot of people participated.

10. (A) The book should be returned to the library within a week.
    (B) The man isn't able to do his work in this book.
    (C) The man is due for a raise this week.
    (D) The book was due last week.

11. (A) She spent a lot of time finding the bracelet.
    (B) It wasn't a difficult project.
    (C) The bracelet was hard to make.
    (D) It wasn't worth the time it took.

12. (A) She believes the cost was reasonable.
    (B) The cost was unbelievably low.
    (C) She believes she'll stay overnight.
    (D) The cost was rather high.

13. (A) Perhaps the woman left the checks in her suitcase.
    (B) He doesn't know why the woman is looking in her suitcase.
    (C) The woman should check her purse again.
    (D) The woman could've left her purse in the suitcase.

14. (A) Mr. Milton pointed to the dean of the college.
    (B) The dean of the college pointed out Mr. Milton.
    (C) Mr. Milton's appointment was deemed unnecessary.
    (D) Mr. Milton received a new position a month ago.

15. (A) His intuition was not very good.
    (B) He was scared that he hadn't studied enough.
    (C) He couldn't pay tuition because money was scarce.
    (D) He had just enough to pay his school fees.

**GO ON TO THE NEXT PAGE**

16. (A) If Eric wants to play basketball.
    (B) If Eric's walking to the basketball game.
    (C) If Eric's still hurt.
    (D) If Eric's uncle's playing basketball.

17. (A) He thinks the housing deadline hasn't passed.
    (B) He's accepting the housing that's been offered.
    (C) He doesn't have a place to stay.
    (D) He supposes that his application's been accepted.

18. (A) She thinks the homework's easy.
    (B) She doesn't know about the homework assignment.
    (C) She's worked hard on her biology homework.
    (D) The homework was due yesterday.

19. (A) He didn't read Stan's article.
    (B) He read the article when it appeared in the paper.
    (C) He helped Stan with the article.
    (D) Stan read the article in the school paper.

20. (A) The woman should not have given him the gift.
    (B) It was a problem to pick those things up.
    (C) The woman should be more realistic about the situation.
    (D) The woman should keep trying.

21. (A) Ten dollars was too much to pay for the perfume.
    (B) It was unfortunate that she didn't like the perfume.
    (C) Fortunately, she got the perfume for ten dollars.
    (D) She didn't have enough money to buy the perfume.

22. (A) Only Eric can play the piano so well.
    (B) Eric can't play the piano very well.
    (C) Eric's the only one who plays the piano.
    (D) Others play the piano better than Eric.

23. (A) He never likes to play tennis.
    (B) He's unable to play tennis with them.
    (C) He isn't a very good tennis player.
    (D) He is in town for a game of tennis.

24. (A) She could not believe how hard it snowed.
    (B) The surprise trip really pleased her.
    (C) She was unable to go because of the snow.
    (D) She expected more snow.

25. (A) He's disappointed about the promotion.
    (B) He made some extra motions.
    (C) He's heard a lot of static.
    (D) He's very pleased.

26. (A) Both shirts are made exactly the same.
    (B) It doesn't matter to her which shirt the man gets.
    (C) The man shouldn't get either one.
    (D) She doesn't like either shirt.

27. (A) He got the job he wanted.
    (B) He doesn't want a part-time job.
    (C) He's no longer looking for a job.
    (D) He did not get a position.

28. (A) The dean will listen to the circumstances of the complaint.
    (B) The dean never complains about the circumstances.
    (C) The dean never hears any complaints.
    (D) The dean always listens to any complaints.

29. (A) She did not know how to cook.
    (B) She would never invite people to her house.
    (C) She was busy doing something else that evening.
    (D) She was a really good cook.

30. (A) He has put off going to Texas.
    (B) He completed them long ago.
    (C) He put the money for his taxes away in the bank.
    (D) His taxes are not done.

**GO ON TO THE NEXT PAGE**

**Part B**

**Directions:** In this part of the test, you will hear longer conversations. After each conversation, you will hear several questions. The conversations and questions will not be repeated.

After you hear a question, read the four possible answers in your test book and choose the best answer. Then, on your answer sheet, find the number of the question and fill in the space that corresponds to the letter of the answer you have chosen.

Remember, you are <u>not</u> allowed to take notes or write in your test book.

31. (A) The price of textbooks.
    (B) History 101.
    (C) The university bookstore.
    (D) Ways to sell used books.

32. (A) He desperately needs the money.
    (B) Reading doesn't interest him.
    (C) He's finished using them.
    (D) He'd rather have cheaper books.

33. (A) The bookstore doesn't want to buy them.
    (B) He wouldn't get enough money.
    (C) He doesn't like the bookstore's advertisements.
    (D) It's too late to sell them to the bookstore.

34. (A) Post some advertisements.
    (B) Take History 101.
    (C) Give the books to the bookstore for nothing.
    (D) Keep the books.

35. (A) That babies sleep thirteen hours a day.
    (B) That the woman was taking a psychology class.
    (C) That more mature people required so much sleep.
    (D) That the need for sleep decreases with age.

36. (A) In psychology class.
    (B) In a discussion with the man.
    (C) From an article that she read.
    (D) From the class textbook.

37. (A) Teens.
    (B) Twenties.
    (C) Thirties.
    (D) Fifties.

38. (A) Thirteen hours.
    (B) Nine hours.
    (C) Eight hours.
    (D) Six hours.

GO ON TO THE NEXT PAGE

## Part C

**Directions:** In this part of the test, you will hear several talks. After each talk, you will hear some questions. The talks and questions will not be repeated.

After you hear a question, read the four possible answers in your test book and choose the best answer. Then, on your answer sheet, find the number of the question and fill in the space that corresponds to the letter of the answer you have chosen.

Here is an example.

On the recording, you hear:

(narrator)   *Listen to an instructor talk to his class about painting.*

(man)   *Artist Grant Wood was a guiding force in the school of painting known as American regionalist, a style reflecting the distinctive characteristics of art from rural areas of the United States. Wood began drawing animals on the family farm at the age of three, and when he was thirty-eight one of his paintings received a remarkable amount of public notice and acclaim. This painting, called* American Gothic, *is a starkly simple depiction of a serious couple staring directly out at the viewer.*

Now listen to a sample question.                   **Sample Answer**

(narrator)   *What style of painting is known as American regionalist?*   Ⓐ
                                                                          Ⓑ
                                                                          Ⓒ
In your test book, you read:   (A)   Art from America's inner cities.      ●
                               (B)   Art from the central region of the U.S.
                               (C)   Art from various urban areas in the U.S.
                               (D)   Art from rural sections of America.

The best answer to the question, "What style of painting is known as American regionalist?" is (D), "Art from rural sections of America." Therefore, the correct choice is (D).

Now listen to another sample question.               **Sample Answer**

(narrator)   *What is the name of Wood's most successful painting?*   Ⓐ
                                                                      Ⓑ
                                                                      ●
In your test book, you read:   (A)   "American Regionalist."            Ⓓ
                               (B)   "The Family Farm in Iowa."
                               (C)   "American Gothic."
                               (D)   "A Serious Couple."

The best answer to the question, "What is the name of Wood's most successful painting?" is (C), "American Gothic." Therefore, the correct choice is (C).

Remember, you are <u>not</u> allowed to take notes or write in your test book.

39. (A) How to get a professor's signature.
    (B) The procedure for dropping courses.
    (C) When to come and see the advisor.
    (D) The effect of officially dropping a
        course.

40. (A) Any time, if the professor is willing to
        sign.
    (B) Only on the day of thc talk.
    (C) During the first three weeks of the
        semester.
    (D) Up to three weeks before the end of
        the semester.

41. (A) None.
    (B) One.
    (C) Two.
    (D) Three.

42. (A) The student fails the course.
    (B) The course is removed from the
        student's schedule.
    (C) The student needs to get the advisor's
        signature.
    (D) The student receives a warning.

43. (A) A woodcarving business.
    (B) A lumber business.
    (C) A construction business.
    (D) A jewelry business.

44. (A) During the construction of a sawmill.
    (B) After prospectors had arrived.
    (C) Sometime after Sutter's death.
    (D) Before Sutter had the rights to the
        land.

45. (A) Increased prosperity.
    (B) A large share of gold.
    (C) A healthier lumber business.
    (D) Little or nothing.

46. (A) To show what a terrible life John
        Sutter had led.
    (B) To show the folly of trying to develop
        a business.
    (C) To show the effect that the discovery
        of gold has on individuals.
    (D) To show that the development of the
        West happened partly by chance.

47. (A) Becoming a university student.
    (B) Managing time.
    (C) Majoring in management.
    (D) Spending a week in a management
        training program.

48. (A) Relaxation techniques.
    (B) Homework assignments.
    (C) A personal time-management study.
    (D) Keeping an appointment calendar.

49. (A) Ninety-six days.
    (B) Twenty-four days.
    (C) Seven days.
    (D) Fifteen minutes.

50. (A) Make an appointment.
    (B) Begin the time study.
    (C) Write down how they spend their
        time.
    (D) Attend another seminar.

**This is the end of Section 1.**
**Stop work on Section 1.**

**Turn off your cassette player.**

**Read the directions for Section 2 and begin work.**
**Do NOT read or work on any other section**
**of the test during the next 25 minutes.**

## SECTION 2
## STRUCTURE AND WRITTEN EXPRESSION
### Time—25 minutes
### (including the reading of the directions)
### Now set your clock for 25 minutes.

This section is designed to measure your ability to recognize language that is appropriate for standard written English. There are two types of questions in this section, with special directions for each type.

### Structure

**Directions:** Questions 1–15 are incomplete sentences. Beneath each sentence you will see four words or phrases, marked (A), (B), (C), and (D). Choose the <u>one</u> word or phrase that best completes the sentence. Then, on your answer sheet, find the number of the question and fill in the space that corresponds to the letter of the answer you have chosen. Fill in the space so that the letter inside the oval cannot be seen.

Look at the following examples.

*Example I*                                                                 **Sample Answer**

The president _____ the election by a landslide.

(A)   won
(B)   he won
(C)   yesterday
(D)   fortunately

The sentence should read, "The president won the election by a landslide." Therefore, you should choose (A).

*Example II*                                                                **Sample Answer**

When _____ the conference?

(A)   the doctor attended
(B)   did the doctor attend
(C)   the doctor will attend
(D)   the doctor's attendance

The sentence should read, "When did the doctor attend the conference?" Therefore, you should choose (B).

Now begin work on the questions.

GO ON TO THE NEXT PAGE

1.  In medieval times _____ his enemy by throwing down his gauntlet.

    (A) the challenge
    (B) a man challenged
    (C) a man made a challenge
    (D) his challenge

2.  In 1885 photography changed dramatically _____ introduced paper-based film.

    (A) Eastman
    (B) Eastman was
    (C) when it was Eastman
    (D) when Eastman

3.  _____ antitrust laws did not exist in the U.S., there would not be as much competition in certain industries.

    (A) So
    (B) If
    (C) For
    (D) Also

4.  A bat will often spend the daylight hours _____ upside down in a tree or cave.

    (A) hanging
    (B) which hangs
    (C) that is
    (D) hangs

5.  Geomorphology is the study of the changes that _____ on the surface of the earth.

    (A) taking place
    (B) takes place
    (C) take place
    (D) they take place

6.  A hero of the war of 1812, _____ president of the United States.

    (A) Andrew Jackson later became
    (B) that Andrew Jackson later became
    (C) who was Andrew Jackson
    (D) later became Andrew Jackson

7.  _____ jellies, jams are made by retaining the pulp with the fruit juice.

    (A) No likeness to
    (B) Not alike
    (C) Unlike
    (D) Dislike

8.  An elephant can lift _____ a ton with its tusks.

    (A) so much that
    (B) it
    (C) most
    (D) as much as

9.  The electric eel uses its electric shock to capture food and _____.

    (A) for protection
    (B) protect itself
    (C) protecting itself
    (D) it protects itself

10. Rarely _____ acorns until the trees are more than twenty years old.

    (A) when oak trees bear
    (B) oak trees that bear
    (C) do oak trees bear
    (D) oak trees bear

11. The Andromeda Nebula, _____ more than two million light years away, can be seen from the Northern Hemisphere.

    (A) a galaxy
    (B) is a galaxy
    (C) a galaxy is
    (D) a galaxy which

GO ON TO THE NEXT PAGE

12. The closer to one of the Earth's poles, the greater _____ gravitational force.

    (A) is
    (B) the
    (C) has
    (D) it has

13. Baboons eat a variety of foods, _____ eggs, fruits, grass, insects, plant leaves, and roots.

    (A) they include
    (B) among them are
    (C) among
    (D) including

14. The flamingo uses its bill _____ feeding to filter mud and water from the tiny plants and animals that it finds in shallow ponds.

    (A) when
    (B) is
    (C) that it is
    (D) was

15. The first nuclear-powered ship in the world, the *Nautilus*, _____ by the U.S. Navy in 1954.

    (A) when it was launched
    (B) that was launched
    (C) was launched
    (D) launched

GO ON TO THE NEXT PAGE

## Written Expression

**Directions:** In questions 16–40, each sentence has four underlined words or phrases. The four underlined parts of the sentence are marked (A), (B), (C), and (D). Identify the <u>one</u> underlined word or phrase that must be changed in order for the sentence to be correct. Then, on your answer sheet, find the number of the question and fill in the space that corresponds to the letter of the answer you have chosen.

Look at the following examples.

*Example I*                                                                                    **Sample Answer**

The four string on a violin are tuned
 A      B                    C    D

in fifths.

Ⓐ
●
Ⓒ
Ⓓ

The sentence should read, "The four strings on a violin are tuned in fifths." Therefore, you should choose (B).

*Example II*                                                                                   **Sample Answer**

The research for the book *Roots* taking
       A        B              C

Alex Haley twelve years.
                    D

Ⓐ
Ⓑ
●
Ⓓ

The sentence should read, "The research for the book *Roots* took Alex Haley twelve years." Therefore, you should choose (C).

Now begin work on the questions.

**GO ON TO THE NEXT PAGE**

16. The winter storm that raced through the area for the last two day moved east today.
　　　　　　　　　　 A　　 B　　　　　　　　　 C　　　 D

17. In the 1800's botanist Asa Gray worked to describe and classifying the plants found in North
　　　　　　　　 A　　　　　 B　　　　　　　　　　 C　　　　　　 D

America.

18. Bryce Canyon National Park, where is there oddly shaped and magnificently colored rock
　　　　　　　　　　　　　　　　 A　　　　　 B

formations, is located in southern Utah.
　　 C　　　　　　　　 D

19. After talks in Copenhagen yesterday, the secretary of state returning to Washington.
　　 A　 B　　　　　　　　 C　　　　　　　　　　　　　 D

20. Lava, rock fragments, and gaseous may all erupt from a volcano.
　　　　 A　　　　　　　 B　　 C　 D

21. Many of the characters portrayed by writer Joyce Carol Oats is mentally ill.
　　 A　　　　　　　 B　　　　　　　　　　　　 C　　　 D

22. The two types of nucleic acids, known as DNA and RNA, are not like.
　　　　 A　　　　　　　 B　　　　　　　　　 C　　 D

23. Of all the states in the United States, Rhode Island is a smallest.
　　　 A　　　　 B　　　　　　　　　　 C D

24. The classification of a dinosaur as either saurischian nor ornithischian depends on the structure
　　　　　　　　　　　　　　 A　　　　　　　 B　　　　　　 C

of the hip.
　　 D

25. An octopus has three hearts to pump blood throughout their body.
　 A　　　　　　　　 B　　　　　 C　　　 D

26. Studies show that the new strategy is not very effective as the previous one.
　 A　　　 B　　　　　　　　　 C　　　　　　 D

27. Most the newspapers depend on the wire services for their international stories and photographs.
　 A　　　　　　　 B　　　　　　　 C　 D

28. The new system responds at seconds to any emergency.
　 A　　　　　 B　 C　　 D

29. Landscape painting was a dominant art forms during much of the nineteenth century.
　　　　 A　　　　　 B　　　 C　 D

30. While his racing days, racehorse John Henry earned a record $6.5 million, $2.3 million more than
　　 A　　　　　　　　　　　　　 B

his closest competitor.
　 C　　 D

31. Cartilage covers the ends of bones helps to protect the joints from wear and tear.
　　　 A　 B　　　　　　　 C　　　　　　 D

32. The Alaskan malamute, used extensively to pull sleds, is closely related to the wolves.
　　　　　　　　 A　　　　　 B　　　　 C　　　　　　 D

**GO ON TO THE NEXT PAGE**

33. The 1890's in America were known as a Gay Nineties.
    ‾A‾  ‾B‾                              ‾C‾ ‾D‾

34. The General Agreement on Tariffs and Trades (GATT) is an international agreement designing to
                                                                ‾‾‾‾‾‾‾‾‾‾‾             ‾‾‾‾‾‾‾‾‾
                                                                    A                      B

    increase trade among member nations.
                    ‾‾‾‾‾ ‾‾‾‾‾‾‾
                      C      D

35. Like a small child, a victim of Alzheimer's Disease who is left lone may get lost and not know
        ‾‾‾‾‾‾‾‾‾‾‾                                               ‾‾‾‾               ‾‾‾‾‾‾‾
             A                                                      B                   C

    the way home.
        ‾‾‾‾‾‾‾‾
           D

36. Death Valley is 130 miles length and no more than 14 miles wide.
                ‾‾      ‾‾‾‾‾‾    ‾‾‾‾‾‾‾‾‾‾‾            ‾‾‾‾
                A          B           C                  D

37. The theory of natural selection is used to explain which animals of a species will die
                                     ‾‾‾‾‾‾‾         ‾‾‾‾‾
                                        A              B

    prematurely and which will survival.
    ‾‾‾‾‾‾‾‾‾‾              ‾‾‾‾‾‾‾‾
        C                      D

38. There are thousands of kinds of bacteria, most of which is harmless to humans.
    ‾‾‾‾‾‾‾‾                               ‾‾‾‾‾‾‾‾‾‾ ‾‾ ‾‾‾‾‾‾‾‾
        A                                      B      C    D

39. An invention best known for the development of the Gatling Gun, Richard Gatling actually put
       ‾‾‾‾‾‾‾‾                                                                    ‾‾‾‾‾‾‾‾
          A                                                                          B

    most of his effort into improving agricultural methods.
    ‾‾‾‾‾‾‾                        ‾‾‾‾‾‾‾‾‾‾‾
       C                               D

40. Dorothea Dix worked extensively during the second half of the nineteenth century to improve
                        ‾‾‾‾‾‾‾‾‾‾ ‾‾‾‾‾‾                                              ‾‾‾‾‾‾‾
                             A        B                                                  C

    conditions in mental health facilities and the prisons.
                                             ‾‾‾
                                              D

**This is the end of Section 2.
If you finish before 25 minutes has ended,
check your work on Section 2 only.**

STOP  STOP  STOP  STOP  STOP  STOP  STOP

**At the end of 25 minutes, go on to Section 3.
Use exactly 55 minutes to work on Section 3.**

## SECTION 3
## READING COMPREHENSION
**Time—55 minutes**
**(including the reading of the directions)**
**Now set your clock for 55 minutes.**

This section is designed to measure your ability to read and understand short passages similar in topic and style to those that students are likely to encounter in North American universities and colleges.

**Directions:** In this section you will read several passages. Each one is followed by a number of questions about it. You are to choose the <u>one</u> best answer, (A), (B), (C), or (D), to each question. Then, on your answer sheet, find the number of the question and fill in the space that corresponds to the letter of the answer you have chosen.

Answer all questions about the information in a passage on the basis of what is <u>stated</u> or <u>implied</u> in that passage.

Read the following passage:

> John Quincy Adams, who served as the sixth president of the United States from 1825 to 1829, is today recognized for his masterful statesmanship and diplomacy. He dedicated his life to public service, both in the presidency and in the various other political offices that he
> *Line* held. Throughout his political career he demonstrated his unswerving belief in freedom of
> *(5)* speech, the antislavery cause, and the right of Americans to be free from European and Asian domination.

*Example I*                                                                    **Sample Answer**

To what did John Quincy Adams devote his life?                                Ⓐ ● Ⓒ Ⓓ

(A)   Improving his personal life
(B)   Serving the public
(C)   Increasing his fortune
(D)   Working on his private business

According to the passage, John Quincy Adams "dedicated his life to public service." Therefore, you should choose (B).

*Example II*                                                                   **Sample Answer**

In line 4, the word "unswerving" is closest in meaning to                     Ⓐ Ⓑ ● Ⓓ

(A)   moveable
(B)   insignificant
(C)   unchanging
(D)   diplomatic

The passage states that John Quincy Adams demonstrated his unswerving belief "throughout his career." This implies that the belief did not change. Therefore, you should choose (C).

Now begin work on the questions.

**GO ON TO THE NEXT PAGE** ➔

## Questions 1–10

In west-central New York State there is a group of eleven long, narrow, glacial lakes known as the Finger Lakes. From east to west these lakes are Otisco, Skaneateles, Owasco, Cayuga, Seneca, Keuka, Canandaigua, Honeoye, Canadice, Hemlock, and Conesus.

*Line*
(5) These lakes have been aptly named because of their resemblance to the fingers of a hand. Two of the largest of the Finger Lakes, Seneca and Cayuga, exemplify the selection of the name: Seneca is thirty-seven miles long and four miles across at its widest point, and Cayuga is forty miles long and two miles across.

Although scientists are not completely certain as to how these lakes were formed, most believe that successive sheets of glacial ice carved out the long, narrow valleys. The glaciers most probably
(10) moved along the paths of preexisting stream valleys and further deepened these valleys to depths well below sea level. With the melting of the glaciers at the end of the Ice Age, the lakes were filled.

1. The topic of this passage is

   (A) west-central New York State
   (B) Seneca and Cayuga
   (C) the description and origin of the Finger Lakes
   (D) the scientific findings about the Finger Lakes

2. The word "glacial" in line 1 is closest in meaning to which of the following?

   (A) Icy
   (B) Thin
   (C) Shallow
   (D) Wide

3. According to the passage, why are these lakes known as the Finger Lakes?

   (A) They are the same size as fingers.
   (B) Their shape is similar to a finger's.
   (C) Their composition is the same as a finger's.
   (D) There are as many lakes as there are fingers.

4. Why does the author mention Seneca and Cayuga in the second paragraph?

   (A) They are the only two Finger Lakes.
   (B) They are the two largest lakes in the United States.
   (C) They are good examples of long and narrow lakes.
   (D) They are long and wide.

5. The word "selection" in line 5 is closest in meaning to

   (A) sound
   (B) choice
   (C) feeling
   (D) presentation

6. The passage implies that Seneca Lake is

   (A) a constant four miles wide
   (B) at least four miles wide at each point
   (C) wider than it is long
   (D) narrower than four miles at certain points

GO ON TO THE NEXT PAGE

7. What do most scientists believe caused the formation of the Finger Lakes?

   (A) The sea level decreased.
   (B) Heavy rainfalls flooded the area.
   (C) Melted glaciers carved out the valleys.
   (D) Glaciers cut into the land and then melted to fill the valleys.

8. The word "successive" in line 9 could best be replaced by

   (A) timely
   (B) duplicate
   (C) sequential
   (D) simultaneous

9. The word "paths" in line 10 is closest in meaning to which of the following?

   (A) Waves
   (B) Routes
   (C) Sands
   (D) Highways

10. What is the tone of this passage?

   (A) Informative
   (B) Accusatory
   (C) Humorous
   (D) Calculating

GO ON TO THE NEXT PAGE

**Questions 11–20**

Popular architecture in the United States in the beginning of the twentieth century continued as it had at the end of the nineteenth century, with elaborately ornate historical motifs. The new skyscrapers sprouting up at the time were often ornately finished with elements of Gothic or Roman detailing.
Line During this period of emphasis on intricate ornamentation, certain architects began moving in a
(5) different direction, from the historic attention to ornate detailing toward more modern design typified by simplified flowing lines.

Frank Lloyd Wright, the best known of these early modern architects, developed a style that he termed *organic architecture,* a building style based on natural forms rather than on the intricately detailed styles that had been popular. Wright started work in Chicago designing "prairie houses," long,
(10) low buildings featuring flowing horizontal lines and simplistic unity of design. These buildings often centered around massive stone fireplaces with rooms open to each other and space flowing from one room to the next; they were intended to fit the wide open expanses of the Midwest Plains that served as a setting for Chicago. These "prairie houses," found in Chicago's suburban areas, served to tie the rapidly developing neighborhoods of Chicago with its Plains heritage.

11. The paragraph preceding this passage most probably discussed

   (A) popular music
   (B) simpler forms of architecture
   (C) the development of Chicago
   (D) architecture in the nineteenth century

12. What is the main idea of this passage?

   (A) The architectural style of Frank Lloyd Wright represented a change from earlier styles.
   (B) Architecture in the twentieth century was very ornate.
   (C) Frank Lloyd Wright's architecture was more elaborate than previous styles.
   (D) Frank Lloyd Wright's "prairie houses" were well known in Chicago.

13. According to the passage, the new skyscrapers built at the beginning of the twentieth century were

   (A) elementary
   (B) elaborately ornamented
   (C) in a very modern style
   (D) completely Gothic

14. The expression "sprouting up" in line 3 could best be replaced by

   (A) being grown
   (B) dominating
   (C) popularized
   (D) being built

15. The word "simplified" in line 6 is closest in meaning to

   (A) basic
   (B) not difficult
   (C) straight
   (D) recent

16. Which of the following statements about Frank Lloyd Wright is supported in the passage?

   (A) He was extremely popular prior to the twentieth century.
   (B) He used elements of Gothic and Roman detailing in his work.
   (C) His architectural style can be seen in Chicago's skyscrapers.
   (D) His "prairie houses" were very different from the elaborately ornamented skyscrapers.

**GO ON TO THE NEXT PAGE**

17. The "prairie houses" built by Frank Lloyd Wright were

    (A) ornately detailed
    (B) built in the Roman style
    (C) skyscrapers
    (D) flowing and simple

18. The word "fit" in line 12 could best be replaced by

    (A) match
    (B) wear
    (C) try
    (D) fill

19. It is implied that Frank Lloyd Wright's "prairie houses" resembled the prairies around Chicago in that

    (A) they were covered with grass
    (B) they were rapidly developing
    (C) they were long and low
    (D) they were in Chicago

20. The word "heritage" in line 14 is closest in meaning to which of the following?

    (A) Ambiance
    (B) Tradition
    (C) Appearance
    (D) Surroundings

GO ON TO THE NEXT PAGE

**Questions 21–30**

Louisa May Alcott, an American author best known for her children's books *Little Women, Little Men,* and *Jo's Boys,* was profoundly influenced by her family, particularly her father. She was the daughter of Bronson Alcott, a well-known teacher, intellectual, and free thinker who advocated
*Line* abolitionism, women's rights, and vegetarianism long before they were popular. He was called a man of
(5) unparalleled intellect by his friend Ralph Waldo Emerson. Bronson Alcott instilled in his daughter his lofty and spiritual values and in return was idolized by his daughter.

The financial situation of the Alcott family during Louisa's childhood was not good, mainly due to the fact that her father made unsound investments in projects that reflected his idealistic view of the world. As a result, Louisa had to begin helping to support her family at a young age, by taking a variety
(10) of low-paying jobs as a seamstress, a maid, and a tutor.

Her novel *Little Women* was patterned after her own family, and Louisa used her father as a model for the impractical yet serenely wise and adored father in *Little Women.* With the success of this novel she was able to provide for her family, giving her father the financial security that until then he had never experienced.

21. The passage mainly discusses

    (A) Louisa May Alcott's famous books
    (B) how Bronson Alcott implemented his educational philosophies
    (C) the success of *Little Women*
    (D) Bronson Alcott's influence on his daughter

22. The word "particularly" in line 2 is closest in meaning to

    (A) in part by
    (B) strangely
    (C) except for
    (D) especially

23. The passage implies that vegetarianism

    (A) was more popular than abolitionism
    (B) was the reason for Louisa's adoration for her father
    (C) became popular in a later period
    (D) was one of the reasons for Bronson Alcott's unparalleled intellect

24. In line 6, the word "lofty" is closest in meaning to

    (A) commonplace
    (B) high-minded
    (C) self-serving
    (D) sympathetic

25. The word "unsound" in line 8 is closest in meaning to which of the following?

    (A) Noiseless
    (B) Unprepared
    (C) Unsafe
    (D) Unheard

26. Which of the following is NOT implied as something that Louisa did to earn money as a youth?

    (A) She did some sewing.
    (B) She cleaned houses.
    (C) She taught.
    (D) She worked in a store.

**GO ON TO THE NEXT PAGE**

27. The expression "provide for" in line 13 could best be replaced by

   (A) support
   (B) identify with
   (C) buy presents for
   (D) manage

28. It can be inferred from the passage that Louisa May Alcott used the success of *Little Women* to

   (A) buy herself anything she had ever wanted
   (B) achieve personal financial success
   (C) give her father tangible proof of her love
   (D) detach herself from her family

29. The author's purpose in the passage is to

   (A) explain how an author becomes famous
   (B) describe the influence of family on a writer
   (C) support Bronson Alcott's educational theories
   (D) show the success that can be achieved by an author

30. Where in the passage does the author mention examples of the beliefs of Louisa's father?

   (A) Lines 1–2
   (B) Lines 2–4
   (C) Lines 7–9
   (D) Line 11–12

GO ON TO THE NEXT PAGE

## Questions 31–41

In the American colonies there was little money. England did not supply the colonies with coins and it did not allow the colonies to make their own coins, except for the Massachusetts Bay Colony, which received permission for a short period in 1652 to make several kinds of silver coins. England
*Line* wanted to keep money out of America as a means of controlling trade: America was forced to trade
(5) only with England if it did not have the money to buy products from other countries. The result during this prerevolutionary period was that the colonists used various goods in place of money: beaver pelts, Indian wampum, and tobacco leaves were all commonly used substitutes for money. The colonists also made use of any foreign coins they could obtain. Dutch, Spanish, French, and English coins were all in use in the American colonies.

(10)     During the Revolutionary War, funds were needed to finance the war, so each of the individual states and the Continental Congress issued paper money. So much of this paper money was printed that by the end of the war, almost no one would accept it. As a result, trade in goods and the use of foreign coins still flourished during this period.

By the time the Revolutionary War had been won by the American colonists, the monetary system
(15) was in a state of total disarray. To remedy this situation, the new Constitution of the United States, approved in 1789, allowed Congress to issue money. The individual states could no longer have their own money supply. A few years later, the Coinage Act of 1792 made the dollar the official currency of the United States and put the country on a bimetallic standard. In this bimetallic system, both gold and silver were legal money, and the rate of exchange of silver to gold was fixed by the government at
(20) sixteen to one.

31.  The passage mainly discusses

(A)  American money from past to present
(B)  the English monetary policies in colonial America
(C)  the effect of the Revolution on American money
(D)  the American monetary system of the seventeenth and eighteenth centuries

32.  The passage indicates that during the colonial period, money was

(A)  supplied by England
(B)  coined by the colonists
(C)  scarce
(D)  used extensively for trade

33.  The Massachusetts Bay Colony was allowed to make coins

(A)  continuously from the inception of the colony
(B)  throughout the seventeenth century
(C)  from 1652 until the Revolutionary War
(D)  for a short time during one year

34.  The expression "a means of" in line 4 could best be replaced by

(A)  an example of
(B)  a method for
(C)  a result of
(D)  a punishment for

35.  Which of the following is NOT mentioned in the passage as a substitute for money during the colonial period?

(A)  Wampum
(B)  Cotton
(C)  Tobacco
(D)  Beaver furs

36.  The pronoun "it" in line 12 refers to which of the following?

(A)  The Continental Congress
(B)  Paper money
(C)  The war
(D)  Trade in goods

**GO ON TO THE NEXT PAGE**

37. It is implied in the passage that at the end of the Revolutionary War, a paper dollar was worth

    (A) exactly one dollar
    (B) just under one dollar
    (C) just over one dollar
    (D) almost nothing

38. The word "remedy" in line 15 is closest in meaning to

    (A) resolve
    (B) understand
    (C) renew
    (D) medicate

39. How was the monetary system arranged in the Constitution?

    (A) Only the U.S. Congress could issue money.
    (B) The U.S. officially went on a bimetallic monetary system.
    (C) Various state governments, including Massachusetts, could issue money.
    (D) The dollar was made the official currency of the U.S.

40. According to the passage, which of the following is NOT true about the bimetallic monetary system?

    (A) Either gold or silver could be used as official money.
    (B) Gold could be exchanged for silver at a rate of sixteen to one.
    (C) The monetary system was based on two metals.
    (D) It was established in 1792.

41. The word "fixed" in line 19 is closest in meaning to

    (A) discovered
    (B) repaired
    (C) valued
    (D) set

**GO ON TO THE NEXT PAGE**

**Questions 42–50**

The human brain, with an average weight of 1.4 kilograms, is the control center of the body. It receives information from the senses, processes the information, and rapidly sends out responses; it also stores the information that is the source of human thoughts and feelings. Each of the three main
*Line* parts of the brain—the cerebrum, the cerebellum, and the brain stem—has its own role in carrying out
(5) these functions.

The cerebrum is by far the largest of the three parts, taking up 85 percent of the brain by weight. The outside layer of the cerebrum, the cerebral cortex, is a grooved and bumpy surface covering the nerve cells beneath. The various sections of the cerebrum are the sensory cortex, which is responsible for receiving and decoding sensory messages from throughout the body; the motor cortex, which sends
(10) action instructions to the skeletal muscles; and the association cortex, which receives, monitors, and processes information. It is in the association cortex that the processes that allow humans to think take place.

The cerebellum, located below the cerebrum in the back part of the skull, is made of masses of bunched up nerve cells. It is the cerebellum that controls human balance, coordination, and posture.
(15) The brain stem, which connects the cerebrum and the spinal cord, controls various body processes such as breathing and heartbeat. It is the major motor and sensory pathway connecting the body and the cerebrum.

42. What is the author's main purpose?

   (A) To describe the functions of the parts of the brain
   (B) To explain how the brain processes information
   (C) To demonstrate the physical composition of the brain
   (D) To give examples of human body functions

43. The word "stores" in line 3 is closest in meaning to

   (A) shops
   (B) processes
   (C) releases
   (D) stockpiles

44. The passage states that the most massive part of the brain is the

   (A) cerebrum
   (B) cerebellum
   (C) cerebral cortex
   (D) brain stem

45. The expression "grooved and bumpy" in line 7 means that the cerebral cortex is

   (A) smooth
   (B) rigid
   (C) layered
   (D) ridged

46. The sensory cortex

   (A) senses that messages should be sent out to the muscles
   (B) provides a surface covering for nerve cells
   (C) is where the human process of thinking occurs
   (D) receives and processes information from the senses

**GO ON TO THE NEXT PAGE**

47. The word "monitors" in line 10 is closest in meaning to which of the following?

    (A) Keeps track of
    (B) Keeps hold of
    (C) Gets away with
    (D) Gets rid of

48. Which of the following is true about the cerebellum?

    (A) It is located above the cerebrum.
    (B) It controls breathing.
    (C) It is responsible for balance.
    (D) It is the outside layer of the cerebrum.

49. What shape does the brain stem most likely have?

    (A) Small and round
    (B) Long and thin
    (C) Large and formless
    (D) Short and flat

50. Which of the following could best be used in place of "pathway" in line 16?

    (A) Driveway
    (B) Roadway
    (C) Route
    (D) Street

**This is the end of Section 3.**

**If you finish in less than 55 minutes, check your work on Section 3 only. Do NOT read or work on any other section of the test.**

# TEST OF WRITTEN ENGLISH
## TWE ESSAY TOPIC
### Time—30 minutes

*Some people prefer to spend their leisure time in individual sports and activities, while others prefer group sports or activities. Discuss the advantages of each. Then state which you prefer and why.*

Write your answer on the answer sheet for the Test of Written English (TWE), Practice Test Four, on pages 193–194.

# 1 □ 1 □ 1 □ 1 □ 1 □ 1 □ 1 □ 1 □ 1 □ 1 □ 1 □ 1 □ 1

# PRACTICE TEST FIVE

## SECTION 1
## LISTENING COMPREHENSION
### Time—approximately 35 minutes
### (including the reading of the directions for each part)

In this section of the test, you will have an opportunity to demonstrate your ability to understand conversations and talks in English. There are three parts to this section. Answer all the questions on the basis of what is <u>stated</u> or <u>implied</u> by the speakers you hear. Do <u>not</u> take notes or write in your test book at any time. Do not turn the pages until you are told to do so.

## Part A

**Directions:** In Part A you will hear short conversations between two people. After each conversation, you will hear a question about the conversation. The conversations and questions will not be repeated. After you hear a question, read the four possible answers in your test book and choose the best answer. Then, on your answer sheet, find the number of the question and fill in the space that corresponds to the letter of the answer you have chosen.

Listen to an example.

On the recording, you hear:

**Sample Answer**

Ⓐ Ⓑ Ⓒ ⬤

|  |  |
|---|---|
| (man) | *That exam was just awful.* |
| (woman) | *Oh, it could have been worse.* |
| (narrator) | *What does the woman mean?* |

In your test book, you read:
- (A) The exam was really awful.
- (B) It was the worst exam she had ever seen.
- (C) It couldn't have been more difficult.
- (D) It wasn't that hard.

You learn from the conversation that the man thought the exam was very difficult and that the woman disagreed with the man. The best answer to the question, "What does the woman mean?" is (D), "It wasn't that hard." Therefore, the correct choice is (D).

**Wait**

1. (A) It's time to go home.
   (B) He's late for an appointment.
   (C) His home's far away.
   (D) He's ready to leave home.

2. (A) She only spent a few cents.
   (B) She couldn't find a lot of money in her purse.
   (C) She spent all she had.
   (D) It wasn't fair to spend the money in her purse.

3. (A) In a bookstore.
   (B) In a library.
   (C) In a classroom.
   (D) In a newspaper office.

4. (A) She just delivered the clothes.
   (B) The clothes were ordered just this morning.
   (C) She recently received the clothes.
   (D) She got just some of the order.

5. (A) It's too dark where she usually studies.
   (B) She doesn't like working with a lamp on the desk.
   (C) She isn't working in the living room.
   (D) There's no lamp on her desk.

6. (A) He himself did something wrong.
   (B) He believes in firmness.
   (C) He believes that Jack was not really wrong.
   (D) He agrees with the woman.

7. (A) A maid.
   (B) A real estate agent.
   (C) A supermarket cashier.
   (D) A hotel desk clerk.

8. (A) Hospital visiting hours begin at 10:00.
   (B) This hospital doesn't allow visitors.
   (C) Visitors must leave before 10:00.
   (D) People may visit only the hospital's lower floors.

9. (A) The man should find some new clothes.
   (B) The man should have his clothes cleaned in a different place.
   (C) The man should look for a way to do his own laundry.
   (D) The man should give the laundry another chance.

10. (A) He thinks he knows when the meeting begins.
    (B) The meeting will not start when it's supposed to.
    (C) The meeting is not at 3 o'clock.
    (D) They are not supposed to attend the meeting.

11. (A) She doubts that the weather will be bad.
    (B) She probably won't go skiing.
    (C) She thinks the weather won't be as bad as predicted.
    (D) The weather forecaster didn't do a good job.

12. (A) That she should sit down in psychology class.
    (B) That she should go to class before trying to read the chapter.
    (C) That she should provide a chapter to read.
    (D) That she should prepare for class.

13. (A) She knows Tim's not seriously injured.
    (B) She hopes Tim'll get to the emergency room quickly.
    (C) She's heard all about Tim's illness.
    (D) She doesn't know how Tim's doing.

14. (A) She really enjoys the language lab.
    (B) She doesn't always do what she's supposed to do.
    (C) She isn't supposed to attend the lab.
    (D) She attends the lab regularly.

15. (A) She thinks the roses are lovely.
    (B) She doesn't like the roses.
    (C) She wonders if the roses are blooming.
    (D) She prefers other types of flowers.

**GO ON TO THE NEXT PAGE** →

16. (A) He doesn't think it's enough medicine.
    (B) Taking pills every day should help the woman a lot.
    (C) It seems like too much medicine.
    (D) Maybe there aren't enough pills.

17. (A) He was unaware of the tornado.
    (B) A tornado came dangerously close to him.
    (C) The tornado came in through the window.
    (D) He climbed out of the window when the tornado came in.

18. (A) He never wants it to stop.
    (B) He'd like it to rain again.
    (C) He thinks it's finally stopped.
    (D) He's tired of it.

19. (A) She'd really like some ice cream.
    (B) She doesn't want to do anything.
    (C) She's trying to limit desserts.
    (D) She never eats sweets.

20. (A) He's going to open a bank account.
    (B) He's going to the mountains.
    (C) He has quite a few dollars in his account.
    (D) The trip is impossible for him.

21. (A) The printer was supposed to arrive weeks ago.
    (B) Everyone's talking excitedly about the new printer.
    (C) The new printer should arrive in a few weeks.
    (D) The computer lab is four weeks old now.

22. (A) He's unable to go to the opera.
    (B) He isn't very fond of opera.
    (C) He likes going to the opera occasionally.
    (D) He has a dentist appointment tonight.

23. (A) The sales staff only sold the minimum amount.
    (B) The sales staff almost reached their goal.
    (C) The sales staff rarely used quotes in their research.
    (D) This month the sales staff reached its highest sales level ever.

24. (A) He can wait for a short time.
    (B) He went to the post office a few minutes ago.
    (C) He can help her with the letters for a few minutes.
    (D) He can hold the letters for her.

25. (A) He must study about turtles for his exam.
    (B) He's not accomplishing very much.
    (C) He'll prepare for his exams after he moves.
    (D) He comprehends that he must prepare for his exams.

26. (A) He was not taking the physics course.
    (B) He did not like physics because of the homework.
    (C) He would never do the physics homework.
    (D) He was registered in physics.

27. (A) It is impossible to install the program on the computer.
    (B) He is not the one who installed the computer.
    (C) He doesn't know how to use the program.
    (D) He would help if he had time.

28. (A) This report is better than the last.
    (B) It's better to publish the report annually.
    (C) He feels better about the report.
    (D) The report isn't too good.

29. (A) The man shouldn't speak when he's standing on his feet.
    (B) It was not polite for the man to talk about his feet.
    (C) The man put his foot where he shouldn't have.
    (D) The man said something embarrassing.

30. (A) Marla won the competition fairly.
    (B) It was advantageous for Marla to win.
    (C) The competition was not fair.
    (D) The judge provided Marla with an advantage.

**GO ON TO THE NEXT PAGE**

## Part B

**Directions:** In this part of the test, you will hear longer conversations. After each conversation, you will hear several questions. The conversations and questions will not be repeated.

After you hear a question, read the four possible answers in your test book and choose the best answer. Then, on your answer sheet, find the number of the question and fill in the space that corresponds to the letter of the answer you have chosen.

Remember, you are <u>not</u> allowed to take notes or write in your test book.

31. (A) To a doctor's appointment.
    (B) To an exercise club.
    (C) To a swimming pool.
    (D) To a school.

32. (A) They're both regular members.
    (B) He likes to go there occasionally.
    (C) She wants him to try it out.
    (D) She hates to exercise alone.

33. (A) A limited number.
    (B) Racquetball courts and a swimming pool.
    (C) Exercise machines, but not classes.
    (D) Just about anything.

34. (A) Visit the club once.
    (B) Take out a membership.
    (C) Try the club unless he hurts himself.
    (D) See if he has time to go.

35. (A) A presentation for political science class.
    (B) How quickly time passes.
    (C) The differences between the various types of courts.
    (D) A schedule for preparing for a political science exam.

36. (A) Three levels of courts.
    (B) Only the municipal courts.
    (C) The state but not the federal courts.
    (D) Only the state and federal courts.

37. (A) On Thursday.
    (B) On Monday.
    (C) In a week.
    (D) Before Monday.

38. (A) Plenty of time.
    (B) Until Monday.
    (C) One week.
    (D) Until a week from Monday.

**GO ON TO THE NEXT PAGE**

## Part C

**Directions:** In this part of the test, you will hear several talks. After each talk, you will hear some questions. The talks and questions will not be repeated.

After you hear a question, read the four possible answers in your test book and choose the best answer. Then, on your answer sheet, find the number of the question and fill in the space that corresponds to the letter of the answer you have chosen.

Here is an example.

On the recording, you hear:

(narrator)  *Listen to an instructor talk to his class about painting.*

(man)  *Artist Grant Wood was a guiding force in the school of painting known as American regionalist, a style reflecting the distinctive characteristics of art from rural areas of the United States. Wood began drawing animals on the family farm at the age of three, and when he was thirty-eight one of his paintings received a remarkable amount of public notice and acclaim. This painting, called American Gothic, is a starkly simple depiction of a serious couple staring directly out at the viewer.*

Now listen to a sample question.                    **Sample Answer**

(narrator)  *What style of painting is known as American regionalist?*

In your test book, you read:   (A)   Art from America's inner cities.
                               (B)   Art from the central region of the U.S.
                               (C)   Art from various urban areas in the U.S.
                               (D)   Art from rural sections of America.

The best answer to the question, "What style of painting is known as American regionalist?" is (D), "Art from rural sections of America." Therefore, the correct choice is (D).

Now listen to another sample question.                    **Sample Answer**

(narrator)  *What is the name of Wood's most successful painting?*

In your test book, you read:   (A)   "American Regionalist."
                               (B)   "The Family Farm in Iowa."
                               (C)   "American Gothic."
                               (D)   "A Serious Couple."

The best answer to the question, "What is the name of Wood's most successful painting?" is (C), "American Gothic." Therefore, the correct choice is (C).

Remember, you are <u>not</u> allowed to take notes or write in your test book.

39. (A) A university administrator.
    (B) A student.
    (C) A librarian.
    (D) A registrar.

40. (A) How to use the library.
    (B) The university registration procedure.
    (C) Services offered by the Student Center.
    (D) Important locations on campus.

41. (A) To provide students with assistance and amusement.
    (B) To assist students in the registration process.
    (C) To allow students to watch movies.
    (D) To provide textbooks for university courses.

42. (A) In administrators' offices.
    (B) In the Student Center.
    (C) In an auditorium.
    (D) In the Student Records Office.

43. (A) Natural soaps.
    (B) Synthetic detergents.
    (C) Biodegradable detergents.
    (D) Phosphates.

44. (A) Synthetic detergents.
    (B) A major cause of water pollution.
    (C) Substances that break down into simpler forms.
    (D) The reason for the foaming water supply.

45. (A) They broke down into simpler forms.
    (B) They caused the water to become foamy.
    (C) They released phosphates into the water.
    (D) They damaged only the underground water supply.

46. (A) Water pollution in the 1950's.
    (B) Nonbiodegradable synthetic detergents.
    (C) The foamy water supply.
    (D) Problems caused by the phosphates.

47. (A) The static atmosphere.
    (B) The cause of changes in the atmosphere.
    (C) The evolution of plant life.
    (D) The process of photosynthesis.

48. (A) Two hundred million years ago.
    (B) Twenty million years ago.
    (C) Two hundred thousand years ago.
    (D) Twenty thousand years ago.

49. (A) The evolution of plants and photosynthesis.
    (B) The variety of gases in the atmosphere.
    (C) The high percentage of nitrogen.
    (D) The ammonia and methane in the original atmosphere.

50. (A) Read about the composition of the atmosphere.
    (B) Study the notes of today's lecture.
    (C) Prepare for a quiz.
    (D) Read the following chapter.

**This is the end of Section 1.**
**Stop work on Section 1.**

**Turn off your cassette player.**

**Read the directions for Section 2 and begin work.**
**Do NOT read or work on any other section**
**of the test during the next 25 minutes.**

## SECTION 2
## STRUCTURE AND WRITTEN EXPRESSION
### Time—25 minutes
### (including the reading of the directions)
### Now set your clock for 25 minutes.

This section is designed to measure your ability to recognize language that is appropriate for standard written English. There are two types of questions in this section, with special directions for each type.

### Structure

**Directions:** Questions 1–15 are incomplete sentences. Beneath each sentence you will see four words or phrases, marked (A), (B), (C), and (D). Choose the <u>one</u> word or phrase that best completes the sentence. Then, on your answer sheet, find the number of the question and fill in the space that corresponds to the letter of the answer you have chosen. Fill in the space so that the letter inside the oval cannot be seen.

Look at the following examples.

*Example I*                                   **Sample Answer**

The president _____ the election by a landslide.        ● Ⓑ Ⓒ Ⓓ

(A)  won
(B)  he won
(C)  yesterday
(D)  fortunately

The sentence should read, "The president won the election by a landslide." Therefore, you should choose (A).

*Example II*                                  **Sample Answer**

When _____ the conference?                      Ⓐ ● Ⓒ Ⓓ

(A)  the doctor attended
(B)  did the doctor attend
(C)  the doctor will attend
(D)  the doctor's attendance

The sentence should read, "When did the doctor attend the conference?" Therefore, you should choose (B).

Now begin work on the questions.

**GO ON TO THE NEXT PAGE**

1. Jackson, _____ capital of Mississippi, is the largest city in the state.

   (A) the
   (B) where is the
   (C) is the
   (D) it is the

2. Valley Forge National Park commemorates the time that Washington _____ in Valley Forge with his troops.

   (A) spend
   (B) spent
   (C) was spent
   (D) has been spent

3. In New England _____ picturesque fishing villages and manufacturing towns.

   (A) has
   (B) many
   (C) about
   (D) there are

4. In 1774 delegates from all the colonies _____ attended the First Continental Congress.

   (A) Georgia
   (B) the exception was Georgia
   (C) except Georgia
   (D) except that Georgia was

5. It is the recommendation of the U.S. Public Health Service _____ children be vaccinated against a variety of diseases.

   (A) suggestion to all
   (B) that all
   (C) to all
   (D) suggests that all

6. The pirate Jean Lafitte offered his services to the U.S. government in the War of 1812, _____ in 1815, and received a full pardon from President James Madison.

   (A) fought in the Battle of New Orleans
   (B) the Battle of New Orleans was
   (C) he fought in the Battle of New Orleans
   (D) the Battle of New Orleans

7. Although fish do not have outer ears, _____ have a simple inner ear on either side of the head.

   (A) there are varieties
   (B) they are varieties
   (C) some varieties
   (D) which varieties

8. Jamestown, the first permanent English settlement in America, _____ in 1607.

   (A) it was founded
   (B) colonists arrived there
   (C) was established
   (D) founded

9. _____ through a telescope, Venus appears to go through changes in size and shape.

   (A) It is seen
   (B) Seeing
   (C) When seen
   (D) It has seen

10. The various types of bacteria are classified according to _____ shaped.

   (A) they are
   (B) having
   (C) how they are
   (D) whose

**GO ON TO THE NEXT PAGE**

11. Beavers have been known to use logs, branches, rocks, and mud to build dams that are more than a thousand ____ .

 (A) foot in length
 (B) feet long
 (C) long feet
 (D) lengthy feet

12. ____ stone tools and animal remains found with human fossils, anthropologists have determined that Neanderthal Man was a successful hunter.

 (A) When the
 (B) The
 (C) Both the
 (D) From the

13. ____ as the most important crop in Hawaii is sugar cane.

 (A) It ranks
 (B) It is ranked
 (C) What ranks
 (D) The rank

14. Under the educational plan proposed by the school board of Rocklyn County, ____ unhappy with a particular school, they could simply move their children to another.

 (A) were parents
 (B) when parents
 (C) parents who were
 (D) parents were

15. In the U.S. more than 60 percent of all high school students who ____ continue their education.

 (A) do not
 (B) graduate
 (C) will
 (D) can

GO ON TO THE NEXT PAGE

**Written Expression**

**Directions:** In questions 16–40, each sentence has four underlined words or phrases. The four underlined parts of the sentence are marked (A), (B), (C), and (D). Identify the <u>one</u> underlined word or phrase that must be changed in order for the sentence to be correct. Then, on your answer sheet, find the number of the question and fill in the space that corresponds to the letter of the answer you have chosen.

Look at the following examples.

> *Example I*                                                    **Sample Answer**

>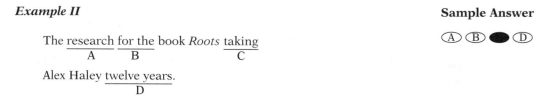

> The sentence should read, "The four strings on a violin are tuned in fifths." Therefore, you should choose (B).

> *Example II*                                                   **Sample Answer**

> The sentence should read, "The research for the book *Roots* took Alex Haley twelve years." Therefore, you should choose (C).

Now begin work on the questions.

**GO ON TO THE NEXT PAGE**

16. J. Edgar Hoover <u>has served</u> as <u>director</u> of the FBI <u>from</u> 1924 until <u>his death</u> in 1972.
                 A             B                 C             D

17. Denver is <u>call</u> the "Mile High City" because <u>it is</u> at <u>an altitude</u> of 5,280 <u>feet</u>, or 1 mile, above sea
          A                              B   C         D

level.

18. A neutrino is <u>a subatomic</u> particle <u>it</u> <u>has</u> <u>no</u> electrical charge.
                   A             B  C  D

19. <u>While</u> the Sun is <u>the major</u> source of ultraviolet rays, <u>it is</u> not the <u>source only</u>.
   A             B                        C       D

20. Gamma globulin, a protein <u>found in</u> blood plasma, <u>is</u> used to prevent such infectious diseases <u>for</u>
                          A              B                            C

measles <u>and</u> viral hepatitis.
       D

21. <u>Together</u> Rogers and Hammerstein wrote nine <u>musicals</u>, the <u>first</u> of <u>whose</u> was *Oklahoma*.
     A                                 B      C    D

22. A dam <u>stops</u> the <u>flow</u> of water, creating a reservoir and <u>raise</u> the <u>level</u> of water.
         A     B                           C       D

23. <u>Authors</u> Samuel Morison <u>won</u> two Pulitzer Prizes, one in 1943 for <u>a biography</u> of Columbus and
    A                 B                             C

the other in 1960 for a biography of John Paul Jones.
    D

24. The United States is the <u>world's</u> largest cheese producer, <u>making</u> more than two million <u>tons</u> of
                          A                       B                 C

cheese <u>annual</u>.
       D

25. According to the 1978 Bakke decision by the Supreme Court, <u>an</u> university may not <u>use</u>
                                               A                    B

admissions <u>quotas</u> to obtain <u>a racially</u> balanced student body.
           C            D

26. The system <u>for helping</u> slaves escape to the North was called the "Underground Railroad,"
             A

though <u>it</u> <u>was</u> neither underground <u>or</u> a railroad.
    B    C                     D

27. <u>Unlike</u> light from other sources, <u>which</u> travels in all <u>direction</u>, the light from a laser is
   A                             B             C

<u>highly directional</u>.
     D

28. Natural gas is composed of hydrocarbon molecules <u>that breaks</u> <u>apart</u> into hydrogen and carbon
          A                                  B    C

atoms <u>when heated</u>.
     D

**GO ON TO THE NEXT PAGE** ➡

29. Nuclear <u>powers</u> production in the U.S. <u>is</u> <u>controlled</u> by <u>the</u> Nuclear Regulatory Commission.
    A                    B   C     D

30. Diamonds <u>are evaluated</u> on <u>the basis</u> of <u>their</u> <u>weigh</u>, purity, and color.
             A          B        C  D

31. Ships are able to <u>move through</u> canals <u>by means</u> locks, <u>rectangular</u> areas with <u>variable</u> water
                  A             B          C          D
    levels.

32. Harvard University <u>was</u> established <u>just</u> <u>after sixteen years</u> the Pilgrims <u>arrived</u>.
                    A       B        C            D

33. Patients <u>suffering</u> <u>from</u> encephalitis have an <u>inflame</u> <u>of the</u> brain.
            A     B                  C    D

34. About twenty-eight million Americans suffer serious hearing <u>loss</u>, and the <u>likely</u> cause in more
                                                    A           B
    than a third of the cases <u>are</u> too much <u>exposure</u> to loud noise.
                              C           D

35. <u>Because</u> helicopters are capable <u>of hovering</u> in midair, they are <u>particularly</u> useful for rescue
      A                             B                         C
    missions, military <u>operates</u>, and transportation.
                      D

36. Many states <u>do</u> laws regulating <u>production processes</u> for different <u>types</u> of food <u>products</u>.
                A                  B                    C     D

37. For photosynthesis <u>to occur</u>, a leaf <u>requires</u> carbon dioxide, water, and <u>lightness</u>.
     A               B        C                    D

38. Ester Forbes <u>won</u> the 1943 Pulitzer Prize <u>in</u> American history for <u>her</u> <u>biographer</u> of Paul Revere.
                A                      B            C   D

39. The Bill of Rights <u>was added</u> to the Constitution <u>specifically</u> to guarantee <u>the certain</u> individual
                        A                           B                  C
    rights.
    D

40. The <u>longer a noise</u> <u>lasts</u>, the <u>damaging it</u> <u>becomes</u>.
           A      B        C       D

**This is the end of Section 2.**
**If you finish before 25 minutes has ended,**
**check your work on Section 2 only.**

**At the end of 25 minutes, go on to Section 3.**
**Use exactly 55 minutes to work on Section 3.**

## SECTION 3
## READING COMPREHENSION
**Time—55 minutes**
**(including the reading of the directions)**
**Now set your clock for 55 minutes.**

This section is designed to measure your ability to read and understand short passages similar in topic and style to those that students are likely to encounter in North American universities and colleges.

**Directions:** In this section you will read several passages. Each one is followed by a number of questions about it. You are to choose the <u>one</u> best answer, (A), (B), (C), or (D), to each question. Then, on your answer sheet, find the number of the question and fill in the space that corresponds to the letter of the answer you have chosen.

Answer all questions about the information in a passage on the basis of what is <u>stated</u> or <u>implied</u> in that passage.

Read the following passage:

  John Quincy Adams, who served as the sixth president of the United States from 1825 to 1829, is today recognized for his masterful statesmanship and diplomacy. He dedicated his life to public service, both in the presidency and in the various other political offices that he
*Line* held. Throughout his political career he demonstrated his unswerving belief in freedom of
*(5)* speech, the antislavery cause, and the right of Americans to be free from European and Asian domination.

*Example I*                 **Sample Answer**

                               Ⓐ ● Ⓒ Ⓓ

  To what did John Quincy Adams devote his life?

  (A) Improving his personal life
  (B) Serving the public
  (C) Increasing his fortune
  (D) Working on his private business

According to the passage, John Quincy Adams "dedicated his life to public service." Therefore, you should choose (B).

*Example II*                **Sample Answer**

                               Ⓐ Ⓑ ● Ⓓ

  In line 4, the word "unswerving" is closest in meaning to

  (A) moveable
  (B) insignificant
  (C) unchanging
  (D) diplomatic

The passage states that John Quincy Adams demonstrated his unswerving belief "throughout his career." This implies that the belief did not change. Therefore, you should choose (C).

Now begin work on the questions.

**GO ON TO THE NEXT PAGE**

**Questions 1–9**

The next famous woman writer to be considered is Dorothy Parker, an American poet, short story writer, and literary critic who became famous in the early twentieth century for her witty but cynical observations on life. She got her first paying job as a writer in 1916 at the age of twenty-three when she
*Line* began working for a women's magazine, and nine years later she became a contributor to *The New*
(5) *Yorker* and regularly had her book reviews appear in "Constant Reader," a column in that magazine.

In addition to her magazine work, she published volumes of poetry and short stories with the recurrent themes of disappointment with life and the loss of idealism; these pessimistic themes, however, were presented with biting wit. One of her most famous observations, "Men seldom make passes / At girls who wear glasses," came from the poem "News Item," which was published in the
(10) volume *Enough Rope* (1926). This volume of poetry was followed by *Sunset Gun* (1928), *Death and Taxes* (1931), and a collection of short stories, *Here Lies* (1939). Her book reviews were published in 1970 in a volume entitled "Constant Reader."

1. What topic does the paragraph preceding the passage most likely discuss?

   (A) Dorothy Parker's early childhood
   (B) American literature of the nineteenth century
   (C) An introduction to literary criticism
   (D) A well-known female author other than Dorothy Parker

2. According to the passage, Dorothy Parker was NOT famous for

   (A) poetry
   (B) humor
   (C) book reviews
   (D) autobiography

3. The word "observations" in line 3 could best be replaced by

   (A) looks
   (B) scenes
   (C) views
   (D) jokes

4. Dorothy Parker's first job was

   (A) for a women's magazine
   (B) as a literary critic
   (C) for *The New Yorker*
   (D) as a short story writer

5. In line 7, the word "recurrent" is closest in meaning to which of the following?

   (A) Related
   (B) Repeated
   (C) Flowing
   (D) Negative

6. The word "pessimistic" in line 7 is closest in meaning to

   (A) negative
   (B) impractical
   (C) forgotten
   (D) unattained

**GO ON TO THE NEXT PAGE**

7. The expression "biting wit" in line 8 could best be replaced by which of the following?

(A) Intelligence
(B) Sadness
(C) Sharp humor
(D) Hunger

8. In what year did "News Item" appear?

(A) 1916
(B) 1926
(C) 1928
(D) 1931

9. It can be inferred from the passage that the title of Parker's volume of book reviews came from

(A) some earlier work she had done
(B) a favorite expression of hers
(C) a title of one of her poems
(D) her biting sense of humor

**GO ON TO THE NEXT PAGE**

**Questions 10–19**

Fog occurs when moisture from the surface of the Earth evaporates; as this evaporated moisture moves upward, it cools and condenses into the familiar phenomenon of fog. Fog differs from clouds in that fog touches the surface of the Earth, while clouds do not.

*Line*
*(5)*
Of the two types of fog, advection fog occurs along the ocean coast or near rivers and lakes. This type of fast-moving fog, which may cover vast areas, occurs when the temperature of the wind blowing over a body of water differs from the temperature of the body of water itself. This kind of fog can occur when warm air moves over a cold surface of water; this commonly occurs along the ocean coastline or along the shores of large lakes. Advection fog can also occur when cooler air moves over the surface of warmer water; this is very common in the winter in an area such as Florida, where the temperature of
*(10)* the lakes is quite warm in relation to the temperature of the air.

Radiation fog, quite different from advection fog, is immobile, cloudlike moisture generally found hovering over wintertime valleys. It occurs on clear nights when the Earth's warmth escapes into the upper atmosphere; the ground gives off heat through radiation. As the land becomes cooler, the air above it also becomes cooler. This cooler air is unable to hold as much water vapor as it had when it
*(15)* was warmer; in this manner fog is created.

10. According to the passage, fog is formed when wetness in the air is

    (A) vaporized
    (B) cooled
    (C) dampened
    (D) heated

11. The word "familiar" in line 2 could best be replaced by

    (A) friendly
    (B) confidential
    (C) common
    (D) parental

12. According to the passage, advection fog is found

    (A) in valleys
    (B) in the ocean
    (C) near bodies of water
    (D) only in small, enclosed areas

13. The word "vast" in line 5 is closest in meaning to

    (A) immense
    (B) flat
    (C) humid
    (D) windy

14. In the passage, radiation fog is said to be

    (A) similar to advection fog
    (B) found in coastal areas
    (C) fast-moving
    (D) trapped moisture hanging over inland valleys

15. The word "immobile" in line 11 is closest in meaning to

    (A) unmotivated
    (B) unsteady
    (C) variable
    (D) unmoving

**GO ON TO THE NEXT PAGE**

16.  The pronoun "It" in line 12 refers to which of the following?

    (A)   Radiation fog
    (B)   Advection fog
    (C)   Cloudlike moisture
    (D)   The Earth's warmth

17.  The word "manner" in line 15 could best be replaced by

    (A)   politeness
    (B)   way
    (C)   period of time
    (D)   example

18.  According to the passage, which of the following statements about fog is NOT true?

    (A)   Advection fog occurs when the cooled atmosphere meets with heat from the Earth.
    (B)   Advection fog generally moves quickly across vast areas of land.
    (C)   Radiation fog often starts on clear nights.
    (D)   Radiation fog is the type of fog that occurs in small valleys on clear nights.

19.  The author's purpose in this passage is to

    (A)   explain the different types of fog
    (B)   describe where different types of fog are found
    (C)   discuss advection fog
    (D)   give a scientific description of various types of precipitation

**GO ON TO THE NEXT PAGE**

**Questions 20–30**

Harvard University, today recognized as part of the top echelon of the world's universities, came from very inauspicious and humble beginnings.

*Line*
(5)

This oldest of American universities was founded in 1636, just sixteen years after the Pilgrims landed at Plymouth. Included in the Puritan emigrants to the Massachusetts colony during this period were more than 100 graduates of England's prestigious Oxford and Cambridge Universities, and these university graduates in the New World were determined that their sons would have the same educational opportunities that they themselves had had. Because of this support in the colony for an institution of higher learning, the General Court of Massachusetts appropriated 400 pounds for a college in October of 1636 and early the following year decided on a parcel of land for the school; this

(10)
land was in an area called Newetowne, which was later renamed Cambridge after its English cousin and is the site of the present-day university.

When a young minister named John Harvard, who came from the neighboring town of Charlestowne, died from tuberculosis in 1638, he willed half of his estate of 1,700 pounds to the fledgling college. In spite of the fact that only half of the bequest was actually paid, the General Court

(15)
named the college after the minister in appreciation for what he had done. The amount of the bequest may not have been large, particularly by today's standards, but it was more than the General Court had found it necessary to appropriate in order to open the college.

Henry Dunster was appointed the first president of Harvard in 1640, and it should be noted that in addition to serving as president, he was also the entire faculty, with an entering freshman class of four

(20)
students. Although the staff did expand somewhat, for the first century of its existence the entire teaching staff consisted of the president and three or four tutors.

20. The main idea of this passage is that

(A) Harvard is one of the world's most prestigious universities
(B) what is today a great university started out small
(C) John Harvard was key to the development of a great university
(D) Harvard University developed under the auspices of the General Court of Massachusetts

21. The passage indicates that Harvard is

(A) one of the oldest universities in the world
(B) the oldest university in the world
(C) one of the oldest universities in America
(D) the oldest university in America

22. It can be inferred from the passage that the Puritans who traveled to the Massachusetts colony were

(A) rather well educated
(B) rather rich
(C) rather supportive of the English government
(D) rather undemocratic

23. The pronoun "they" in line 7 refers to

(A) Oxford and Cambridge Universities
(B) university graduates
(C) sons
(D) educational opportunities

24. A "pound" in line 8 is probably

(A) a type of book
(B) a type of student
(C) a type of money
(D) a type of college

**GO ON TO THE NEXT PAGE** ➡

25. The "English cousin" in line 10 refers to a

    (A)  city
    (B)  relative
    (C)  person
    (D)  court

26. Which of the following is NOT mentioned about John Harvard?

    (A)  What he died of
    (B)  Where he came from
    (C)  Where he was buried
    (D)  How much he bequeathed to Harvard

27. The word "fledgling" in line 14 could best be replaced by which of the following?

    (A)  Newborn
    (B)  Flying
    (C)  Winged
    (D)  Established

28. The passage implies that

    (A)  Henry Dunster was an ineffective president
    (B)  someone else really served as president of Harvard before Henry Dunster
    (C)  Henry Dunster spent much of his time as president managing the Harvard faculty
    (D)  the position of president of Harvard was not merely an administrative position in the early years

29. The word "somewhat" in line 20 could best be replaced by

    (A)  back and forth
    (B)  to and fro
    (C)  side by side
    (D)  more or less

30. Where in the passage does it indicate how much money Minister Harvard was really responsible for giving to the university?

    (A)  Lines 3–7
    (B)  Lines 7–11
    (C)  Lines 12–15
    (D)  Lines 15–17

GO ON TO THE NEXT PAGE

**Questions 31–40**

A binary star is actually a pair of stars that are held together by the force of gravity. Although occasionally the individual stars that compose a binary star can be distinguished, they generally appear as one star. The gravitational pull between the individual stars of a binary star causes one to orbit
*Line* around the other. From the orbital pattern of a binary, the mass of its stars can be determined: the
(5) gravitational pull of a star is in direct proportion to its mass, and the strength of the gravitational force of one star on another determines the orbital pattern of the binary.

Scientists have discovered stars that seem to orbit around an empty space. It has been suggested that such a star and the empty space really composed a binary star. The empty space is known as a "black hole," a star with such strong gravitational force that no light is able to get through. Although
(10) the existence of black holes has not been proven, the theory of their existence has been around for about two centuries, since the French mathematician Pierre Simon de Laplace first proposed the concept at the end of the eighteenth century. Scientific interest in this theory has been intense in the last few decades. However, currently the theory is unproven. Black holes can only be potentially identified based on the interactions of objects around them, as happens when a potential black hole is
(15) part of a binary star; they of course cannot be seen because of the inability of any light to escape the star's powerful gravity.

31. A binary star could best be described as

    (A) stars that have been forced apart
    (B) a star with a strong gravitational force
    (C) two stars pulled together by gravity
    (D) a large number of attached stars

32. The word "distinguished" in line 2 is closest in meaning to

    (A) renowned
    (B) tied
    (C) celebrated
    (D) differentiated

33. According to the passage, what happens as a result of the gravitational force between the stars?

    (A) One star circles the other.
    (B) The mass of the binary star increases.
    (C) A black hole is destroyed.
    (D) The gravitational force decreases.

34. The word "proportion" in line 5 is closest in meaning to which of the following?

    (A) Contrast
    (B) Ratio
    (C) Inversion
    (D) Force

35. According to the passage, what is a "black hole"?

    (A) An empty space around which nothing orbits
    (B) A star with close to zero gravity
    (C) A star whose gravitational force blocks the passage of light
    (D) An empty space so far away that no light can reach it

36. Which of the following statements about black holes is NOT supported by the passage?

    (A) A black hole can have a star orbiting around it.
    (B) A binary star can be composed of a black hole and a visible star.
    (C) All empty space contains black holes.
    (D) The gravitational pull of a black hole is strong.

37. The word "get" in line 9 could best be replaced by

    (A) pass
    (B) sink
    (C) jump
    (D) see

**GO ON TO THE NEXT PAGE**

38. Which of the following is implied in the passage about the theory of black holes?

    (A) No reputable scientists believe it.
    (B) It has only recently been hypothesized.
    (C) At least some scientists find it credible.
    (D) Scientists are hoping to see a black hole in order to prove the theory.

39. The word "intense" in line 12 is closest in meaning to

    (A) brilliant
    (B) intermittent
    (C) bright
    (D) strong

40. This passage would probably be assigned reading in a course on

    (A) botany
    (B) astrophysics
    (C) geology
    (D) astrology

GO ON TO THE NEXT PAGE

## Questions 41–50

It is the role of the Federal Reserve, known simply as the Fed, to control the supply of money in the U.S. through its system of twelve regional Federal Reserve Banks, each with its own Federal Reserve District Bank. Many commercial banks belong to the Federal Reserve System and as members
*Line* must follow the Fed's reserve requirements, a ruling by the Fed on the percentage of deposits that a
(5) member bank must keep either in its own vaults or on deposit at the Fed. If the Fed wants to change the money supply, it can change reserve requirements to member banks; for example, an increase in the percentage of deposits required to be kept on hand would reduce the available money supply. Member banks can also borrow money from the Fed, and an additional way that the Fed can control the money supply is to raise or lower the discount rate, the interest rate at which commercial banks
(10) borrow from the Fed. An increase in the discount rate would reduce the funds available to commercial banks and thus shrink the money supply. In addition to using reserve requirements and the discount rate to control the money supply, the Fed has another powerful tool: open-market operations.

41. This passage is mainly about

    (A) the functions of the Federal Reserve
    (B) the organization of the Federal Reserve
    (C) reserve requirements
    (D) the effect of lowering the discount rate

42. According to the passage, the main purpose of the Federal Reserve System is to

    (A) increase reserve requirements
    (B) increase or decrease the amount of money available
    (C) increase the number of Federal Reserve Banks
    (D) increase the money kept on deposit by member banks

43. The word "regional" in line 2 is closest in meaning to

    (A) dozen
    (B) similar
    (C) separate
    (D) area

44. When the Fed controls the percentage of deposits kept on hand by member banks, it controls

    (A) district banks
    (B) the discount rate
    (C) the reserve requirement
    (D) borrowing by commercial banks

45. "Vaults" in line 5 are

    (A) accounts
    (B) cash drawers
    (C) compartments for safekeeping
    (D) personal safety deposit boxes

46. The expression "on hand" in line 7 is closest in meaning to

    (A) tightly held
    (B) in current supplies
    (C) under control
    (D) locked up

**GO ON TO THE NEXT PAGE**

47. The word "shrink" in line 11 could best be replaced by

    (A) reduce
    (B) inflate
    (C) support
    (D) increase

48. The passage implies that a lowering of the discount rate would lead to

    (A) an increase in the money supply
    (B) a decrease in borrowing from the Fed by commercial banks
    (C) a decrease in the money available
    (D) an increase in the reserve requirement

49. Where in the passage does the author discuss the organization of the Fed?

    (A) Lines 1–3
    (B) Lines 5–7
    (C) Lines 8–10
    (D) Lines 11–12

50. The paragraph following the passage most likely discusses

    (A) the need for controlling the money supply
    (B) the structure of the Federal Reserve System
    (C) recent changes in reserve requirements
    (D) open-market purchases and sales

**This is the end of Section 3.**

**If you finish in less than 55 minutes, check your work on Section 3 only. Do NOT read or work on any other section of the test.**

# TEST OF WRITTEN ENGLISH
## TWE ESSAY TOPIC
**Time—30 minutes**

Do you agree or disagree with the following statement?

*It is important to be as careful as you can with money and save every penny that you can.*

Use specific reasons and details to support your answer. Write your answer on the answer sheet for the Test of Written English (TWE), Practice Test Five, on pages 197–198.

# TAPESCRIPT

# PRACTICE TEST ONE TAPESCRIPT

## SECTION 1
## LISTENING COMPREHENSION

In this section of the test, you will have an opportunity to demonstrate your ability to understand conversations and talks in English. There are three parts to this section. Answer all the questions on the basis of what is <u>stated</u> or <u>implied</u> by the speakers you hear. Do <u>not</u> take notes or write in your test book at any time. Do not turn the pages until you are told to do so.

### Part A

**<u>Directions:</u>** In Part A you will hear short conversations between two people. After each conversation, you will hear a question about the conversation. The conversations and questions will not be repeated. After you hear a question, read the four possible answers in your test book and choose the best answer. Then, on your answer sheet, find the number of the question and fill in the space that corresponds to the letter of the answer you have chosen.

Listen to an example.

On the recording, you hear:

| | |
|---|---|
| (man) | *That exam was just awful.* |
| (woman) | *Oh, it could have been worse.* |
| (narrator) | *What does the woman mean?* |

In your test book, you read:

(A) The exam was really awful.
(B) It was the worst exam she had ever seen.
(C) It couldn't have been more difficult.
(D) It wasn't that hard.

You learn from the conversation that the man thought the exam was very difficult and that the woman disagreed with the man. The best answer to the question, "What does the woman mean?" is (D), "It wasn't that hard." Therefore, the correct choice is (D).

1. (woman) Is there any more typing paper?
   (man) Not that I know of.
   (narrator) WHAT DOES THE MAN MEAN?

2. (man) What's the matter? You don't look too good.
   (woman) I was frightened by a loud noise.
   (narrator) WHAT DOES THE WOMAN MEAN?

3. (man) Will this take very long? I have to get to a meeting at work.
   (woman) Well, you need to have your teeth cleaned and a cavity filled.
   (narrator) WHERE DOES THIS CONVERSATION PROBABLY TAKE PLACE?

4. (woman) Is Tina going to work on the science project with us?
   (man) She prefers not to work on group projects.
   (narrator) WHAT DOES THE MAN SAY ABOUT TINA?

5. (woman) Been working long?
   (man) Not really. Only since last week.
   (narrator) WHAT DOES THE MAN MEAN?

6. (man) Did Mel and Amy really prepare for the exam?
   (woman) Mel studied thoroughly for the exam, and Amy did, too.
   (narrator) WHAT DOES THE WOMAN MEAN?

7. (woman) How often do you watch television?
   (man) Only an hour or two a week.
   (narrator) WHAT DOES THE MAN MEAN?

8. (woman) I'd like to see the personnel manager, please.
   (man) He'll be in tomorrow at 10:00. Would you like to make an appointment?
   (narrator) WHAT WILL THE WOMAN PROBABLY DO?

141

9.  (woman)    Bob, what are you doing with that budgetary report?
    (man)      I keep adding and re-adding the numbers, but they just don't balance.
    (narrator) WHAT IS BOB'S PROFESSION MOST LIKELY TO BE?

10. (man)      This television cost me fifty dollars.
    (woman)    Only fifty dollars? Mine cost a fortune.
    (narrator) WHAT DOES THE WOMAN IMPLY?

11. (woman)    Can you tell me how to get to the administration building?
    (man)      The administration building is next to the bookstore, isn't it?
    (narrator) WHAT DOES THE MAN MEAN?

12. (man)      There's a symphony concert tomorrow night. Do you want to go?
    (woman)    What a good idea! I haven't been to one in a long time.
    (narrator) WHAT WILL THE WOMAN PROBABLY DO?

13. (woman)    Greg just arrived at the airport.
    (man)      And not a minute too soon.
    (narrator) WHAT DOES THE MAN MEAN?

14. (woman)    Did you or Sally finish the assignment? I know she didn't want to do it.
    (man)      I made Sally finish the assignment.
    (narrator) WHAT DOES THE MAN MEAN?

15. (man)      Can you show me how to use the word processor?
    (woman)    I doubt I know more than you, but I'll try.
    (narrator) WHAT DOES THE WOMAN MEAN?

16. (woman)    I hope you were able to be really productive today.
    (man)      It was so hot that I couldn't get any work done.
    (narrator) WHAT DOES THE MAN MEAN?

17. (man)      Have you seen the school play?
    (woman)    Seen it? I have the lead role.
    (narrator) WHAT DOES THE WOMAN MEAN?

18. (woman)    Did Margaret ever figure out what that word meant?
    (man)      She had to look it up in an unabridged dictionary.
    (narrator) WHAT DOES THE MAN SAY ABOUT MARGARET?

19. (woman)    There's a great movie on television tonight. Do you want to watch it?
    (man)      Not if it's on at the same time as the game.
    (narrator) WHAT DOES THE MAN IMPLY?

20. (man)      Does everyone in the house help with the laundry?
    (woman)    Pat doesn't mind doing the laundry, nor does Jim.
    (narrator) WHAT DOES THE WOMAN MEAN?

21. (woman)    I can't believe that it's snowing again today.
    (man)      Two weeks without a change is pretty boring.
    (narrator) WHAT DOES THE MAN IMPLY?

22. (man)      The bookstore's out of texts for American History, and the first exam is next week.
    (woman)    You'd better borrow one from a friend, because the new order won't arrive by then.
    (narrator) WHAT DOES THE WOMAN MEAN?

23. (woman)    I hope you enjoyed the movie.
    (man)      It couldn't have been any funnier.
    (narrator) WHAT DOES THE MAN MEAN?

24. (man)      I don't know if Steve liked the apartment or not.
    (woman)    He said he liked it, but then he didn't want to sign the lease.
    (narrator) WHAT CAN BE CONCLUDED ABOUT STEVE?

25. (man)      Are you going to see the dentist this afternoon?
    (woman)    I wish I didn't have to.
    (narrator) WHAT DOES THE WOMAN MEAN?

26. (woman)    Lucky Tom. He just bought a new car.
    (man)      Lucky? He had to buy it because he wrecked his other car in an accident.
    (narrator) WHAT DOES THE MAN MEAN?

27.  (man)  It's the first of the month, and the rent is due.

(woman)  I'll take care of it this month.

(narrator)  WHAT DOES THE WOMAN MEAN?

28.  (man)  Here's the book that you asked me about.

(woman)  So you <u>did</u> remember that I wanted to borrow it.

(narrator)  WHAT HAD THE WOMAN ASSUMED?

29.  (woman)  Did you pay the electric company on time?

(man)  If I hadn't, we wouldn't have any lights now.

(narrator)  WHAT DOES THE MAN MEAN?

30.  (man)  I thought that we were having an exam today.

(woman)  Didn't you hear what the professor said yesterday? You really missed the boat!

(narrator)  WHAT DOES THE WOMAN IMPLY ABOUT THE MAN?

---

## Part B

**Directions:** In this part of the test, you will hear longer conversations. After each conversation, you will hear several questions. The conversations and questions will not be repeated.

After you hear a question, read the four possible answers in your test book and choose the best answer. Then, on your answer sheet, find the number of the question and fill in the space that corresponds to the letter of the answer you have chosen.

Remember, you are <u>not</u> allowed to take notes or write in your test book.

**Questions 31 through 34.** Listen to a conversation about a research project.

(woman)  Have you started your research project for management class?

(man)  Well, I've decided on a topic: I want to write about motivation. But I haven't actually started the research yet.

(woman)  When are you going to begin the research? You don't have that much time to complete the paper.

(man)  I went to the library, but I wasn't sure where to look.

(woman)  Well, you can try the card catalogue if you want to find books about motivation.

(man)  The professor said that we shouldn't use just books as references for our papers. We should also use journal articles as references. Would I find those in the card catalogue also?

(woman)  No, for journal articles you should look in an index. There's an index for almost every subject; I'm sure there's an index for management topics.

(man)  Well, I guess I should get started today. I think I'll head to the library now. Thanks for your help.

(narrator)  31.  WHAT IS THE TOPIC OF THE CONVERSATION?

32.  WHY HAS THE MAN NOT COMPLETED THE RESEARCH?

33.  WHAT TYPES OF RESOURCES SHOULD THE MAN USE IN HIS RESEARCH PROJECT?

34.  WHAT WILL THE MAN PROBABLY DO NEXT?

**Questions 35 through 38.** Listen to a conversation about a trip.

(man)  This trip next week to Crested Butte is going to be fantastic!

(woman)  I just can't believe we're going to Colorado, of all places.

(man)  Well, why not?

(woman)  It's summertime. I thought people only took trips to Crested Butte in the winter, for skiing.

(man)  Oh, it's a great place to go in the summer, too. There's lots to do.

(woman)  Like what?

(man)  It's a beautiful outdoor area, and it's great for hiking. Or, if you don't feel like traveling on foot, you can rent horses or mountain bikes for some trips through the wilderness areas.

(woman)  Oh, I don't think I could get very far on a mountain bike if the hills are very steep.

(man)  They can be!

(woman)  Maybe a horseback ride sounds pretty good, except that the horse might get a little wild. I guess I'd better stick to hiking.

(man)  You can't go wrong. You'll love the hiking in the beautiful weather we're going to find there.

(woman)　What _is_ the weather like in July?

(man)　You know, the snow often doesn't melt until June since the elevation of the area is so high. The days are warm, but not too hot, and the nights can be rather cool.

(woman)　I guess I understand why we're going now. This actually does sound like a great trip.

(man)　Trust me. It is.

(narrator)　35.　WHEN IS THE TRIP?

36.　WHAT SEASON IS IT?

37.　HOW WILL THE WOMAN PROBABLY GET AROUND THE CRESTED BUTTE AREA?

38.　WHAT TYPE OF WEATHER WILL THEY PROBABLY ENCOUNTER?

---

## Part C

**Directions:** In this part of the test, you will hear several talks. After each talk, you will hear some questions. The talks and questions will not be repeated.

After you hear a question, read the four possible answers in your test book and choose the best answer. Then, on your answer sheet, find the number of the question and fill in the space that corresponds to the letter of the answer you have chosen.

Here is an example.

On the recording, you hear:

(narrator)　_Listen to an instructor talk to his class about painting._

(man)　_Artist Grant Wood was a guiding force in the school of painting known as American regionalist, a style reflecting the distinctive characteristics of art from rural areas of the United States. Wood began drawing animals on the family farm at the age of three, and when he was thirty-eight one of his paintings received a remarkable amount of public notice and acclaim. This painting, called_ American Gothic, _is a starkly simple depiction of a serious couple staring directly out at the viewer._

Now listen to a sample question.

(narrator)　_What style of painting is known as American regionalist?_

In your test book, you read:

(A)　Art from America's inner cities.
(B)　Art from the central region of the U.S.
(C)　Art from various urban areas in the U.S.
(D)　Art from rural sections of America.

The best answer to the question, "What style of painting is known as American regionalist?" is (D), "Art from rural sections of America." Therefore, the correct choice is (D).

Now listen to another sample question.

(narrator)　_What is the name of Wood's most successful painting?_

In your test book, you read:

(A)　"American Regionalist."
(B)　"The Family Farm in Iowa."
(C)　"American Gothic."
(D)　"A Serious Couple."

The best answer to the question, "What is the name of Wood's most successful painting?" is (C), "American Gothic." Therefore, the correct choice is (C).

Remember, you are _not_ allowed to take notes or write in your test book.

**Questions 39 through 42.** Listen to a talk given by a university advisor to a group of students.

(woman)　Now, I would like to explain to you about some special grades: satisfactory and unsatisfactory grades. You understand that the basic grading system at this university is the standard letter grading system of A, B, C, D, or F, and most of the courses that you take during your graduate program will use this standard system of grading. However, certain of the courses may be taken on a satisfactory/unsatisfactory basis. This means that you do not get a standard grade of A, B, C, D, or F in the course. Instead, you will receive either an S for "satisfactory" or a U for "unsatisfactory." Only two of your elective courses may be taken on a satisfactory/ unsatisfactory basis during your graduate program; the remaining elective courses and all required courses must be taken for a regular grade.

(narrator)    39.    WHAT IS THE TOPIC OF THIS TALK?

40.    WHAT IS TRUE ABOUT A STUDENT WHO RECEIVES A GRADE OF U?

41.    HOW MANY COURSES MAY BE TAKEN ON A SATISFACTORY/ UNSATISFACTORY BASIS?

42.    WHICH COURSES MAY BE TAKEN ON A SATISFACTORY/UNSATISFACTORY BASIS?

**Questions 43 through 46.** Listen to a talk about Native Americans.

(man)    The next topic in this course on the history of Native Americans is communication. Have you ever wondered how the various tribes were able to communicate when these tribes spoke such different languages? The answer is sign language, which is a language based on hand movements. Sign language developed from a need to improve communications among the various tribes on the plains of North America. There were many different tribes on the plains, and each tribe had its own language. Because these tribes often came into contact, there was a strong need to develop some form of communication. Sign language arose from this need. With sign language, tribes who spoke widely differing languages were able to communicate at least on a basic level, by using hand gestures.

(narrator)    43.    WHAT IS SIGN LANGUAGE?

44.    WHY DID SIGN LANGUAGE DEVELOP?

45.    HOW OFTEN DID VARIOUS TRIBES MEET?

46.    HOW COULD SIGN LANGUAGE BE CHARACTERIZED?

**Questions 47 through 50.** Listen to a talk about a famous American writer.

(woman)    Up to now in this course on American authors we have studied American novelists, but next class we will move on to short story writers. We will begin with a man who is probably the most famous American short story writer of all, Edgar Allan Poe. To truly understand an author, it is important to have knowledge of events in his life and times and how they affected his works. In Poe's case, we will see that the major tragedies in his life, particularly the untimely death of his wife after a long illness, exerted a major influence on his work. In addition to studying Poe's life and times, we will read several of his short stories, including "The Fall of the House of Usher" and "The Masque of the Red Death," and write a short analysis of one of the stories. Poe is best known for his symbolism, his impressionistic style, and his ability to create and maintain an eerie tone, and those two short stories are excellent examples of his style. For the next class, you should read "The Fall of the House of Usher" thoroughly, and be prepared for a discussion.

(narrator)    47.    WHAT SUBJECT HAVE THE STUDENTS JUST FINISHED STUDYING?

48.    ACCORDING TO THE SPEAKER, WHAT KIND OF LIFE DID POE HAVE?

49.    WHICH IS NOT A CHARACTERISTIC OF POE'S WORK?

50.    WHAT SHOULD THE STUDENTS DO TO PREPARE FOR THE NEXT CLASS?

# PRACTICE TEST TWO TAPESCRIPT

## SECTION 1
## LISTENING COMPREHENSION

In this section of the test, you will have an opportunity to demonstrate your ability to understand conversations and talks in English. There are three parts to this section. Answer all the questions on the basis of what is stated or implied by the speakers you hear. Do not take notes or write in your test book at any time. Do not turn the pages until you are told to do so.

### Part A

**Directions:** In Part A you will hear short conversations between two people. After each conversation, you will hear a question about the conversation. The conversations and questions will not be repeated. After you hear a question, read the four possible answers in your test book and choose the best answer. Then, on your answer sheet, find the number of the question and fill in the space that corresponds to the letter of the answer you have chosen.

Listen to an example.

On the recording, you hear:

| | |
|---|---|
| (man) | *That exam was just awful.* |
| (woman) | *Oh, it could have been worse.* |
| (narrator) | *What does the woman mean?* |

In your test book, you read:

(A) The exam was really awful.
(B) It was the worst exam she had ever seen.
(C) It couldn't have been more difficult.
(D) It wasn't that hard.

You learn from the conversation that the man thought the exam was very difficult and that the woman disagreed with the man. The best answer to the question, "What does the woman mean?" is (D), "It wasn't that hard." Therefore, the correct choice is (D).

1. (woman) How much of a tip should we leave?
   (man) Not more than a dollar. The service was slow and the soup was cold.
   (narrator) WHERE DOES THIS CONVERSATION PROBABLY TAKE PLACE?

2. (man) What time's the mail delivered?
   (woman) It usually comes by lunchtime, but not always.
   (narrator) WHAT DOES THE WOMAN MEAN?

3. (man) Would you like me to get you some coffee?
   (woman) Not now, thanks. Maybe later.
   (narrator) WHAT DOES THE WOMAN WANT?

4. (man) Let's go for a walk at the beach today.
   (woman) Why not? It's too nice to stay indoors.
   (narrator) WHAT DOES THE WOMAN MEAN?

5. (woman) Wasn't the anthropology lecture fascinating?
   (man) Fascinating? It was too long and drawn out for me.
   (narrator) HOW DID THE MAN FEEL ABOUT THE LECTURE?

6. (man) I found my briefcase.
   (woman) Just a moment. That's my briefcase. Yours is smaller, isn't it?
   (narrator) WHAT DOES THE WOMAN MEAN?

7. (man) That's a nice cake. Did you make it yourself?
   (woman) Not exactly. My roommate helped with the frosting.
   (narrator) WHAT DOES THE WOMAN MEAN?

8. (woman) The board is really going to regret its decision.
   (man) I'll say!
   (narrator) WHAT DOES THE MAN MEAN?

9.    (man)    Are you attending the planning committee meeting later?

   (woman)    Only if I have to.

   (narrator)    WHAT DOES THE WOMAN MEAN?

10.    (man)    Have you completed the paper for history class?

   (woman)    No, I just can't seem to get things done on time.

   (narrator)    WHAT DOES THE WOMAN MEAN?

11.    (woman)    Was Pam able to get some sleep last night? I know she was really tired.

   (man)    She was disturbed by the noisy traffic.

   (narrator)    WHAT DOES THE MAN SAY ABOUT PAM?

12.    (man)    Why do you want to go into this store?

   (woman)    They sell shoes here, don't they?

   (narrator)    WHAT DOES THE WOMAN IMPLY?

13.    (woman)    Alice was so angry when the toaster that she bought didn't work.

   (man)    She certainly was. And she made the salesclerk refund her money.

   (narrator)    WHAT DOES THE MAN SAY ABOUT ALICE?

14.    (man)    Would you tell me what time the dormitory doors will be locked?

   (woman)    No problem. In fact, I can give you a copy of the dormitory rulebook.

   (narrator)    WHAT DOES THE MAN WANT TO KNOW?

15.    (woman)    The history assignment was difficult. I worked all night and couldn't finish it.

   (man)    You worked all night? It took me only thirty minutes.

   (narrator)    WHY IS THE MAN SURPRISED?

16.    (woman)    You must be able to type fifty words per minute for this job.

   (man)    Oh, I can do that easily.

   (narrator)    WHAT DOES THE MAN MEAN?

17.    (man)    I've run out of time. Can we finish this tomorrow?

   (woman)    Great. I'll see you then.

   (narrator)    WHAT IS THE MAN'S PROBLEM?

18.    (woman)    Are there enough drinks in the refrigerator?

   (man)    Enough? Any more and we'll need another refrigerator.

   (narrator)    WHAT DOES THE MAN IMPLY?

19.    (woman)    Do you think Carla's guilty or innocent?

   (man)    She insists that she didn't take the money, but that's hard to believe.

   (narrator)    WHAT DOES THE MAN MEAN?

20.    (woman)    Do you know which students have completed the assignment?

   (man)    I should check off the names of the students as they turn it in.

   (narrator)    WHAT DOES THE MAN MEAN?

21.    (man)    You don't really seem to care about how you do in this class.

   (woman)    But nothing's more important to me than this class!

   (narrator)    WHAT DOES THE WOMAN MEAN?

22.    (man)    Are you going to the football game on Saturday? It's going to be a great game!

   (woman)    I really wish I were.

   (narrator)    WHAT DOES THE WOMAN MEAN?

23.    (woman)    The technology of microcomputers is increasing at a rapid pace.

   (man)    This means that the prices should come down as a result.

   (narrator)    WHAT DOES THE MAN MEAN?

24.    (man)    I hope Paul's graduate research project is going well.

   (woman)    He isn't <u>at all</u> dissatisfied with his findings.

   (narrator)    WHAT DOES THE WOMAN SAY ABOUT PAUL?

25.    (woman)    Can I still get dinner in the cafeteria tonight?

   (man)    If you get in line quickly.

   (narrator)    WHAT WILL PROBABLY HAPPEN SOON?

26.    (woman)    Is the security guard going to let us in?

    (man)    I doubt it. His job is to prohibit unauthorized personnel from entering the test site.

    (narrator)    WHAT DOES THE MAN MEAN?

27.    (man)    Do you think that it was Sally who broke the vase?

    (woman)    If she had done it, I'm sure she would have told you.

    (narrator)    WHAT DOES THE WOMAN MEAN?

28.    (woman)    Was Roger upset when he heard the news?

    (man)    Oh, he really fell apart!

    (narrator)    HOW DID ROGER FEEL?

29.    (man)    I haven't taken the introductory course, but I've decided to take the advanced course anyway.

    (woman)    I think you're putting the cart before the horse.

    (narrator)    WHAT DOES THE WOMAN MEAN?

30.    (woman)    It took me almost an hour to get here on that bicycle.

    (man)    So you haven't sold your bicycle.

    (narrator)    WHAT HAD THE MAN ASSUMED?

---

## Part B

**Directions:** In this part of the test, you will hear longer conversations. After each conversation, you will hear several questions. The conversations and questions will not be repeated.

After you hear a question, read the four possible answers in your test book and choose the best answer. Then, on your answer sheet, find the number of the question and fill in the space that corresponds to the letter of the answer you have chosen.

Remember, you are not allowed to take notes or write in your test book.

**Questions 31 through 34.** Listen to a conversation about a college course.

(woman)    Hi, Mike. I've been trying to get in touch with you. I wanted to ask you about the Introduction to Sociology course you took last semester with Professor Patterson.

(man)    Why did you want to know about that course?

(woman)    Well, Professor Patterson is teaching it again next semester, and I think I might take it.

(man)    I wouldn't do that if I were you.

(woman)    Why not? Was it a terrible course?

(man)    All the professor did was lecture day after day after day. He's a good enough lecturer, but I prefer courses where the students can participate more. I found it quite boring.

(woman)    That course doesn't sound so bad to me. In fact, I like that kind of course. You can listen to the professor's ideas and not feel any pressure to come up with something to say.

(man)    Well, then, maybe this course is for you.

(narrator)    31.    WHO IS TAKING PART IN THIS CONVERSATION?

    32.    WHY DOES THE WOMAN WANT TO TALK WITH MIKE?

    33.    WHAT KIND OF COURSE DOES THE MAN PREFER?

    34.    HOW DOES THE WOMAN FEEL ABOUT PROFESSOR PATTERSON'S COURSE?

**Questions 35 through 38.** Listen to a conversation about a new solar energy plant.

(man)    I was reading in last night's paper that the utility company wants to build a solar energy plant in the desert not far from here.

(woman)    Do you think that's a good idea?

(man)    A good idea? It's a great idea! Solar energy is the energy of the future. It's clean, it's safe, and it's abundant. What could be better?

(woman)    Won't the utility company just raise our rates to pay for this new plant?

(man)    The newspaper said that the utility company would need extra money to get the plant going, but in the long run rates would be lower. And to have a constant supply of energy, that's a small price to pay.

(woman)    I'm not convinced that the price will be small.

(narrator)    35.    HOW DID THE MAN LEARN ABOUT THE NEW SOLAR ENERGY PLANT?

    36.    WHERE WILL THE SOLAR ENERGY PLANT BE CONSTRUCTED?

37. ACCORDING TO THE MAN, WHAT IS A BENEFIT OF SOLAR ENERGY?

38. HOW DOES THE WOMAN FEEL ABOUT THE PROPOSED SOLAR ENERGY PLANT?

---

## Part C

**Directions:** In this part of the test, you will hear several talks. After each talk, you will hear some questions. The talks and questions will not be repeated.

After you hear a question, read the four possible answers in your test book and choose the best answer. Then, on your answer sheet, find the number of the question and fill in the space that corresponds to the letter of the answer you have chosen.

Here is an example.

On the recording, you hear:

(narrator)   *Listen to an instructor talk to his class about painting.*

(man)   *Artist Grant Wood was a guiding force in the school of painting known as American regionalist, a style reflecting the distinctive characteristics of art from rural areas of the United States. Wood began drawing animals on the family farm at the age of three, and when he was thirty-eight one of his paintings received a remarkable amount of public notice and acclaim. This painting, called* American Gothic, *is a starkly simple depiction of a serious couple staring directly out at the viewer.*

Now listen to a sample question.

(narrator)   *What style of painting is known as American regionalist?*

In your test book, you read:

(A)   Art from America's inner cities.
(B)   Art from the central region of the U.S.
(C)   Art from various urban areas in the U.S.
(D)   Art from rural sections of America.

The best answer to the question, "What style of painting is known as American regionalist?" is (D), "Art from rural sections of America." Therefore, the correct choice is (D).

Now listen to another sample question.

(narrator)   *What is the name of Wood's most successful painting?*

In your test book, you read:

(A)   "American Regionalist."
(B)   "The Family Farm in Iowa."
(C)   "American Gothic."
(D)   "A Serious Couple."

The best answer to the question, "What is the name of Wood's most successful painting?" is (C), "American Gothic." Therefore, the correct choice is (C).

Remember, you are **not** allowed to take notes or write in your test book.

**Questions 39 through 42.** Listen to a man talking to a group of students.

(*man*)   Hello, I'm John Rogers, the manager of the Student Bookstore. All of you have been selected to work part-time in the bookstore while you are completing your university studies. One of the first things I need to do is prepare a work schedule, and I need two pieces of information from each of you in order to make up the schedule.
First of all, I need to know the hours you are free to work. Each of you will be assigned twenty hours of work per week, and those hours could be anytime that the bookstore is open, on weekdays, in the evenings, or on weekends. I would like each of you to write down for me the hours when you have classes so that I will know when you are free to work.

The second piece of information that I need is your job preference. Most of the jobs that are available are working as a cashier or stocking shelves with books. There are also a few positions working in the business office.

Please write down which jobs you would prefer. I cannot promise that everyone will get the first choice when I make the schedule, but I will do what I can.

(narrator)    39.    WHO IS JOHN ROGERS?

40.    WHAT DOES JOHN ROGERS NEED TO DO NOW?

41.    WHAT DOES JOHN ROGERS NEED TO KNOW?

42.    WHICH IS NOT MENTIONED AS A POSSIBLE JOB OPEN TO THE STUDENTS?

**Questions 43 through 46.** Listen to a talk given by a woman.

(woman)    Did you know that those large plastic soda bottles that are so common today can actually get recycled into soft, warm, cuddly jackets and blankets with the feel of fleece? These bottles have generally been dumped into landfill rather than recycled, but now that's beginning to change. In this recycling process, the bottles are gathered at a plant, cleaned, and then crushed into tiny chips. The chips are melted and then shaped into long threads. These threads are spun into yarn and knit into cloth. It can then be dyed and made into fabric. The outcome of this process is a soft and warm cloth that can be made into items of clothing or blankets. It seems rather incredible that plastic soda bottles can be turned into something so soft and warm! I think that all of you should look for some of these products in stores and purchase them. They are great products, and they are great for the environment at the same time.

(narrator)    43.    WHAT IS THE TOPIC OF THE TALK?

44.    IN THE PAST, WHAT COMMONLY HAPPENED TO THE SODA BOTTLES?

45.    WHAT CAN BE MADE OUT OF THE SODA BOTTLES?

46.    WHAT DOES THE SPEAKER RECOMMEND?

**Questions 47 through 50.** Listen to a talk on the first transcontinental railroad.

(man)    The importance to the United States of the first transcontinental railroad cannot be overrated. This railroad had a profound effect on many aspects of American life, on communication, on transportation of agricultural products and livestock to market, and the settlement of the West, to name a few. But it was no easy feat to build such a railroad. The first transcontinental railroad was undertaken in 1862 by two competing railroad companies. The Union Pacific started in Omaha, Nebraska, and moved westward; the Central Pacific began in Sacramento, California, and moved eastward. Of the two, the Central Pacific had the more difficult task because it was faced with traversing the Sierra Nevadas. To lay tracks across these mountains, workers had to carve out footpaths on steep mountain faces and then use dynamite to blast out access for the railroad tracks. After years of dangerous and exhausting labor, the workers from the Central Pacific met up with the workers from the Union Pacific near Ogden, Utah, on May 10, 1869. In an exuberant ceremony, the last of the tracks was nailed to the ground with a golden spike. The completion of the railroad marked the beginning of a new era in transportation.

(narrator)    47.    WHO BUILT THE FIRST TRANSCONTINENTAL RAILROAD?

48.    WHAT WAS DIFFICULT ABOUT THE JOB THE CENTRAL PACIFIC WORKERS HAD TO COMPLETE?

49.    HOW LONG DID IT TAKE TO COMPLETE THE FIRST TRANSCONTINENTAL RAILROAD?

50.    WHAT HAPPENED AT THE CEREMONY MARKING THE COMPLETION OF THE RAILROAD?

# PRACTICE TEST THREE TAPESCRIPT

## SECTION 1
## LISTENING COMPREHENSION

In this section of the test, you will have an opportunity to demonstrate your ability to understand conversations and talks in English. There are three parts to this section. Answer all the questions on the basis of what is <u>stated</u> or <u>implied</u> by the speakers you hear. Do <u>not</u> take notes or write in your test book at any time. Do not turn the pages until you are told to do so.

### Part A

<u>Directions:</u> In Part A you will hear short conversations between two people. After each conversation, you will hear a question about the conversation. The conversations and questions will not be repeated. After you hear a question, read the four possible answers in your test book and choose the best answer. Then, on your answer sheet, find the number of the question and fill in the space that corresponds to the letter of the answer you have chosen.

Listen to an example.

On the recording, you hear:

| (man) | *That exam was just awful.* |
| (woman) | *Oh, it could have been worse.* |
| (narrator) | *What does the woman mean?* |

In your test book, you read:

(A) The exam was really awful.
(B) It was the worst exam she had ever seen.
(C) It couldn't have been more difficult.
(D) It wasn't that hard.

You learn from the conversation that the man thought the exam was very difficult and that the woman disagreed with the man. The best answer to the question, "What does the woman mean?" is (D), "It wasn't that hard." Therefore, the correct choice is (D).

1. (man) Did you get the tickets?
   (woman) Yes, I did. Let's go on in because the film's about to start.
   (narrator) WHERE DOES THIS CONVERSATION PROBABLY TAKE PLACE?

2. (woman) I'm ready for the therapy session.
   (man) Would you mind taking a seat?
   (narrator) WHAT DOES THE MAN WANT THE WOMAN TO DO?

3. (man) Can we meet later to work on our presentation?
   (woman) How about noon?
   (narrator) WHAT DOES THE WOMAN MEAN?

4. (woman) I never want to take another test like that again.
   (man) You can say that again.
   (narrator) WHAT DOES THE MAN MEAN?

5. (woman) Are you going to be finished with the yard work soon?
   (man) I just have one part of the lawn still to mow and a couple of bushes to trim.
   (narrator) WHO IS THE MAN?

6. (woman) Can we sit anywhere?
   (man) No, this section is reserved.
   (narrator) WHAT DOES THE MAN MEAN?

7. (man) Do you think we should bring the camera with us?
   (woman) That doesn't sound like a bad idea.
   (narrator) WHAT DOES THE WOMAN IMPLY?

8. (woman) Have you finished washing the dishes?

(man) I've been working on my term paper instead.

(narrator) WHAT DOES THE MAN MEAN?

9. (man) Is it possible to drop a class in the third week of the semester?

(woman) As far as I know.

(narrator) WHAT DOES THE WOMAN MEAN?

10. (woman) Can you turn off the lights when you leave?

(man) No problem. Our utility bill is high enough as it is.

(narrator) WHAT IS THE MAN CONCERNED ABOUT?

11. (man) Was the lecture easy to understand?

(woman) I'm glad I taped it, because I didn't understand a single word.

(narrator) WHAT DOES THE WOMAN MEAN?

12. (woman) I'm leaving for New York tomorrow at noon. Could you take me to the airport?

(man) Sorry. I'm working then. Why not see if Mike can help you out.

(narrator) WHAT DOES THE MAN SUGGEST TO THE WOMAN?

13. (man) Let's shut down for tonight. It's late.

(woman) Shut down? But we have so much more to do.

(narrator) WHAT DOES THE WOMAN MEAN?

14. (woman) Why don't we spend our vacation in the Bahamas?

(man) I don't make enough to do that.

(narrator) WHAT DOES THE MAN MEAN?

15. (woman) Did Bob fix the radio?

(man) He took it apart and then left it.

(narrator) WHAT DOES THE MAN SAY ABOUT THE RADIO?

16. (man) The anthem just finished and the game's about to start.

(woman) Let's get drinks _later_, then.

(narrator) WHAT DOES THE WOMAN PROBABLY WANT TO DO?

17. (woman) Have you seen the announcement in the lobby?

(man) What announcement is that?

(narrator) WHAT DOES THE MAN MEAN?

18. (man) I heard you were taking a nice vacation next week.

(woman) Oh, no, you're mistaken. I rarely take time off from work.

(narrator) WHAT DOES THE WOMAN MEAN?

19. (man) Is the lecture tonight worth attending?

(woman) Without a doubt!

(narrator) WHAT DOES THE WOMAN SAY ABOUT THE LECTURE?

20. (woman) Can you believe how many people were crowded into the stadium?

(man) Only once has a larger crowd attended a football game!

(narrator) WHAT DOES THE MAN MEAN?

21. (man) The travel agent told me about a really good deal on a skiing trip.

(woman) We'll have to look into that.

(narrator) WHAT DOES THE WOMAN SUGGEST?

22. (woman) It never occurred to me that you were an athlete.

(man) Most people who meet me don't think so, either.

(narrator) WHAT CAN BE SAID ABOUT THE MAN?

23. (woman) Barbara only told me that she wouldn't be in today.

(man) That couldn't be all she said!

(narrator) WHAT DOES THE MAN SAY ABOUT BARBARA?

24. (man) I can't believe it! All of my exams are finally over.

(woman) I wish mine were.

(narrator) WHAT DOES THE WOMAN IMPLY?

25. (man) The prices on this airline are rather high, don't you think?

(woman) They seem reasonable, for a trip to the Moon.

(narrator) WHAT DOES THE WOMAN MEAN?

26.    (man)   You know, Gary really didn't do a good job on his presentation.

   (woman)   I couldn't believe that he was unprepared!

   (narrator)   WHAT DOES THE WOMAN SAY ABOUT GARY?

27.    (man)   Did the report get finished before you left last night?

   (woman)   I wouldn't have left had it not been finished.

   (narrator)   WHAT DOES THE WOMAN MEAN?

28.    (woman)   I asked Roger if he was going to help us, but he really didn't answer my question.

   (man)   Oh, he's always beating around the bush.

   (narrator)   WHAT DOES THE MAN SAY ABOUT ROGER?

29.    (man)   Are you still interested in selling those concert tickets?

   (woman)   Then you _do_ want to buy them.

   (narrator)   WHAT HAD THE WOMAN ASSUMED?

30.    (woman)   Is it time for the meeting to start?

   (man)   You're here? I didn't think you were going to show up.

   (narrator)   WHY IS THE MAN SURPRISED?

---

## Part B

**Directions:** In this part of the test, you will hear longer conversations. After each conversation, you will hear several questions. The conversations and questions will not be repeated.

After you hear a question, read the four possible answers in your test book and choose the best answer. Then, on your answer sheet, find the number of the question and fill in the space that corresponds to the letter of the answer you have chosen.

Remember, you are <u>not</u> allowed to take notes or write in your test book.

**Questions 31 through 34.** Listen to a conversation between two students.

   (man)   Dora, could you please give me some help?

   (woman)   With what?

   (man)   I kept putting off my History 101 paper, and it's due next week.

   (woman)   If you want to pass the course, you've got to write that paper.

   (man)   I know. I thought that since you're a history major, you could help me come up with a topic for my paper.

   (woman)   History 101 is about American history. You could write about the Revolutionary War, or the Civil War, or World War I.

   (man)   Oh, I don't want to write about wars. I don't want to think about killing and death. Can you think of something else?

   (woman)   Why don't you write about technology, inventions that changed American history?

   (man)   That topic seems a little broad. Maybe I should narrow it down a bit.

   (woman)   Well, you could choose one invention, the telephone or the airplane, for example, and write about its effect on history.

   (man)   I know. My favorite topic is cars. I'll write about the invention of the automobile and its effect on American history.

   (woman)   That sounds like a good topic for you. Now, you'd better get busy. You only have one week.

   (narrator)   31.   WHAT DOES THE MAN ASK THE WOMAN TO DO?

            32.   WHEN IN THE SEMESTER DOES THIS CONVERSATION PROBABLY TAKE PLACE?

            33.   WHY WON'T THE MAN CHOOSE "TECHNOLOGY" AS A TOPIC?

            34.   HOW MUCH TIME DOES THE MAN HAVE TO WRITE THE PAPER?

**Questions 35 through 38.** Listen to a conversation about a tragic event.

   (woman)   Did you hear the story on the news this morning about the apartment fire down the street?

   (man)   I heard something about it. What happened exactly?

   (woman)   A fire started about three o'clock in the morning in an apartment complex with about twenty apartments. One of the apartments was completely destroyed, and several of the others were damaged.

(man)    Do they know how the fire started?

(woman)   They're not sure at this point, but they believe that it was started by someone smoking in bed. It's a shame that one careless person can cause so much trauma for others, not to mention the thousands and thousands of dollars of damage.

(man)    Even more serious than the damage to property is the harm to the apartments' occupants. I hear that several residents were rushed to the hospital, but at least none of them died.

(woman)   It's all so frightening. Do you know of anything I can do to keep this from happening to me?

(man)    I guess the best thing to protect yourself is to make sure that you have a smoke alarm and a fire extinguisher in good working condition. The smoke alarm will give you an early warning that a fire has started, so you can call the fire department. If it is a small fire, maybe you can use the fire extinguisher to help put out the fire before the fire trucks arrive.

(woman)   That's good advice. I think I'll go home and check my smoke alarm.

(narrator)   35.   WHAT IS THE TOPIC OF THIS CONVERSATION?

36.   ACCORDING TO THE WOMAN, HOW EXTENSIVELY WERE THE APARTMENTS DAMAGED?

37.   WHAT DID THE MAN SAY ABOUT SOME OF THE APARTMENT RESIDENTS?

38.   WHAT ADVICE DOES THE MAN GIVE TO THE WOMAN TO PROTECT HERSELF FROM FIRES?

---

## Part C

**Directions:** In this part of the test, you will hear several talks. After each talk, you will hear some questions. The talks and questions will not be repeated.

After you hear a question, read the four possible answers in your test book and choose the best answer. Then, on your answer sheet, find the number of the question and fill in the space that corresponds to the letter of the answer you have chosen.

Here is an example.

On the recording, you hear:

(narrator)   *Listen to an instructor talk to his class about painting.*

(man)    *Artist Grant Wood was a guiding force in the school of painting known as American regionalist, a style reflecting the distinctive characteristics of art from rural areas of the United States. Wood began drawing animals on the family farm at the age of three, and when he was thirty-eight one of his paintings received a remarkable amount of public notice and acclaim. This painting, called* American Gothic, *is a starkly simple depiction of a serious couple staring directly out at the viewer.*

Now listen to a sample question.

(narrator)   *What style of painting is known as American regionalist?*

In your test book, you read:

(A)   Art from America's inner cities.
(B)   Art from the central region of the U.S.
(C)   Art from various urban areas in the U.S.
(D)   Art from rural sections of America.

The best answer to the question, "What style of painting is known as American regionalist?" is (D), "Art from rural sections of America." Therefore, the correct choice is (D).

Now listen to another sample question.

(narrator)   *What is the name of Wood's most successful painting?*

In your test book, you read:

(A)   "American Regionalist."
(B)   "The Family Farm in Iowa."
(C)   "American Gothic."
(D)   "A Serious Couple."

The best answer to the question, "What is the name of Wood's most successful painting?" is (C), "American Gothic." Therefore, the correct choice is (C).

Remember, you are <u>not</u> allowed to take notes or write in your test book.

**Questions 39 through 42.** Listen to a talk to university students.

*(woman)*  Welcome to the orientation meeting for dance majors. All of you in the room should be students who want to be dance majors. Oh, please let me introduce myself—I am Dean Peterson, the head of the dance department.

If you are majoring in dance, the most important decision you have to make is which degree you will get. Let me explain. There are two possible degrees for dance majors, and the programs are quite different; one is geared toward performance and one is not.

The first possible major in dance is the Bachelor of Performance Arts. This is a performance-oriented degree. It is intended for students who wish to pursue a professional performance career in dance, or in choreography.

The second possible major in dance is the Bachelor of Art Studies. This major is intended for those of you who are interested in nonperformance dance careers, in areas such as dance therapy, dance history, dance administration, or dance education.

Either major is a four-year program, but many of the courses that you take along the way are different, so you will have to specify your degree choice early. I hope this information will help you to decide.

*(narrator)*  39.  WHO IS THE SPEAKER?

40.  WHAT DECISION DO THE STUDENTS HAVE TO MAKE?

41.  A DANCE MAJOR WITH A BACHELOR OF PERFORMANCE ARTS DEGREE MIGHT BE INTERESTED IN WHICH AREA OF WORK?

42.  WHAT IS TRUE ABOUT THE DANCE DEGREES DISCUSSED IN THE TALK?

**Questions 43 through 46.** Listen to a talk about Cajun country.

*(man)*  Now that we're all on the bus, I'd like to tell you a little bit about what we're going to be seeing today. The area that we're visiting is called Cajun country. The Cajuns are descended from the Acadians, French settlers who came from the Acadia region of present-day Canada. They came in the eighteenth century, during the French and Indian War, when they were driven from Acadia by the British. They settled in southern Louisiana in the areas around New Orleans. They brought their French culture with them, and today approximately a quarter of a million people in Louisiana still speak French as a result.

We'll be driving by some sugar plantations and alligator farms, and then we'll be stopping at Avery Island. There is a factory there that has been producing tabasco since 1868. Are you familiar with tabasco? It's one of the best-known spicy sauces in Cajun cooking, and it's very hot. I hope you like spicy food, because any Cajun food that you eat on this trip is going to be spicy.

After Avery Island, we'll continue on to Lafayette, which is the largest city in Cajun country. When we arrive in Lafayette, we're going to visit Acadian Village, which is a Cajun theme park. This theme park offers rides, exhibits, shopping, and restaurants, all with a Cajun theme.

Now settle back, relax, and enjoy the ride. I'll point out the interesting sights as we come to them.

*(narrator)*  43.  WHO IS THE SPEAKER?

44.  WHAT IS TRUE ABOUT THE CAJUNS?

45.  WHAT IS CAJUN FOOD LIKE?

46.  WHAT WILL PROBABLY HAPPEN NEXT?

**Questions 47 through 50.** Listen to a lecture given in a college course.

*(woman)* The development of the radio into a worldwide force occurred relatively quickly. In 1920, only nineteen years after Marconi sent the first wireless signal across the Atlantic, the world's first radio station was established in Pittsburgh, Pennsylvania, and by 1923 nationwide broadcasting was possible in the United States. Radio broadcasting was initially totally uncontrolled, and each of the dozens of existing stations broadcasted its programs whenever and on whatever wavelength it wanted. The result for listeners, as you can imagine, was often a garbled mess. This confused situation in radio broadcasting lasted until the Federal Communications Commission, which is often referred to as the FCC, was created in 1930 by the United States government. The initial purpose of the FCC was to regulate radio broadcasting; each station was assigned a wavelength for its broadcasts to minimize interference from other radio stations.

*(narrator)*  47.  WHAT IS THE TOPIC OF THIS TALK?

48.  THIS LECTURE WOULD PROBABLY BE GIVEN IN WHICH COURSE?

49.  HOW COULD THE SITUATION IN EARLY RADIO BROADCASTING BEST BE DESCRIBED?

50.  WHAT DO THE INITIALS FCC STAND FOR?

# PRACTICE TEST FOUR TAPESCRIPT

## SECTION 1
## LISTENING COMPREHENSION

In this section of the test, you will have an opportunity to demonstrate your ability to understand conversations and talks in English. There are three parts to this section. Answer all the questions on the basis of what is <u>stated</u> or <u>implied</u> by the speakers you hear. Do <u>not</u> take notes or write in your test book at any time. Do not turn the pages until you are told to do so.

### Part A

**Directions:** In Part A you will hear short conversations between two people. After each conversation, you will hear a question about the conversation. The conversations and questions will not be repeated. After you hear a question, read the four possible answers in your test book and choose the best answer. Then, on your answer sheet, find the number of the question and fill in the space that corresponds to the letter of the answer you have chosen.

Listen to an example.

On the recording, you hear:

| (man) | *That exam was just awful.* |
|---|---|
| (woman) | *Oh, it could have been worse.* |
| (narrator) | *What does the woman mean?* |

In your test book, you read:

(A) The exam was really awful.
(B) It was the worst exam she had ever seen.
(C) It couldn't have been more difficult.
(D) It wasn't that hard.

You learn from the conversation that the man thought the exam was very difficult and that the woman disagreed with the man. The best answer to the question, "What does the woman mean?" is (D), "It wasn't that hard." Therefore, the correct choice is (D).

1. (man) I'd like two tickets to Vancouver.
   (woman) You'd better hurry. The flight takes off in just a few minutes.
   (narrator) WHERE DOES THIS CONVERSATION PROBABLY TAKE PLACE?

2. (man) The car won't start. Maybe I should call a service station.
   (woman) Did you check to see if there's any gas?
   (narrator) WHAT DOES THE WOMAN WANT TO KNOW?

3. (woman) How can I finish all these problems before midnight?
   (man) Why not leave some for the morning?
   (narrator) WHAT DOES THE MAN SUGGEST?

4. (man) The roads are really clogged with traffic today!
   (woman) Aren't they!
   (narrator) WHAT DOES THE WOMAN MEAN?

5. (woman) Why don't you water the plants, Mark?
   (man) But I watered them yesterday.
   (narrator) WHAT DOES MARK IMPLY?

6. (woman) Have you seen the results of the music competition?
   (man) Unfortunately, I have. I didn't do very well, and neither did you.
   (narrator) WHAT DOES THE MAN MEAN?

7. (man) I don't think there's enough time to go to the market now.
   (woman) It's not too late, is it?
   (narrator) WHAT DOES THE WOMAN MEAN?

8. (man) Why are you looking so worried?
   (woman) I can't find my wallet. I hope it wasn't stolen.
   (narrator) WHAT DOES THE WOMAN MEAN?

9. (woman) That sure was a loud meeting.
   (man) Everyone seemed to have something to say.
   (narrator) WHAT DO THEY IMPLY ABOUT THE MEETING?

10. (man) I need to take this book back to the library right away.
    (woman) But it isn't due for a week!
    (narrator) WHAT DOES THE WOMAN MEAN?

11. (man) I can't believe that you made that bracelet.
    (woman) It's really not too hard. It just takes a lot of time.
    (narrator) WHAT IS THE WOMAN SAYING ABOUT THE BRACELET?

12. (man) Did it cost very much to stay overnight at the hotel?
    (woman) More than you would believe.
    (narrator) WHAT DOES THE WOMAN MEAN?

13. (woman) The checks aren't in my purse.
    (man) Why don't you look in your suitcase?
    (narrator) WHAT DOES THE MAN MEAN?

14. (man) I heard that Mr. Milton has a new position now.
    (woman) He was appointed dean of the college last month.
    (narrator) WHAT DOES THE WOMAN MEAN?

15. (man) Was Roger able to pay his tuition this semester?
    (woman) He scarcely had enough money.
    (narrator) WHAT DOES THE WOMAN SAY ABOUT ROGER?

16. (woman) Eric twisted his ankle playing basketball.
    (man) Can he walk on it now?
    (narrator) WHAT DOES THE MAN WANT TO KNOW?

17. (woman) We are unable to accept your housing application because it's well past the deadline.
    (man) But what am I supposed to do about housing?
    (narrator) WHAT DOES THE MAN IMPLY?

18. (man) Have you been working on your biology homework?
    (woman) What homework is that?
    (narrator) WHY IS THE WOMAN SURPRISED?

19. (woman) Have you read the article Stan wrote for the school newspaper?
    (man) Read it? I typed it for him.
    (narrator) WHAT DOES THE MAN MEAN?

20. (woman) These problems are really difficult!
    (man) Don't give up.
    (narrator) WHAT DOES THE MAN MEAN?

21. (man) Did you buy the perfume that you liked so much?
    (woman) Unfortunately, I only had ten dollars with me.
    (narrator) WHAT DOES THE WOMAN SUGGEST?

22. (man) I saw you at the piano recital last night. What did you think of it?
    (woman) No one plays the piano better than Eric!
    (narrator) WHAT DOES THE WOMAN MEAN?

23. (woman) Do you think Paul will come play tennis with us this afternoon?
    (man) I believe he's out of town.
    (narrator) WHAT DOES THE MAN IMPLY ABOUT PAUL?

24. (man) Did you enjoy your trip to the mountains last weekend?
    (woman) I was surprised that there was hardly any snow.
    (narrator) WHAT DOES THE WOMAN MEAN?

25. (man) Did Bob get the promotion he wanted?
    (woman) Yes, and he's really ecstatic!
    (narrator) WHAT IS THE WOMAN SAYING ABOUT BOB?

26. (man) Should I get the plaid shirt or the striped one?
    (woman) It's all the same to me.
    (narrator) WHAT DOES THE WOMAN MEAN?

27. (woman) Did you get the part-time job in the library?
    (man) If I had gotten it, I wouldn't still be looking for a job.
    (narrator) WHAT DOES THE MAN MEAN?

28.   (man)    I'm having a problem with my advisor, and some other students suggested that I see the dean about this. Do you think I should?

(woman)    Under no circumstances will the dean listen to any complaints.

(narrator)    WHAT DOES THE WOMAN MEAN?

29.   (woman)    Do you want to come over tonight? I'm fixing dinner for a group of friends.

(man)    So you _can_ cook after all!

(narrator)    WHAT HAD THE MAN ASSUMED ABOUT THE WOMAN?

30.   (woman)    Are you finished with your taxes yet?

(man)    I wish I hadn't put them off until the last moment.

(narrator)    WHAT DOES THE MAN IMPLY?

---

## Part B

**Directions:** In this part of the test, you will hear longer conversations. After each conversation, you will hear several questions. The conversations and questions will not be repeated.

After you hear a question, read the four possible answers in your test book and choose the best answer. Then, on your answer sheet, find the number of the question and fill in the space that corresponds to the letter of the answer you have chosen.

Remember, you are _not_ allowed to take notes or write in your test book.

**Questions 31 through 34.** Listen to a conversation between two students.

(man)    Hey, Gloria. How would you like to increase the extent of your educational and historical background?

(woman)    Steve, I don't understand what you're saying at all.

(man)    I just took my final in History 101 this morning, and I'm trying to get rid of the books. They cost eighty dollars.

(woman)    Why don't you try to sell them back to the bookstore?

(man)    I tried, but they'd only refund twenty dollars, and I paid so much more for them. I'd like to get at least forty dollars.

(woman)    Well, I'm not going to take History 101, so I'm not really interested in those books. Maybe you should ask some other friends.

(man)    I already have. Everyone I know has already taken History 101 and doesn't want those books.

(woman)    Why don't you put up some advertisements in the history building? Maybe someone you don't know will call you and buy them.

(man)    I'll try, but I don't think that'll work.

(woman)    Then you'll have to go back to the bookstore. After all, twenty dollars is better than nothing.

(narrator)    31.    WHAT IS THE TOPIC OF THIS CONVERSATION?

32.    WHY IS THE MAN INTERESTED IN SELLING HIS BOOKS?

33.    WHY DOES THE MAN NOT WANT TO SELL THE BOOKS TO THE BOOKSTORE?

34.    WHAT DOES THE WOMAN SUGGEST THAT THE MAN DO?

**Questions 35 through 38.** Listen to a conversation about sleeping habits.

(woman)    Did you know that the average time that people spend sleeping decreases considerably as they get older?

(man)    Really? I would have thought that the opposite was true, that people needed more sleep when they were older.

(woman)    No, studies clearly show that the need for sleep decreases rather than increases with age. I was just reading a journal article for my psychology class, and it contained some really interesting information about sleep.

(man)    Really? What did you find out?

(woman)    Well, young babies required the most sleep, and that should come as no surprise; the average one-year-old sleeps about thirteen hours a day. People in their twenties need about eight hours of sleep a night.

(man)    That sounds about right to me. That's my age group, and I know I'm at my best when I'm able to sleep that much each night. What about older people?

(woman)    Well, the average amount of sleep decreases with age, and in the study I read the average amount of sleep for people in their fifties was between five and six hours a night.

(man)    That's really surprising to me! I expected the opposite to be true.

(narrator)    35.    WHAT INFORMATION SURPRISED THE MAN?

36.    WHERE DID THE WOMAN LEARN THIS INFORMATION ABOUT SLEEP?

37.    WHAT IS THE MAN'S AGE GROUP?

38.    APPROXIMATELY HOW MANY HOURS OF SLEEP PER NIGHT DO FIFTY-YEAR-OLDS REQUIRE?

---

## Part C

**Directions:** In this part of the test, you will hear several talks. After each talk, you will hear some questions. The talks and questions will not be repeated.

After you hear a question, read the four possible answers in your test book and choose the best answer. Then, on your answer sheet, find the number of the question and fill in the space that corresponds to the letter of the answer you have chosen.

Here is an example.

On the recording, you hear:

(narrator)    *Listen to an instructor talk to his class about painting.*

(man)    *Artist Grant Wood was a guiding force in the school of painting known as American regionalist, a style reflecting the distinctive characteristics of art from rural areas of the United States. Wood began drawing animals on the family farm at the age of three, and when he was thirty-eight one of his paintings received a remarkable amount of public notice and acclaim. This painting, called*

*American Gothic, is a starkly simple depiction of a serious couple staring directly out at the viewer.*

Now listen to a sample question.

(narrator)    *What style of painting is known as American regionalist?*

In your test book, you read:

(A)    Art from America's inner cities.
(B)    Art from the central region of the U.S.
(C)    Art from various urban areas in the U.S.
(D)    Art from rural sections of America.

The best answer to the question, "What style of painting is known as American regionalist?" is (D), "Art from rural sections of America." Therefore, the correct choice is (D).

Now listen to another sample question.

(narrator)    *What is the name of Wood's most successful painting?*

In your test book, you read:

(A)    "American Regionalist."
(B)    "The Family Farm in Iowa."
(C)    "American Gothic."
(D)    "A Serious Couple."

The best answer to the question, "What is the name of Wood's most successful painting?" is (C), "American Gothic." Therefore, the correct choice is (C).

Remember, you are **not** allowed to take notes or write in your test book.

**Questions 39 through 42.** Listen to a talk by a student advisor on campus.

(woman)    I'm Ms. Morton, your advisor. I'd like to explain the policies for dropping classes at this school. It's important to understand these policies, or your grades can suffer.

The policy at this school is that you can drop a course within the first three weeks of the semester. To drop a course, you first need to get the signature of the professor of the course you want to drop on an official drop card; then you need to come to me to get the signature of your advisor.

Let me give you a couple of strong warnings. First, you cannot officially drop a course after the first three weeks of the semester. If you are having problems in a course and you decide later on that you want to drop the course, it is impossible to do so. Second, if you stop attending a course without going through the official "drop" procedures, the course will remain on your schedule, and you will receive a failing grade.

It is important for you to understand these procedures and follow them. If you do so, you will not have any problems. Any questions?

(*narrator*) 39. WHAT IS THE PRIMARY TOPIC OF THE TALK?

40. WHEN CAN A STUDENT OFFICIALLY DROP A COURSE?

41. HOW MANY SIGNATURES ARE NECESSARY TO DROP A COURSE?

42. WHAT HAPPENS IF A STUDENT STOPS ATTENDING A COURSE WITHOUT OFFICIALLY DROPPING IT?

**Questions 43 through 46.** Listen to a talk about the California Gold Rush.

(*man*) The California Gold Rush, which figured so prominently in the development of the West, was actually the result of a chance happening. Captain John Sutter received the rights to a large piece of land near what is today Sacramento, in northern California. Sutter's main purpose was to develop a lumber business from the huge expanses of trees on his property. It was during the construction of a sawmill for his lumber business that gold was found on the bank of the American River. As news about the gold spread, thousands of gold prospectors descended on Sutter's property. Sutter's business was destroyed by the prospectors, and Sutter received little from the gold that was found there. Although Sutter died a poor and disheartened man, the population of California increased tremendously because of what was found on his property.

(*narrator*) 43. WHAT KIND OF BUSINESS WAS SUTTER UNDERTAKING?

44. WHEN WAS GOLD DISCOVERED ON SUTTER'S FARM?

45. WHAT BENEFIT DID SUTTER RECEIVE FROM THE DISCOVERY OF GOLD ON HIS PROPERTY?

46. WHAT IS THE SPEAKER'S MAIN POINT IN THIS LECTURE?

**Questions 47 through 50.** Listen to a talk to university students.

(*woman*) This lecture series is intended to help students at this university benefit more from their studies here. The topic of tonight's talk is how to manage your time.

Time is a very important commodity when you are a university student; there simply never seems to be enough of it to go around. You will need to attend classes, study, complete homework assignments, work on research, eat, sleep, perhaps hold down a part-time job, and maybe actually find time to relax for a moment or two.

So a very important skill for you to learn is to manage your time. If you manage your time wisely, I think that you'll find that there is enough of it to go around.

One valuable tool in time management is to monitor how you spend your time for a week. Then, after you spend this week monitoring your time, you can evaluate what you have done with your time and learn to make the best use of it.

During this week of personal time monitoring, you should divide each twenty-four-hour day into fifteen-minute blocks, so each day has ninety-six blocks of time. Then, write down how you spend each fifteen-minute period. I know that it is bothersome to write all of this information down for a week, but the benefits of such a study can be great. At the end of a week, you will see just how much time you have spent productively and how much time you have not.

The specific assignment that I have for each one of you is to spend the next week conducting your personal time-monitoring study. At the end of this week you should make an appointment with me to discuss your results.

(*narrator*)   47.   WHAT IS THE TOPIC OF THIS TALK?

48.   WHAT VALUABLE TOOL IN TIME MANAGEMENT IS DISCUSSED HERE?

49.   HOW LONG SHOULD THIS STUDY TAKE?

50.   WHAT SHOULD THE STUDENTS DO AT THE END OF THE STUDY?

# PRACTICE TEST FIVE TAPESCRIPT

## SECTION 1
## LISTENING COMPREHENSION

In this section of the test, you will have an opportunity to demonstrate your ability to understand conversations and talks in English. There are three parts to this section. Answer all the questions on the basis of what is <u>stated</u> or <u>implied</u> by the speakers you hear. Do <u>not</u> take notes or write in your test book at any time. Do not turn the pages until you are told to do so.

### Part A

**<u>Directions:</u>** In Part A you will hear short conversations between two people. After each conversation, you will hear a question about the conversation. The conversations and questions will not be repeated. After you hear a question, read the four possible answers in your test book and choose the best answer. Then, on your answer sheet, find the number of the question and fill in the space that corresponds to the letter of the answer you have chosen.

Listen to an example.

On the recording, you hear:

| (man) | *That exam was just awful.* |
| (woman) | *Oh, it could have been worse.* |
| (narrator) | *What does the woman mean?* |

In your test book, you read:

(A)   The exam was really awful.
(B)   It was the worst exam she had ever seen.
(C)   It couldn't have been more difficult.
(D)   It wasn't that hard.

You learn from the conversation that the man thought the exam was very difficult and that the woman disagreed with the man. The best answer to the question, "What does the woman mean?" is (D), "It wasn't that hard." Therefore, the correct choice is (D).

1.   (woman)   Going home already?
      (man)   Yes. It's late.
     (narrator)   WHAT DOES THE MAN MEAN?

2.   (man)   Did you spend a lot of money at the fair?
     (woman)   Only every cent in my purse.
     (narrator)   WHAT DOES THE WOMAN MEAN?

3.   (woman)   Can I still check out these books?
      (man)   Yes, the circulation desk doesn't close for an hour.
     (narrator)   WHERE DOES THIS CONVERSATION PROBABLY TAKE PLACE?

4.   (man)   Have you gotten the clothes that you ordered?
     (woman)   They were delivered just this morning.
     (narrator)   WHAT DOES THE WOMAN MEAN?

5.   (man)   Why are you studying in the living room?
     (woman)   The lamp on my desk isn't working.
     (narrator)   WHAT DOES THE WOMAN MEAN?

6.   (woman)   I quite firmly believe that what Jack did was wrong.
      (man)   So do I!
     (narrator)   WHAT DOES THE MAN MEAN?

7.   (woman)   I'd like to check in, please. I need a single room.
      (man)   For how many nights?
     (narrator)   WHO IS THE MAN?

8.   (woman)   Is it possible to stay here for a little while more?
      (man)   Visitors aren't allowed in the hospital after 10:00.
     (narrator)   WHAT DOES THE MAN MEAN?

9.   (man)   I'm not really pleased with the way my clothes look when they are cleaned.
     (woman)   Why not find another laundry?
     (narrator)   WHAT DOES THE WOMAN SUGGEST?

10. (woman) Do you know when the staff meeting is supposed to start?

    (man) It's at 3:00, isn't it?

    (narrator) WHAT DOES THE MAN MEAN?

11. (man) Are you going skiing this afternoon?

    (woman) I doubt it. The weather forecast is pretty bad.

    (narrator) WHAT DOES THE WOMAN MEAN?

12. (woman) Do you think I should sit in on the psychology class tomorrow?

    (man) Definitely, provided you read the chapter first.

    (narrator) WHAT DOES THE MAN SUGGEST TO THE WOMAN?

13. (man) Have you heard about Tim? He had to rush to the emergency room.

    (woman) Really? I hope it's not too serious.

    (narrator) WHAT DOES THE WOMAN IMPLY?

14. (man) Aren't we supposed to go to the language lab?

    (woman) Oh, I seldom go there.

    (narrator) WHAT IS IMPLIED ABOUT THE WOMAN?

15. (man) These roses are for you, because it's your birthday.

    (woman) Aren't they beautiful!

    (narrator) WHAT DOES THE WOMAN MEAN?

16. (woman) My doctor's told me to take these pills every day.

    (man) That's a lot of medicine, isn't it?

    (narrator) WHAT DOES THE MAN MEAN?

17. (woman) Did you know there was a tornado yesterday?

    (man) I saw it from my window!

    (narrator) WHAT DOES THE MAN MEAN?

18. (woman) What do you think of the weather?

    (man) Rain again? Sometimes I think it's never going to stop.

    (narrator) HOW DOES THE MAN FEEL ABOUT THE RAIN?

19. (man) Let's go to Gianelli's for some ice cream.

    (woman) How about something else? I'm trying to cut down on sweets.

    (narrator) WHAT DOES THE WOMAN MEAN?

20. (woman) Are you going with us to the mountains this weekend?

    (man) I wish I had a few more dollars in my bank account. Then I would.

    (narrator) WHAT DOES THE MAN MEAN?

21. (woman) The new printer should arrive in the computer lab soon.

    (man) They've been saying that for weeks now.

    (narrator) WHAT DOES THE MAN MEAN?

22. (woman) Would you like to go to the opera tonight?

    (man) I'd prefer a trip to the dentist.

    (narrator) WHAT DOES THE MAN IMPLY?

23. (man) Did the sales staff have a very successful month?

    (woman) They barely reached their quota.

    (narrator) WHAT DOES THE WOMAN MEAN?

24. (woman) Do you have to leave for the post office now? I'm working on some letters, but they're not quite ready.

    (man) I can hold off for a few minutes, but that's all.

    (narrator) WHAT DOES THE MAN MEAN?

25. (man) Has George been preparing for his comprehensive exams?

    (woman) He's been moving at a turtle's pace.

    (narrator) WHAT DOES THE WOMAN SAY ABOUT GEORGE?

26. (man) I can't believe how much physics homework I have to do tonight.

    (woman) Then you _are_ enrolled in that course.

    (narrator) WHAT HAD THE WOMAN ASSUMED ABOUT THE MAN?

27.   (woman)    The new computer program has been installed on the computer. Can you show me how to use it?
      (man)      Sorry. I would if I knew myself.
      (narrator) WHAT DOES THE MAN MEAN?

28.   (woman)    What do you think of the annual report?
      (man)      It could've been better.
      (narrator) WHAT DOES THE MAN MEAN?

29.   (man)      I have to be more careful about what I say in the future.
      (woman)    You really put your foot in your mouth this time.
      (narrator) WHAT DOES THE WOMAN MEAN?

30.   (woman)    Do you think that Marla won the competition because she was one of the judge's friends?
      (man)      I'm sure she didn't win because she had an unfair advantage.
      (narrator) WHAT DOES THE MAN IMPLY?

---

## Part B

**Directions:** In this part of the test, you will hear longer conversations. After each conversation, you will hear several questions. The conversations and questions will not be repeated.

After you hear a question, read the four possible answers in your test book and choose the best answer. Then, on your answer sheet, find the number of the question and fill in the space that corresponds to the letter of the answer you have chosen.

Remember, you are <u>not</u> allowed to take notes or write in your test book.

**Questions 31 through 34.** Listen to a woman talk to a friend about her plans for the afternoon.

(woman)    I'm going to my health club this afternoon. Would you like to come along? You could try it out and see if you want to take out a membership.
(man)      You belong to a health club? It seems that everyone that I meet here is involved in some kind of exercise program!

(woman)    Oh, exercise is very popular nowadays, and this health club's the best in the area. Why don't you try it today?
(man)      I would like to get a little more exercise, but I'm not sure if a health club's the way to go.
(woman)    This club has all kinds of exercise machines and classes, a track, racquetball courts, and a sauna. It has every kind of exercise you could want, except perhaps a swimming pool.
(man)      Well, I guess it can't hurt to try it just once. What time should we go?

(narrator)  31.   WHERE IS THE WOMAN GOING THIS AFTERNOON?

            32.   WHY DOES THE WOMAN ASK THE MAN TO GO?

            33.   ACCORDING TO THE WOMAN, WHAT KINDS OF SERVICES DOES THE HEALTH CLUB OFFER?

            34.   WHAT DOES THE MAN DECIDE TO DO?

**Questions 35 through 38.** Listen to a conversation between two students.

(woman)    We really need to get to work on our oral presentation for political science class.
(man)      We certainly do. You and I have to give the presentation next week, and we've hardly anything done.
(woman)    I can't believe that the presentation is next week. I thought we had so much time to prepare, but the time just seems to have disappeared. The presentation's on Thursday of next week, isn't it?
(man)      That's right, so we have exactly one week to get ready for it. We're going to have to do a lot of work in the next week.
(woman)    In this presentation on the court system, do you think we should talk about all three, the municipal, the state, and the federal court systems?
(man)      It's too much if we talk about all three, and I'm not sure we have enough time to prepare. How about if we only talk about the state and the federal courts?

(woman)    That sounds good to me. I think it's best if we talk about fewer topics and really cover them in depth. Say, I really know a lot about the state courts, and you know a lot about the federal courts. How about if we each work on preparing those parts individually, and then we can get together and put it all into one overall presentation?

(man)    All right. I'll work on the federal courts, and you can work on the state courts, and then we'll get together in a few days. How about if we get together next Monday?

(woman)    That sounds good to me. The presentation is not until Thursday, so if we get together on Monday, we'll have plenty of time to work on it.

(man)    Not exactly plenty of time, but we should be able to get it done. See you on Monday, if not sooner.

(woman)    See you then. Bye.

(narrator)    35.    WHAT ARE THE MAN AND WOMAN DISCUSSING IN THIS CONVERSATION?

36.    WHAT WILL THE MAN AND WOMAN DISCUSS DURING THEIR PRESENTATION?

37.    WHEN DO THEY NEXT PLAN TO MEET?

38.    HOW MUCH TIME DO THEY HAVE TO PREPARE FOR THE PRESENTATION?

---

## Part C

**Directions:** In this part of the test, you will hear several talks. After each talk, you will hear some questions. The talks and questions will not be repeated.

After you hear a question, read the four possible answers in your test book and choose the best answer. Then, on your answer sheet, find the number of the question and fill in the space that corresponds to the letter of the answer you have chosen.

Here is an example.

On the recording, you hear:

(narrator)    *Listen to an instructor talk to his class about painting.*

(man)    *Artist Grant Wood was a guiding force in the school of painting known as American regionalist, a style reflecting the distinctive characteristics of art from rural areas of the United States. Wood began drawing animals on the family farm at the age of three, and when he was thirty-eight one of his paintings received a remarkable amount of public notice and acclaim. This painting, called American Gothic, is a starkly simple depiction of a serious couple staring directly out at the viewer.*

Now listen to a sample question.

(narrator)    *What style of painting is known as American regionalist?*

In your test book, you read:

(A)    Art from America's inner cities.
(B)    Art from the central region of the U.S.
(C)    Art from various urban areas in the U.S.
(D)    Art from rural sections of America.

The best answer to the question, "What style of painting is known as American regionalist?" is (D), "Art from rural sections of America." Therefore, the correct choice is (D).

Now listen to another sample question.

(narrator)    *What is the name of Wood's most successful painting?*

In your test book, you read:

(A)    "American Regionalist."
(B)    "The Family Farm in Iowa."
(C)    "American Gothic."
(D)    "A Serious Couple."

The best answer to the question, "What is the name of Wood's most successful painting?" is (C), "American Gothic." Therefore, the correct choice is (C).

Remember, you are not allowed to take notes or write in your test book.

**Questions 39 through 42.** Listen to a talk given on a college campus.

(man)    Hello and welcome to campus. This morning there will be a short tour of the university before we head to the Administration Complex for registration. I've been selected to be your tour guide because I've been a student on this campus for three years, and I know my way around well.

From the library, we'll move on to the Student Center. In the Student Center you'll find the university bookstore, where you can purchase all the texts for the courses you're taking. You can also find a post office, a bank, a theater, a coffee shop, a travel agency, and a bowling alley in the Student Center. The Student Center's here to provide services and entertainment for the student body.

The first stop on our tour is the library. As you can see, it's a large library, with over 100,000 volumes. Additionally there are journals, newspapers, and magazines from around the world. The library's open seven days a week from 8:00 to midnight.

The final stop on our tour is the Administration Complex. In this area, you'll find the offices of university administrators and the Student Records Office. The auditorium where registration takes place is also in the Administration Complex. Now that we have reached the Administration Complex, the next item on your agenda is registration. Good luck.

(narrator)   39.  WHO IS THE SPEAKER?

         40.  WHAT IS THE MAIN TOPIC OF THE TALK?

         41.  ACCORDING TO THE SPEAKER, WHAT IS THE OVERALL PURPOSE OF THE STUDENT CENTER?

         42.  WHERE WILL REGISTRATION TAKE PLACE?

**Questions 43 through 46.** Listen to a talk on water pollution.

(woman)    A major cause of water pollution in the 1950's was the use of synthetic detergents. Unlike natural soaps, which were biodegradable, synthetic detergents would not break down into simpler substances. When released into the water supply, these nonbiodegradable synthetic detergents caused masses of foam to remain in both surface water and ground water.

In the 1960's new biodegradable detergents came into use, and the problem of foaming lakes, rivers, and streams began to disappear. However, these new biodegradable detergents contained phosphates, and those phosphates presented an entirely different set of problems in maintaining a clean water supply.

(narrator)   43.  WHAT MAJOR CAUSE OF WATER POLLUTION IN THE 1950's WAS PRESENTED IN THIS TALK?

         44.  WHAT ARE BIODEGRADABLE SUBSTANCES?

         45.  WHAT HAPPENED WHEN NONBIODEGRADABLE SYNTHETIC DETERGENTS WERE RELEASED INTO THE WATER SUPPLY?

         46.  WHAT WILL PROBABLY BE THE TOPIC OF THE TALK THAT FOLLOWS?

**Questions 47 through 50.** Listen to a lecture given by a college professor.

(man)    Today's lecture is on the composition of the Earth's atmosphere; by that, I mean which gases actually make up the atmosphere. I hope all of you have read the required textbook chapter on this subject prior to coming to class today.

The key point that I would like you to understand is the changing nature of the atmosphere—the atmosphere has <u>not</u> remained the same throughout the Earth's history.

Scientists believe that the Earth's original atmosphere probably consisted of ammonia and methane. Perhaps 20 million years ago the atmosphere evolved into something resembling the modern composition of 78 percent nitrogen, 20 percent oxygen, and a variety of other gases making up the remaining 2 percent.

One factor that was instrumental in causing the change in the atmosphere was the evolution of plant life; oxygen is part of the modern-day atmosphere because of plant life and the process of photosynthesis that goes along with it.

Well, that's all for today. Before tomorrow's class, you should be sure to read the next chapter in the text, Chapter Ten.

(*narrator*) 47. WHAT IS THE TOPIC OF THIS TALK?

48. WHEN DID THE ATMOSPHERE FIRST EVOLVE INTO THE COMPOSITION THAT EXISTS TODAY?

49. WHAT CAUSED OXYGEN TO DEVELOP IN THE ATMOSPHERE?

50. WHAT IS THE ASSIGNMENT FOR TOMORROW'S CLASS?

# ANSWER KEY

# ANSWERS TO PRACTICE TEST ONE

## SECTION 1: Listening Comprehension

| | | | | | | | | | |
|---|---|---|---|---|---|---|---|---|---|
| 1. | D | 11. | A | 21. | A | 31. | B | 41. | B |
| 2. | B | 12. | D | 22. | B | 32. | D | 42. | D |
| 3. | C | 13. | B | 23. | D | 33. | A | 43. | D |
| 4. | A | 14. | C | 24. | D | 34. | A | 44. | B |
| 5. | D | 15. | B | 25. | A | 35. | B | 45. | A |
| 6. | C | 16. | A | 26. | D | 36. | C | 46. | C |
| 7. | D | 17. | D | 27. | C | 37. | C | 47. | C |
| 8. | C | 18. | C | 28. | B | 38. | D | 48. | C |
| 9. | C | 19. | A | 29. | D | 39. | C | 49. | D |
| 10. | A | 20. | C | 30. | C | 40. | D | 50. | B |

## SECTION 2: Structure and Written Expression

| | | | | | | | | | |
|---|---|---|---|---|---|---|---|---|---|
| 1. | B | 9. | B | 17. | C | 25. | B | 33. | C |
| 2. | D | 10. | C | 18. | D | 26. | B | 34. | B |
| 3. | A | 11. | D | 19. | A | 27. | B | 35. | A |
| 4. | B | 12. | B | 20. | D | 28. | C | 36. | C |
| 5. | A | 13. | C | 21. | D | 29. | C | 37. | A |
| 6. | D | 14. | C | 22. | A | 30. | C | 38. | C |
| 7. | A | 15. | A | 23. | C | 31. | D | 39. | B |
| 8. | B | 16. | D | 24. | D | 32. | B | 40. | A |

## SECTION 3: Reading Comprehension

| | | | | | | | | | |
|---|---|---|---|---|---|---|---|---|---|
| 1. | C | 11. | B | 21. | A | 31. | B | 41. | B |
| 2. | D | 12. | A | 22. | C | 32. | B | 42. | C |
| 3. | C | 13. | D | 23. | D | 33. | D | 43. | D |
| 4. | B | 14. | B | 24. | B | 34. | D | 44. | D |
| 5. | D | 15. | C | 25. | C | 35. | A | 45. | A |
| 6. | A | 16. | B | 26. | B | 36. | A | 46. | A |
| 7. | C | 17. | B | 27. | D | 37. | B | 47. | A |
| 8. | D | 18. | D | 28. | A | 38. | D | 48. | C |
| 9. | B | 19. | A | 29. | C | 39. | C | 49. | C |
| 10. | A | 20. | C | 30. | A | 40. | D | 50. | C |

# ANSWERS TO PRACTICE TEST TWO

## SECTION 1:  Listening Comprehension

| | | | | | | | | | |
|---|---|---|---|---|---|---|---|---|---|
| 1. | A | 11. | C | 21. | D | 31. | A | 41. | B |
| 2. | B | 12. | A | 22. | C | 32. | C | 42. | D |
| 3. | A | 13. | D | 23. | B | 33. | D | 43. | D |
| 4. | C | 14. | A | 24. | A | 34. | C | 44. | A |
| 5. | D | 15. | B | 25. | B | 35. | B | 45. | B |
| 6. | C | 16. | C | 26. | D | 36. | B | 46. | C |
| 7. | B | 17. | D | 27. | A | 37. | D | 47. | D |
| 8. | D | 18. | C | 28. | B | 38. | A | 48. | A |
| 9. | C | 19. | C | 29. | C | 39. | C | 49. | D |
| 10. | B | 20. | C | 30. | A | 40. | A | 50. | B |

## SECTION 2:  Structure and Written Expression

| | | | | | | | | | |
|---|---|---|---|---|---|---|---|---|---|
| 1. | D | 9. | C | 17. | B | 25. | B | 33. | D |
| 2. | B | 10. | A | 18. | D | 26. | A | 34. | D |
| 3. | B | 11. | A | 19. | B | 27. | C | 35. | C |
| 4. | A | 12. | B | 20. | C | 28. | D | 36. | C |
| 5. | D | 13. | C | 21. | B | 29. | A | 37. | D |
| 6. | D | 14. | B | 22. | B | 30. | D | 38. | C |
| 7. | D | 15. | C | 23. | A | 31. | D | 39. | B |
| 8. | B | 16. | C | 24. | A | 32. | A | 40. | B |

## SECTION 3:  Reading Comprehension

| | | | | | | | | | |
|---|---|---|---|---|---|---|---|---|---|
| 1. | D | 11. | B | 21. | B | 31. | D | 41. | D |
| 2. | B | 12. | D | 22. | D | 32. | D | 42. | C |
| 3. | B | 13. | C | 23. | A | 33. | B | 43. | B |
| 4. | C | 14. | C | 24. | C | 34. | C | 44. | D |
| 5. | A | 15. | A | 25. | D | 35. | A | 45. | B |
| 6. | D | 16. | B | 26. | B | 36. | B | 46. | A |
| 7. | C | 17. | D | 27. | D | 37. | D | 47. | A |
| 8. | A | 18. | B | 28. | A | 38. | B | 48. | C |
| 9. | B | 19. | C | 29. | C | 39. | A | 49. | B |
| 10. | A | 20. | B | 30. | B | 40. | C | 50. | D |

# ANSWERS TO PRACTICE TEST THREE

### SECTION 1:  Listening Comprehension

| | | | | |
|---|---|---|---|---|
| 1.  C | 11.  B | 21.  C | 31.  B | 41.  C |
| 2.  B | 12.  C | 22.  B | 32.  C | 42.  D |
| 3.  B | 13.  A | 23.  D | 33.  A | 43.  D |
| 4.  D | 14.  C | 24.  D | 34.  C | 44.  C |
| 5.  C | 15.  B | 25.  A | 35.  C | 45.  A |
| 6.  C | 16.  B | 26.  B | 36.  A | 46.  B |
| 7.  D | 17.  D | 27.  D | 37.  B | 47.  B |
| 8.  D | 18.  C | 28.  C | 38.  D | 48.  D |
| 9.  C | 19.  D | 29.  A | 39.  C | 49.  C |
| 10.  A | 20.  A | 30.  B | 40.  A | 50.  D |

### SECTION 2:  Structure and Written Expression

| | | | | |
|---|---|---|---|---|
| 1.  A | 9.  B | 17.  B | 25.  D | 33.  A |
| 2.  C | 10.  A | 18.  C | 26.  D | 34.  C |
| 3.  B | 11.  A | 19.  B | 27.  A | 35.  C |
| 4.  C | 12.  B | 20.  C | 28.  D | 36.  A |
| 5.  A | 13.  D | 21.  C | 29.  A | 37.  D |
| 6.  D | 14.  C | 22.  A | 30.  C | 38.  A |
| 7.  B | 15.  D | 23.  D | 31.  D | 39.  A |
| 8.  C | 16.  A | 24.  A | 32.  B | 40.  D |

### SECTION 3:  Reading Comprehension

| | | | | |
|---|---|---|---|---|
| 1.  A | 11.  C | 21.  A | 31.  D | 41.  C |
| 2.  D | 12.  B | 22.  C | 32.  C | 42.  D |
| 3.  B | 13.  C | 23.  D | 33.  D | 43.  B |
| 4.  C | 14.  A | 24.  A | 34.  D | 44.  C |
| 5.  D | 15.  D | 25.  B | 35.  B | 45.  D |
| 6.  A | 16.  A | 26.  C | 36.  A | 46.  B |
| 7.  B | 17.  C | 27.  D | 37.  D | 47.  A |
| 8.  B | 18.  D | 28.  B | 38.  A | 48.  A |
| 9.  A | 19.  D | 29.  B | 39.  C | 49.  D |
| 10.  D | 20.  D | 30.  A | 40.  D | 50.  C |

# ANSWERS TO PRACTICE TEST FOUR

## SECTION 1:  Listening Comprehension

| | | | | | | | | | |
|---|---|---|---|---|---|---|---|---|---|
| 1. | C | 11. | B | 21. | D | 31. | D | 41. | C |
| 2. | A | 12. | D | 22. | A | 32. | C | 42. | A |
| 3. | D | 13. | A | 23. | B | 33. | B | 43. | B |
| 4. | B | 14. | D | 24. | D | 34. | A | 44. | A |
| 5. | B | 15. | D | 25. | D | 35. | D | 45. | D |
| 6. | D | 16. | C | 26. | B | 36. | C | 46. | D |
| 7. | C | 17. | C | 27. | D | 37. | B | 47. | B |
| 8. | A | 18. | B | 28. | C | 38. | D | 48. | C |
| 9. | D | 19. | C | 29. | A | 39. | B | 49. | C |
| 10. | A | 20. | D | 30. | D | 40. | C | 50. | A |

## SECTION 2:  Structure and Written Expression

| | | | | | | | | | |
|---|---|---|---|---|---|---|---|---|---|
| 1. | B | 9. | B | 17. | C | 25. | D | 33. | D |
| 2. | D | 10. | C | 18. | A | 26. | C | 34. | B |
| 3. | B | 11. | A | 19. | D | 27. | A | 35. | B |
| 4. | A | 12. | B | 20. | B | 28. | C | 36. | B |
| 5. | C | 13. | D | 21. | C | 29. | C | 37. | D |
| 6. | A | 14. | A | 22. | D | 30. | A | 38. | C |
| 7. | C | 15. | C | 23. | D | 31. | A | 39. | A |
| 8. | D | 16. | D | 24. | B | 32. | D | 40. | D |

## SECTION 3:  Reading Comprehension

| | | | | | | | | | |
|---|---|---|---|---|---|---|---|---|---|
| 1. | C | 11. | D | 21. | D | 31. | D | 41. | D |
| 2. | A | 12. | A | 22. | D | 32. | C | 42. | A |
| 3. | B | 13. | B | 23. | C | 33. | D | 43. | D |
| 4. | C | 14. | D | 24. | B | 34. | B | 44. | A |
| 5. | B | 15. | A | 25. | C | 35. | B | 45. | D |
| 6. | D | 16. | D | 26. | D | 36. | B | 46. | D |
| 7. | D | 17. | D | 27. | A | 37. | D | 47. | A |
| 8. | C | 18. | A | 28. | C | 38. | A | 48. | C |
| 9. | B | 19. | C | 29. | B | 39. | A | 49. | B |
| 10. | A | 20. | B | 30. | B | 40. | B | 50. | C |

# ANSWERS TO PRACTICE TEST FIVE

## SECTION 1:  Listening Comprehension

| | | | | | | | | | |
|---|---|---|---|---|---|---|---|---|---|
| 1. | A | 11. | B | 21. | A | 31. | B | 41. | A |
| 2. | C | 12. | D | 22. | B | 32. | C | 42. | C |
| 3. | B | 13. | D | 23. | A | 33. | D | 43. | B |
| 4. | C | 14. | B | 24. | A | 34. | A | 44. | C |
| 5. | A | 15. | A | 25. | B | 35. | A | 45. | B |
| 6. | D | 16. | C | 26. | A | 36. | D | 46. | D |
| 7. | D | 17. | B | 27. | C | 37. | B | 47. | B |
| 8. | C | 18. | D | 28. | D | 38. | C | 48. | B |
| 9. | B | 19. | C | 29. | D | 39. | B | 49. | A |
| 10. | A | 20. | D | 30. | A | 40. | D | 50. | D |

## SECTION 2:  Structure and Written Expression

| | | | | | | | | | |
|---|---|---|---|---|---|---|---|---|---|
| 1. | A | 9. | C | 17. | A | 25. | A | 33. | C |
| 2. | B | 10. | C | 18. | B | 26. | D | 34. | C |
| 3. | D | 11. | B | 19. | D | 27. | C | 35. | D |
| 4. | C | 12. | D | 20. | C | 28. | B | 36. | A |
| 5. | B | 13. | C | 21. | D | 29. | A | 37. | D |
| 6. | A | 14. | A | 22. | C | 30. | D | 38. | D |
| 7. | C | 15. | B | 23. | A | 31. | B | 39. | C |
| 8. | C | 16. | A | 24. | D | 32. | C | 40. | C |

## SECTION 3:  Reading Comprehension

| | | | | | | | | | |
|---|---|---|---|---|---|---|---|---|---|
| 1. | D | 11. | C | 21. | D | 31. | C | 41. | A |
| 2. | D | 12. | C | 22. | A | 32. | D | 42. | B |
| 3. | C | 13. | A | 23. | B | 33. | A | 43. | D |
| 4. | A | 14. | D | 24. | C | 34. | B | 44. | C |
| 5. | B | 15. | D | 25. | A | 35. | C | 45. | C |
| 6. | A | 16. | A | 26. | C | 36. | C | 46. | B |
| 7. | C | 17. | B | 27. | A | 37. | A | 47. | A |
| 8. | B | 18. | A | 28. | D | 38. | C | 48. | A |
| 9. | A | 19. | A | 29. | D | 39. | D | 49. | A |
| 10. | A | 20. | B | 30. | C | 40. | B | 50. | D |

# SCORING INFORMATION

# SCORING YOUR PRACTICE TESTS

When your TOEFL test is scored, you will receive a score between 20 and 68 in each of the three sections (Listening Comprehension, Structure and Written Expression, and Reading Comprehension). You will also receive an overall score between 217 and 677. You can use the following chart to estimate the scores on your Practice Tests.

| NUMBER CORRECT | CONVERTED SCORE SECTION 1 *Listening* | CONVERTED SCORE SECTION 2 *Structure* | CONVERTED SCORE SECTION 3 *Reading* |
|---|---|---|---|
| 50 | 68 | — | 67 |
| 49 | 67 | — | 66 |
| 48 | 66 | — | 65 |
| 47 | 65 | — | 63 |
| 46 | 63 | — | 61 |
| 45 | 62 | — | 60 |
| 44 | 61 | — | 59 |
| 43 | 60 | — | 58 |
| 42 | 59 | — | 57 |
| 41 | 58 | — | 56 |
| 40 | 57 | 68 | 55 |
| 39 | 57 | 67 | 54 |
| 38 | 56 | 65 | 54 |
| 37 | 55 | 63 | 53 |
| 36 | 54 | 61 | 52 |
| 35 | 54 | 60 | 52 |
| 34 | 53 | 58 | 51 |
| 33 | 52 | 57 | 50 |
| 32 | 52 | 56 | 49 |
| 31 | 51 | 55 | 48 |
| 30 | 51 | 54 | 48 |
| 29 | 50 | 53 | 47 |
| 28 | 49 | 52 | 46 |
| 27 | 49 | 51 | 46 |
| 26 | 48 | 50 | 45 |
| 25 | 48 | 49 | 44 |
| 24 | 47 | 48 | 43 |
| 23 | 47 | 47 | 43 |
| 22 | 46 | 46 | 42 |
| 21 | 45 | 45 | 41 |
| 20 | 45 | 44 | 40 |
| 19 | 44 | 43 | 39 |
| 18 | 43 | 42 | 38 |
| 17 | 42 | 41 | 37 |
| 16 | 41 | 40 | 36 |
| 15 | 41 | 40 | 35 |

| NUMBER CORRECT | CONVERTED SCORE SECTION 1 | CONVERTED SCORE SECTION 2 | CONVERTED SCORE SECTION 3 |
|:---:|:---:|:---:|:---:|
| 14 | 37 | 38 | 34 |
| 13 | 38 | 37 | 32 |
| 12 | 37 | 36 | 31 |
| 11 | 35 | 35 | 30 |
| 10 | 33 | 33 | 29 |
| 9 | 32 | 31 | 28 |
| 8 | 32 | 29 | 28 |
| 7 | 31 | 27 | 27 |
| 6 | 30 | 26 | 26 |
| 5 | 29 | 25 | 25 |
| 4 | 28 | 23 | 24 |
| 3 | 27 | 22 | 23 |
| 2 | 26 | 21 | 23 |
| 1 | 25 | 20 | 22 |
| 0 | 24 | 20 | 21 |

You should first use the chart to determine your converted score for each section. Suppose that you got 30 correct in the first section, 28 correct in the second section, and 43 correct in the third section. The 30 correct in the first section means a converted score of 51. The 28 correct in the second section means a converted score of 52. The 43 correct in the third section means a converted score of 58.

|  | SECTION 1 | SECTION 2 | SECTION 3 |
|:---|:---:|:---:|:---:|
| NUMBER CORRECT | 30 | 28 | 43 |
| CONVERTED SCORE | 51 | 52 | 58 |

Next you should determine your overall score in the following way:

1. Add the three converted scores together.

   $51 + 52 + 58 = 161$

2. Divide the sum by 3.

   $161/3 = 53.7$

3. Then multiply by 10.

   $53.7 \times 10 = 537$

The overall TOEFL score in this example is 537.

The score of the TWE is included on the same form as your regular TOEFL score, but it is not part of your overall TOEFL score. It is a separate score on a scale of 1 to 6, where 1 is the worst score and 6 is the best score. The following table outlines what each of the scores essentially means:

---

**TEST OF WRITTEN ENGLISH (TWE) SCORES**

| | |
|---|---|
| 6 | The writer has very strong organizational, structural, and grammatical skills. |
| 5 | The writer has good organizational, structural, and grammatical skills. However, the essay contains some errors. |
| 4 | The writer has adequate organizational, structural, and grammatical skills. The essay contains a number of errors. |
| 3 | The writer shows evidence of organizational, structural, and grammatical skills that still need to be improved. |
| 2 | The writer shows a minimal ability to convey ideas in written English. |
| 1 | The writer is not capable of conveying ideas in written English. |

---

# CHARTING YOUR PROGRESS

Each time you take a practice test, you should record the results in the chart that follows. In this way you will be able to keep track of the progress you make. You will also be aware of the areas of the TOEFL test that you still need to improve.

| | LISTENING COMPREHENSION | STRUCTURE AND WRITTEN EXPRESSION | READING COMPREHENSION | OVERALL SCORE |
|---|---|---|---|---|
| TEST 1 | | | | |
| TEST 2 | | | | |
| TEST 3 | | | | |
| TEST 4 | | | | |
| TEST 5 | | | | |

# TEST OF ENGLISH AS A FOREIGN LANGUAGE

**TOEFL ANSWER SHEET   SIDE 1**

Use a No. 2 (H.B.) pencil only. Do not use ink. Be sure each mark is dark and completely fills the intended oval. Erase errors or stray marks completely.

**1. NAME:** Copy your name from your admission ticket. Use one box for each letter. First print your family name (surname), then your given name, and then your middle name. Leave one box blank between names. Below each box, fill in the oval that contains the same letter.

**2. REGISTRATION NUMBER**
→ Start here

**3. INSTITUTION AND DEPARTMENT CODES:** Give the code numbers of the institutions and departments to which you want your official score report sent. Be sure to fill in the corresponding oval below each box.

INSTITUTION CODE | DEPT. CODE | INSTITUTION CODE | DEPT. CODE | INSTITUTION CODE | DEPT. CODE

**4. DO YOU PLAN TO STUDY FOR A DEGREE IN THE U.S.A. OR CANADA?**
○ YES   ○ NO

**5. REASON FOR TAKING TOEFL (FILL IN ONLY ONE OVAL.)**
1. To enter a college or university as an undergraduate student.
2. To enter a college or university as a graduate student.
3. To enter a school other than a college or university.
4. To become licensed to practice my profession in the U.S.A. or Canada.
5. To demonstrate my proficiency in English to the company for which I work or aspect to work.
6. Other than the above (please specify).

**6. NUMBER OF TIMES YOU HAVE TAKEN TOEFL BEFORE TODAY**
○ NONE   ○ ONE   ○ TWO   ○ THREE   ○ FOUR OR MORE

**7. TEST CENTER (Print.)**
CENTER NUMBER
CITY
COUNTRY

**8. PLEASE PRINT YOUR NAME AND MAILING ADDRESS**
FAMILY NAME (SURNAME)        GIVEN NAME        MIDDLE NAME
STREET ADDRESS OR P. O. BOX NO.
CITY        STATE OR PROVINCE
POSTAL OR ZIP CODE        COUNTRY

**9. SIGNATURE AND DATE:** Copy the statement below; use handwriting. "I hereby agree to the conditions set forth in the Bulletin of Information and affirm that I am the person whose name and address are given on this answer sheet."

SIGNED: _____ (WRITE YOUR NAME IN PENCIL AS IF SIGNING A LEGAL IDENTIFICATION DOCUMENT)

DATE: ____ / ____ / ____    MO.  DAY  YEAR

SAMPLE — DO NOT MARK IN THIS AREA
TEST FORM:

# SIDE 2

**TEST FORM**

**TEST BOOK SERIAL NUMBER**

**ROOM NUMBER** | **SEAT NUMBER**

**SEX** ○ Male ○ Female | **DATE OF BIRTH** MO. DAY YEAR

Choose only one answer for each question. Carefully and completely fill in the oval corresponding to the answer you choose so that the letter inside the oval cannot be seen. Completely erase any other marks you may have made.

| CORRECT | WRONG | WRONG | WRONG | WRONG |
|---------|-------|-------|-------|-------|
| Ⓐ Ⓑ ● Ⓓ | Ⓐ Ⓑ Ⓒ Ⓓ | Ⓐ Ⓑ Ⓒ Ⓓ | Ⓐ Ⓑ Ⓒ Ⓓ | Ⓐ Ⓑ Ⓒ Ⓓ |

**NAME (Print)** _____

FAMILY NAME (SURNAME)　　GIVEN NAME　　MIDDLE NAME

**REGISTRATION NUMBER** | **SIGNATURE**

## SECTION 1

1 Ⓐ Ⓑ Ⓒ Ⓓ
2 Ⓐ Ⓑ Ⓒ Ⓓ
3 Ⓐ Ⓑ Ⓒ Ⓓ
4 Ⓐ Ⓑ Ⓒ Ⓓ
5 Ⓐ Ⓑ Ⓒ Ⓓ
6 Ⓐ Ⓑ Ⓒ Ⓓ
7 Ⓐ Ⓑ Ⓒ Ⓓ
8 Ⓐ Ⓑ Ⓒ Ⓓ
9 Ⓐ Ⓑ Ⓒ Ⓓ
10 Ⓐ Ⓑ Ⓒ Ⓓ
11 Ⓐ Ⓑ Ⓒ Ⓓ
12 Ⓐ Ⓑ Ⓒ Ⓓ
13 Ⓐ Ⓑ Ⓒ Ⓓ
14 Ⓐ Ⓑ Ⓒ Ⓓ
15 Ⓐ Ⓑ Ⓒ Ⓓ
16 Ⓐ Ⓑ Ⓒ Ⓓ
17 Ⓐ Ⓑ Ⓒ Ⓓ
18 Ⓐ Ⓑ Ⓒ Ⓓ
19 Ⓐ Ⓑ Ⓒ Ⓓ
20 Ⓐ Ⓑ Ⓒ Ⓓ
21 Ⓐ Ⓑ Ⓒ Ⓓ
22 Ⓐ Ⓑ Ⓒ Ⓓ
23 Ⓐ Ⓑ Ⓒ Ⓓ
24 Ⓐ Ⓑ Ⓒ Ⓓ
25 Ⓐ Ⓑ Ⓒ Ⓓ
26 Ⓐ Ⓑ Ⓒ Ⓓ
27 Ⓐ Ⓑ Ⓒ Ⓓ
28 Ⓐ Ⓑ Ⓒ Ⓓ
29 Ⓐ Ⓑ Ⓒ Ⓓ
30 Ⓐ Ⓑ Ⓒ Ⓓ
31 Ⓐ Ⓑ Ⓒ Ⓓ
32 Ⓐ Ⓑ Ⓒ Ⓓ
33 Ⓐ Ⓑ Ⓒ Ⓓ
34 Ⓐ Ⓑ Ⓒ Ⓓ
35 Ⓐ Ⓑ Ⓒ Ⓓ
36 Ⓐ Ⓑ Ⓒ Ⓓ
37 Ⓐ Ⓑ Ⓒ Ⓓ
38 Ⓐ Ⓑ Ⓒ Ⓓ
39 Ⓐ Ⓑ Ⓒ Ⓓ
40 Ⓐ Ⓑ Ⓒ Ⓓ
41 Ⓐ Ⓑ Ⓒ Ⓓ
42 Ⓐ Ⓑ Ⓒ Ⓓ
43 Ⓐ Ⓑ Ⓒ Ⓓ
44 Ⓐ Ⓑ Ⓒ Ⓓ
45 Ⓐ Ⓑ Ⓒ Ⓓ
46 Ⓐ Ⓑ Ⓒ Ⓓ
47 Ⓐ Ⓑ Ⓒ Ⓓ
48 Ⓐ Ⓑ Ⓒ Ⓓ
49 Ⓐ Ⓑ Ⓒ Ⓓ
50 Ⓐ Ⓑ Ⓒ Ⓓ

## SECTION 2

1 Ⓐ Ⓑ Ⓒ Ⓓ
2 Ⓐ Ⓑ Ⓒ Ⓓ
3 Ⓐ Ⓑ Ⓒ Ⓓ
4 Ⓐ Ⓑ Ⓒ Ⓓ
5 Ⓐ Ⓑ Ⓒ Ⓓ
6 Ⓐ Ⓑ Ⓒ Ⓓ
7 Ⓐ Ⓑ Ⓒ Ⓓ
8 Ⓐ Ⓑ Ⓒ Ⓓ
9 Ⓐ Ⓑ Ⓒ Ⓓ
10 Ⓐ Ⓑ Ⓒ Ⓓ
11 Ⓐ Ⓑ Ⓒ Ⓓ
12 Ⓐ Ⓑ Ⓒ Ⓓ
13 Ⓐ Ⓑ Ⓒ Ⓓ
14 Ⓐ Ⓑ Ⓒ Ⓓ
15 Ⓐ Ⓑ Ⓒ Ⓓ
16 Ⓐ Ⓑ Ⓒ Ⓓ
17 Ⓐ Ⓑ Ⓒ Ⓓ
18 Ⓐ Ⓑ Ⓒ Ⓓ
19 Ⓐ Ⓑ Ⓒ Ⓓ
20 Ⓐ Ⓑ Ⓒ Ⓓ
21 Ⓐ Ⓑ Ⓒ Ⓓ
22 Ⓐ Ⓑ Ⓒ Ⓓ
23 Ⓐ Ⓑ Ⓒ Ⓓ
24 Ⓐ Ⓑ Ⓒ Ⓓ
25 Ⓐ Ⓑ Ⓒ Ⓓ
26 Ⓐ Ⓑ Ⓒ Ⓓ
27 Ⓐ Ⓑ Ⓒ Ⓓ
28 Ⓐ Ⓑ Ⓒ Ⓓ
29 Ⓐ Ⓑ Ⓒ Ⓓ
30 Ⓐ Ⓑ Ⓒ Ⓓ
31 Ⓐ Ⓑ Ⓒ Ⓓ
32 Ⓐ Ⓑ Ⓒ Ⓓ
33 Ⓐ Ⓑ Ⓒ Ⓓ
34 Ⓐ Ⓑ Ⓒ Ⓓ
35 Ⓐ Ⓑ Ⓒ Ⓓ
36 Ⓐ Ⓑ Ⓒ Ⓓ
37 Ⓐ Ⓑ Ⓒ Ⓓ
38 Ⓐ Ⓑ Ⓒ Ⓓ
39 Ⓐ Ⓑ Ⓒ Ⓓ
40 Ⓐ Ⓑ Ⓒ Ⓓ

## SECTION 3

1 Ⓐ Ⓑ Ⓒ Ⓓ　31 Ⓐ Ⓑ Ⓒ Ⓓ
2 Ⓐ Ⓑ Ⓒ Ⓓ　32 Ⓐ Ⓑ Ⓒ Ⓓ
3 Ⓐ Ⓑ Ⓒ Ⓓ　33 Ⓐ Ⓑ Ⓒ Ⓓ
4 Ⓐ Ⓑ Ⓒ Ⓓ　34 Ⓐ Ⓑ Ⓒ Ⓓ
5 Ⓐ Ⓑ Ⓒ Ⓓ　35 Ⓐ Ⓑ Ⓒ Ⓓ
6 Ⓐ Ⓑ Ⓒ Ⓓ　36 Ⓐ Ⓑ Ⓒ Ⓓ
7 Ⓐ Ⓑ Ⓒ Ⓓ　37 Ⓐ Ⓑ Ⓒ Ⓓ
8 Ⓐ Ⓑ Ⓒ Ⓓ　38 Ⓐ Ⓑ Ⓒ Ⓓ
9 Ⓐ Ⓑ Ⓒ Ⓓ　39 Ⓐ Ⓑ Ⓒ Ⓓ
10 Ⓐ Ⓑ Ⓒ Ⓓ　40 Ⓐ Ⓑ Ⓒ Ⓓ
11 Ⓐ Ⓑ Ⓒ Ⓓ　41 Ⓐ Ⓑ Ⓒ Ⓓ
12 Ⓐ Ⓑ Ⓒ Ⓓ　42 Ⓐ Ⓑ Ⓒ Ⓓ
13 Ⓐ Ⓑ Ⓒ Ⓓ　43 Ⓐ Ⓑ Ⓒ Ⓓ
14 Ⓐ Ⓑ Ⓒ Ⓓ　44 Ⓐ Ⓑ Ⓒ Ⓓ
15 Ⓐ Ⓑ Ⓒ Ⓓ　45 Ⓐ Ⓑ Ⓒ Ⓓ
16 Ⓐ Ⓑ Ⓒ Ⓓ　46 Ⓐ Ⓑ Ⓒ Ⓓ
17 Ⓐ Ⓑ Ⓒ Ⓓ　47 Ⓐ Ⓑ Ⓒ Ⓓ
18 Ⓐ Ⓑ Ⓒ Ⓓ　48 Ⓐ Ⓑ Ⓒ Ⓓ
19 Ⓐ Ⓑ Ⓒ Ⓓ　49 Ⓐ Ⓑ Ⓒ Ⓓ
20 Ⓐ Ⓑ Ⓒ Ⓓ　50 Ⓐ Ⓑ Ⓒ Ⓓ
21 Ⓐ Ⓑ Ⓒ Ⓓ
22 Ⓐ Ⓑ Ⓒ Ⓓ
23 Ⓐ Ⓑ Ⓒ Ⓓ
24 Ⓐ Ⓑ Ⓒ Ⓓ
25 Ⓐ Ⓑ Ⓒ Ⓓ
26 Ⓐ Ⓑ Ⓒ Ⓓ
27 Ⓐ Ⓑ Ⓒ Ⓓ
28 Ⓐ Ⓑ Ⓒ Ⓓ
29 Ⓐ Ⓑ Ⓒ Ⓓ
30 Ⓐ Ⓑ Ⓒ Ⓓ

SAMPLE

### IF YOU DO **NOT** WANT THIS ANSWER SHEET TO BE SCORED

If you want to cancel your scores from this administration, complete A and B below. The scores will not be sent to you or your designated recipients, and they will be removed from your permanent record.

**To cancel your scores from this test administration, you must:**

A. fill in both ovals here ○ — ○ and B. sign your name below

_____

**ONCE A SCORE IS CANCELLED, IT CANNOT BE REPORTED AT ANY TIME.**

| 1R | 2R | 3R | TCS | FOR ETS USE ONLY | F |
|----|----|----|-----|------------------|---|
| 1CS | 2CS | 3CS | | | |

180

**Test Of Written English (TWE) Answer Sheet**

2. REGISTRATION NUMBER
→ Start here

| TEST CENTER | TEST BOOK SERIAL NUMBER | TEST DATE |
|---|---|---|

Begin your essay here. If you need more space, use the other side.

TOPIC

Reprinted by permission.

SAMPLE

ADDITIONAL SPACE IS AVAILABLE ON THE REVERSE SIDE.

DO NOT WRITE BELOW THIS LINE. FOR ETS USE ONLY.

NO ⬤   OFF ⬤

ORS

9

**Continuation of essay**

TEST OF ENGLISH AS A FOREIGN LANGUAGE

**1. NAME:** Copy your name from your admission ticket. Use one box for each letter. First print your family name (surname), then your given name, and then your middle name. Leave one box blank between names. Below each box, fill in the oval that contains the same letter.

TOEFL ANSWER SHEET   SIDE 1

Use a No. 2 (H.B.) pencil only. Do not use ink. Be sure each mark is dark and completely fills the intended oval. Erase errors or stray marks completely.

**2. REGISTRATION NUMBER**
Start here

**3. INSTITUTION AND DEPARTMENT CODES:** Give the code numbers of the institutions and departments to which you want your official score report sent. Be sure to fill in the corresponding oval below each box.

INSTITUTION CODE   DEPT. CODE

**4. DO YOU PLAN TO STUDY FOR A DEGREE IN THE U.S.A. OR CANADA?**
◯ YES   ◯ NO

**5. REASON FOR TAKING TOEFL**
(FILL IN ONLY ONE OVAL.)
1. To enter a college or university as an undergraduate student.
2. To enter a college or university as a graduate student.
3. To enter a school other than a college or university.
4. To become licensed to practice my profession in the U.S.A. or Canada.
5. To demonstrate my proficiency in English to the company for which I work or expect to work.
6. Other than the above (please specify).

**6. NUMBER OF TIMES YOU HAVE TAKEN TOEFL BEFORE TODAY**
◯ NONE   ◯ ONE   ◯ TWO   ◯ THREE   ◯ FOUR OR MORE

**7. TEST CENTER (Print.)**
CENTER NUMBER

**8. PLEASE PRINT YOUR NAME AND MAILING ADDRESS**
FAMILY NAME (SURNAME)   GIVEN NAME   MIDDLE NAME
STREET ADDRESS OR P.O. BOX NO.
CITY   STATE OR PROVINCE
POSTAL OR ZIP CODE   COUNTRY

**9. SIGNATURE AND DATE:** Copy the statement below; use handwriting.
"I hereby agree to the conditions set forth in the Bulletin of Information and affirm that I am the person whose name and address are given on this answer sheet."

SIGNED: _____ (WRITE YOUR NAME IN PENCIL AS IF SIGNING A LEGAL IDENTIFICATION DOCUMENT)

DATE: MO. DAY YEAR

SAMPLE   DO NOT MARK IN THIS AREA.   TEST FORM:

Reprinted by permission.

SIDE 2

TEST FORM

TEST BOOK SERIAL NUMBER

ROOM NUMBER | SEAT NUMBER

SEX
○ Male
○ Female

DATE OF BIRTH
MO. DAY YEAR

Choose only one answer for each question. Carefully and completely fill in the oval corresponding to the answer you choose so that the letter inside the oval cannot be seen. Completely erase any other marks you may have made.

NAME (Print) _____
FAMILY NAME (SURNAME)    GIVEN NAME    MIDDLE NAME

SIGNATURE _____

REGISTRATION NUMBER

| CORRECT | WRONG | WRONG | WRONG | WRONG | WRONG |
|---------|-------|-------|-------|-------|-------|
| Ⓐ | Ⓐ | Ⓐ | Ⓐ | Ⓐ | Ⓐ |
| Ⓑ | Ⓑ | Ⓑ | Ⓑ | Ⓑ | Ⓑ |
| ● | Ⓒ | ⊗ | Ⓒ | Ⓒ | ● |
| Ⓓ | Ⓓ | Ⓓ | Ⓓ | Ⓓ | Ⓓ |

SECTION 1

SECTION 2

SECTION 3

SAMPLE

IF YOU DO NOT WANT THIS ANSWER SHEET TO BE SCORED

If you want to cancel your scores from this administration, complete A and B below. The scores will not be sent to you or your designated recipients, and they will be removed from your permanent record.

To cancel your scores from this test administration, you must:

A. fill in both ovals here    and    B. sign your name below
○ – ○

_____

ONCE A SCORE IS CANCELLED, IT CANNOT BE REPORTED AT ANY TIME.

| FOR ETS USE ONLY | | | |
|---|---|---|---|
| 1R | 2R | 3R | TCS |
| 1CS | 2CS | 3CS | |
| | | | E |

Reprinted by permission.

# Test Of Written English (TWE) Answer Sheet

| TEST CENTER | TEST BOOK SERIAL NUMBER | TEST DATE |
|---|---|---|

**2. REGISTRATION NUMBER** — Start here

**Begin your essay here. If you need more space, use the other side.**

**TOPIC**

ADDITIONAL SPACE IS AVAILABLE ON THE REVERSE SIDE.

DO NOT WRITE BELOW THIS LINE. FOR ETS USE ONLY.

SAMPLE

NO    OFF

ORS

**Continuation of essay**

SAMPLE

**NOTE**

This example of a TWE answer sheet is for practice use only. Do not send it to the TWE office. It cannot be scored. and it will not be returned to you.

# TEST OF ENGLISH AS A FOREIGN LANGUAGE

**1. NAME:** Copy your name from your admission ticket. Use one box for each letter. First print your family name (surname), then your given name, and then your middle name. Leave one box blank between names. Below each box, fill in the oval that contains the same letter.

## TOEFL ANSWER SHEET SIDE 1

Use a No. 2 (H.B.) pencil only. Do not use ink. Be sure each mark is dark and completely fills the intended oval. Erase errors or stray marks completely.

**2. REGISTRATION NUMBER**
Start here

**3. INSTITUTION AND DEPARTMENT CODES:** Give the code numbers of the institutions and departments to which you want your official score report sent. Be sure to fill in the corresponding oval below each box.

INSTITUTION CODE — DEPT. CODE

**4. DO YOU PLAN TO STUDY FOR A DEGREE IN THE U.S.A. OR CANADA?**
○ YES ○ NO

**5. REASON FOR TAKING TOEFL (FILL IN ONLY ONE OVAL).**
1. To enter a college or university as an undergraduate student.
2. To enter a college or university as a graduate student.
3. To enter a school other than a college or university.
4. To become licensed to practice my profession in the U.S.A. or Canada.
5. To demonstrate my proficiency in English to the company for which I work or expect to work.
6. Other than the above (please specify).

**6. NUMBER OF TIMES YOU HAVE TAKEN TOEFL BEFORE TODAY**
○ NONE ○ ONE ○ TWO ○ THREE ○ FOUR OR MORE

**7. TEST CENTER** (Print.)
CENTER NUMBER
CITY
COUNTRY

**8. PLEASE PRINT YOUR NAME AND MAILING ADDRESS**
FAMILY NAME (SURNAME)    GIVEN NAME    MIDDLE NAME
STREET ADDRESS OR P. O. BOX NO.
CITY    STATE OR PROVINCE
POSTAL OR ZIP CODE    COUNTRY

**9. SIGNATURE AND DATE:** Copy the statement below; use handwriting.
"I hereby agree to the conditions set forth in the Bulletin of Information and affirm that I am the person whose name and address are given on this answer sheet."

DATE: ___/___/___    MO. DAY YEAR

SIGNED: _____
(WRITE YOUR NAME IN PENCIL AS IF SIGNING A LEGAL IDENTIFICATION DOCUMENT.)

DO NOT MARK IN THIS AREA.
SAMPLE
TEST FORM:

# SIDE 2

**TEST FORM**

**TEST BOOK SERIAL NUMBER**

**ROOM NUMBER**     **SEAT NUMBER**

**SEX**  ○ Male   ○ Female     **DATE OF BIRTH** ___/___/___  
MO.  DAY  YEAR

Choose only one answer for each question. Carefully and completely fill in the oval corresponding to the answer you choose so that the letter inside the oval cannot be seen. Completely erase any other marks you may have made.

| CORRECT | WRONG | WRONG | WRONG | WRONG |
|---|---|---|---|---|
| Ⓐ Ⓑ ● Ⓓ | Ⓐ Ⓑ Ⓒ̸ Ⓓ | Ⓐ Ⓑ ⊗ Ⓓ | Ⓐ Ⓑ Ⓒ Ⓓ | Ⓐ Ⓑ ◉ Ⓓ |

**NAME (Print)** _____  
FAMILY NAME (SURNAME)          GIVEN NAME          MIDDLE NAME

**REGISTRATION NUMBER**     **SIGNATURE**

## SECTION 1

1 Ⓐ Ⓑ Ⓒ Ⓓ
2 Ⓐ Ⓑ Ⓒ Ⓓ
3 Ⓐ Ⓑ Ⓒ Ⓓ
4 Ⓐ Ⓑ Ⓒ Ⓓ
5 Ⓐ Ⓑ Ⓒ Ⓓ
6 Ⓐ Ⓑ Ⓒ Ⓓ
7 Ⓐ Ⓑ Ⓒ Ⓓ
8 Ⓐ Ⓑ Ⓒ Ⓓ
9 Ⓐ Ⓑ Ⓒ Ⓓ
10 Ⓐ Ⓑ Ⓒ Ⓓ
11 Ⓐ Ⓑ Ⓒ Ⓓ
12 Ⓐ Ⓑ Ⓒ Ⓓ
13 Ⓐ Ⓑ Ⓒ Ⓓ
14 Ⓐ Ⓑ Ⓒ Ⓓ
15 Ⓐ Ⓑ Ⓒ Ⓓ
16 Ⓐ Ⓑ Ⓒ Ⓓ
17 Ⓐ Ⓑ Ⓒ Ⓓ
18 Ⓐ Ⓑ Ⓒ Ⓓ
19 Ⓐ Ⓑ Ⓒ Ⓓ
20 Ⓐ Ⓑ Ⓒ Ⓓ
21 Ⓐ Ⓑ Ⓒ Ⓓ
22 Ⓐ Ⓑ Ⓒ Ⓓ
23 Ⓐ Ⓑ Ⓒ Ⓓ
24 Ⓐ Ⓑ Ⓒ Ⓓ
25 Ⓐ Ⓑ Ⓒ Ⓓ
26 Ⓐ Ⓑ Ⓒ Ⓓ
27 Ⓐ Ⓑ Ⓒ Ⓓ
28 Ⓐ Ⓑ Ⓒ Ⓓ
29 Ⓐ Ⓑ Ⓒ Ⓓ
30 Ⓐ Ⓑ Ⓒ Ⓓ
31 Ⓐ Ⓑ Ⓒ Ⓓ
32 Ⓐ Ⓑ Ⓒ Ⓓ
33 Ⓐ Ⓑ Ⓒ Ⓓ
34 Ⓐ Ⓑ Ⓒ Ⓓ
35 Ⓐ Ⓑ Ⓒ Ⓓ
36 Ⓐ Ⓑ Ⓒ Ⓓ
37 Ⓐ Ⓑ Ⓒ Ⓓ
38 Ⓐ Ⓑ Ⓒ Ⓓ
39 Ⓐ Ⓑ Ⓒ Ⓓ
40 Ⓐ Ⓑ Ⓒ Ⓓ
41 Ⓐ Ⓑ Ⓒ Ⓓ
42 Ⓐ Ⓑ Ⓒ Ⓓ
43 Ⓐ Ⓑ Ⓒ Ⓓ
44 Ⓐ Ⓑ Ⓒ Ⓓ
45 Ⓐ Ⓑ Ⓒ Ⓓ
46 Ⓐ Ⓑ Ⓒ Ⓓ
47 Ⓐ Ⓑ Ⓒ Ⓓ
48 Ⓐ Ⓑ Ⓒ Ⓓ
49 Ⓐ Ⓑ Ⓒ Ⓓ
50 Ⓐ Ⓑ Ⓒ Ⓓ

## SECTION 2

1 Ⓐ Ⓑ Ⓒ Ⓓ
2 Ⓐ Ⓑ Ⓒ Ⓓ
3 Ⓐ Ⓑ Ⓒ Ⓓ
4 Ⓐ Ⓑ Ⓒ Ⓓ
5 Ⓐ Ⓑ Ⓒ Ⓓ
6 Ⓐ Ⓑ Ⓒ Ⓓ
7 Ⓐ Ⓑ Ⓒ Ⓓ
8 Ⓐ Ⓑ Ⓒ Ⓓ
9 Ⓐ Ⓑ Ⓒ Ⓓ
10 Ⓐ Ⓑ Ⓒ Ⓓ
11 Ⓐ Ⓑ Ⓒ Ⓓ
12 Ⓐ Ⓑ Ⓒ Ⓓ
13 Ⓐ Ⓑ Ⓒ Ⓓ
14 Ⓐ Ⓑ Ⓒ Ⓓ
15 Ⓐ Ⓑ Ⓒ Ⓓ
16 Ⓐ Ⓑ Ⓒ Ⓓ
17 Ⓐ Ⓑ Ⓒ Ⓓ
18 Ⓐ Ⓑ Ⓒ Ⓓ
19 Ⓐ Ⓑ Ⓒ Ⓓ
20 Ⓐ Ⓑ Ⓒ Ⓓ
21 Ⓐ Ⓑ Ⓒ Ⓓ
22 Ⓐ Ⓑ Ⓒ Ⓓ
23 Ⓐ Ⓑ Ⓒ Ⓓ
24 Ⓐ Ⓑ Ⓒ Ⓓ
25 Ⓐ Ⓑ Ⓒ Ⓓ
26 Ⓐ Ⓑ Ⓒ Ⓓ
27 Ⓐ Ⓑ Ⓒ Ⓓ
28 Ⓐ Ⓑ Ⓒ Ⓓ
29 Ⓐ Ⓑ Ⓒ Ⓓ
30 Ⓐ Ⓑ Ⓒ Ⓓ
31 Ⓐ Ⓑ Ⓒ Ⓓ
32 Ⓐ Ⓑ Ⓒ Ⓓ
33 Ⓐ Ⓑ Ⓒ Ⓓ
34 Ⓐ Ⓑ Ⓒ Ⓓ
35 Ⓐ Ⓑ Ⓒ Ⓓ
36 Ⓐ Ⓑ Ⓒ Ⓓ
37 Ⓐ Ⓑ Ⓒ Ⓓ
38 Ⓐ Ⓑ Ⓒ Ⓓ
39 Ⓐ Ⓑ Ⓒ Ⓓ
40 Ⓐ Ⓑ Ⓒ Ⓓ

## SECTION 3

1 Ⓐ Ⓑ Ⓒ Ⓓ      31 Ⓐ Ⓑ Ⓒ Ⓓ
2 Ⓐ Ⓑ Ⓒ Ⓓ      32 Ⓐ Ⓑ Ⓒ Ⓓ
3 Ⓐ Ⓑ Ⓒ Ⓓ      33 Ⓐ Ⓑ Ⓒ Ⓓ
4 Ⓐ Ⓑ Ⓒ Ⓓ      34 Ⓐ Ⓑ Ⓒ Ⓓ
5 Ⓐ Ⓑ Ⓒ Ⓓ      35 Ⓐ Ⓑ Ⓒ Ⓓ
6 Ⓐ Ⓑ Ⓒ Ⓓ      36 Ⓐ Ⓑ Ⓒ Ⓓ
7 Ⓐ Ⓑ Ⓒ Ⓓ      37 Ⓐ Ⓑ Ⓒ Ⓓ
8 Ⓐ Ⓑ Ⓒ Ⓓ      38 Ⓐ Ⓑ Ⓒ Ⓓ
9 Ⓐ Ⓑ Ⓒ Ⓓ      39 Ⓐ Ⓑ Ⓒ Ⓓ
10 Ⓐ Ⓑ Ⓒ Ⓓ     40 Ⓐ Ⓑ Ⓒ Ⓓ
11 Ⓐ Ⓑ Ⓒ Ⓓ     41 Ⓐ Ⓑ Ⓒ Ⓓ
12 Ⓐ Ⓑ Ⓒ Ⓓ     42 Ⓐ Ⓑ Ⓒ Ⓓ
13 Ⓐ Ⓑ Ⓒ Ⓓ     43 Ⓐ Ⓑ Ⓒ Ⓓ
14 Ⓐ Ⓑ Ⓒ Ⓓ     44 Ⓐ Ⓑ Ⓒ Ⓓ
15 Ⓐ Ⓑ Ⓒ Ⓓ     45 Ⓐ Ⓑ Ⓒ Ⓓ
16 Ⓐ Ⓑ Ⓒ Ⓓ     46 Ⓐ Ⓑ Ⓒ Ⓓ
17 Ⓐ Ⓑ Ⓒ Ⓓ     47 Ⓐ Ⓑ Ⓒ Ⓓ
18 Ⓐ Ⓑ Ⓒ Ⓓ     48 Ⓐ Ⓑ Ⓒ Ⓓ
19 Ⓐ Ⓑ Ⓒ Ⓓ     49 Ⓐ Ⓑ Ⓒ Ⓓ
20 Ⓐ Ⓑ Ⓒ Ⓓ     50 Ⓐ Ⓑ Ⓒ Ⓓ
21 Ⓐ Ⓑ Ⓒ Ⓓ
22 Ⓐ Ⓑ Ⓒ Ⓓ
23 Ⓐ Ⓑ Ⓒ Ⓓ
24 Ⓐ Ⓑ Ⓒ Ⓓ
25 Ⓐ Ⓑ Ⓒ Ⓓ
26 Ⓐ Ⓑ Ⓒ Ⓓ
27 Ⓐ Ⓑ Ⓒ Ⓓ
28 Ⓐ Ⓑ Ⓒ Ⓓ
29 Ⓐ Ⓑ Ⓒ Ⓓ
30 Ⓐ Ⓑ Ⓒ Ⓓ

SAMPLE

### IF YOU DO NOT WANT THIS ANSWER SHEET TO BE SCORED

If you want to cancel your scores from this administration, complete A and B below. The scores will not be sent to you or your designated recipients, and they will be removed from your permanent record.

**To cancel your scores from this test administration, you must:**

A. fill in both ovals here   and   B. sign your name below

○ — ○     _____

**ONCE A SCORE IS CANCELLED, IT CANNOT BE REPORTED AT ANY TIME.**

| 1R | 2R | 3R | TCS | FOR ETS USE ONLY | F |
|---|---|---|---|---|---|
| 1CS | 2CS | 3CS | | | |

**2. REGISTRATION NUMBER**

→ Start here

| 0 | 1 | 2 | 3 | 4 | 5 | 6 | 7 | 8 | 9 |
| 0 | 1 | 2 | 3 | 4 | 5 | 6 | 7 | 8 | 9 |
| 0 | 1 | 2 | 3 | 4 | 5 | 6 | 7 | 8 | 9 |
| 0 | 1 | 2 | 3 | 4 | 5 | 6 | 7 | 8 | 9 |
| 0 | 1 | 2 | 3 | 4 | 5 | 6 | 7 | 8 | 9 |
| 0 | 1 | 2 | 3 | 4 | 5 | 6 | 7 | 8 | 9 |
| 0 | 1 | 2 | 3 | 4 | 5 | 6 | 7 | 8 | 9 |

® **Test Of Written English (TWE) Answer Sheet**

| TEST CENTER | TEST BOOK SERIAL NUMBER | TEST DATE |
|---|---|---|

**Begin your essay here. If you need more space, use the other side.**

**TOPIC**

Reprinted by permission.

ADDITIONAL SPACE IS AVAILABLE ON THE REVERSE SIDE.

**DO NOT WRITE BELOW THIS LINE. FOR ETS USE ONLY.**

NO ⬭  OFF ⬭

1 | 1 2 3 4 5 6 |
2 | 1 2 3 4 5 6 |
ORS | 1 2 3 4 5 6 |

SAMPLE

9

**Continuation of essay**

SAMPLE

**NOTE**

This example of a TWE answer sheet is for practice use only. Do not send it to the TWE office. It cannot be scored. and it will not be returned to you.

I.N. 678580

# TEST OF ENGLISH AS A FOREIGN LANGUAGE

## TOEFL ANSWER SHEET  SIDE 1

Use a No. 2 (H.B.) pencil only. Do not use ink. Be sure each mark is dark and completely fills the intended oval. Erase errors or stray marks completely.

**1. NAME:** Copy your name from your admission ticket. Use one box for each letter. First print your family name (surname), then your given name, and then your middle name. Leave one box blank between names. Below each box, fill in the oval that contains the same letter.

**2. REGISTRATION NUMBER**
Start here

**3. INSTITUTION AND DEPARTMENT CODES:** Give the code numbers of the institutions and departments to which you want your official score report sent. Be sure to fill in the corresponding oval below each box.

INSTITUTION CODE   DEPT. CODE

**4. DO YOU PLAN TO STUDY FOR A DEGREE IN THE U.S.A. OR CANADA?**
◯ YES  ◯ NO

**5. REASON FOR TAKING TOEFL (FILL IN ONLY ONE OVAL).**
◯ 1. To enter a college or university as an undergraduate student.
◯ 2. To enter a college or university as a graduate student.
◯ 3. To enter a school other than a college or university.
◯ 4. To become licensed to practice my profession in the U.S.A. or Canada.
◯ 5. To demonstrate my proficiency in English to the company for which I work or expect to work.
◯ 6. Other than the above (please specify).

**6. NUMBER OF TIMES YOU HAVE TAKEN TOEFL BEFORE TODAY**
◯ NONE   ◯ THREE
◯ ONE    ◯ FOUR OR MORE
◯ TWO

**7. TEST CENTER (Print.)**

CENTER NUMBER

CITY

COUNTRY

**8. PLEASE PRINT YOUR NAME AND MAILING ADDRESS**

FAMILY NAME (SURNAME)   GIVEN NAME   MIDDLE NAME

STREET ADDRESS OR P. O. BOX NO.

CITY   STATE OR PROVINCE

POSTAL OR ZIP CODE   COUNTRY

**9. SIGNATURE AND DATE:** Copy the statement below; use handwriting.
"I hereby agree to the conditions set forth in the Bulletin of Information and affirm that I am the person whose name and address are given on this answer sheet."

SIGNED: _____ (WRITE YOUR NAME IN PENCIL AS IF SIGNING A LEGAL IDENTIFICATION DOCUMENT)

DATE: ___ / ___ / ___
MO. DAY YEAR

SAMPLE

DO NOT MARK IN THIS AREA.

TEST FORM:

57507 • 02362 • TF35M147e

MH-CW95065

Q2724-09/2   I.N. 203316
F

SIDE 2

Choose only one answer for each question. Carefully and completely fill in the oval corresponding to the answer you choose so that the letter inside the oval cannot be seen. Completely erase any other marks you may have made.

| | CORRECT | WRONG | WRONG | WRONG | WRONG |
|---|---|---|---|---|---|
| | Ⓐ | Ⓐ | Ⓐ | Ⓐ | Ⓐ |
| | Ⓑ | Ⓑ | Ⓑ | Ⓑ | Ⓑ |
| | ● | ⊘ | ⊗ | ⊙ | ⊙ |
| | Ⓓ | Ⓓ | Ⓓ | Ⓓ | Ⓓ |

TEST FORM

SEX
○ Male
○ Female

NAME (Print)

FAMILY NAME (SURNAME)     GIVEN NAME     MIDDLE NAME

TEST BOOK SERIAL NUMBER

REGISTRATION NUMBER

SIGNATURE

ROOM NUMBER     SEAT NUMBER

DATE OF BIRTH
MO. DAY YEAR

SECTION 1

SECTION 2

SECTION 3

SAMPLE

**IF YOU DO NOT WANT THIS ANSWER SHEET TO BE SCORED**
If you want to cancel your scores from this administration, complete A and B below. The scores will not be sent to you or your designated recipients, and they will be removed from your permanent record.
To cancel your scores from this test administration, you must:
A. fill in both ovals here     and     B. sign your name below

○—○

ONCE A SCORE IS CANCELLED, IT CANNOT BE REPORTED AT ANY TIME.

| FOR ETS USE ONLY | | | |
|---|---|---|---|
| 1R | 2R | 3R | TCS |
| 1CS | 2CS | 3CS | E |

Reprinted by permission.

**2. REGISTRATION NUMBER** — Start here →

0 1 2 3 4 5 6 7 8 9
0 1 2 3 4 5 6 7 8 9
0 1 2 3 4 5 6 7 8 9
0 1 2 3 4 5 6 7 8 9
0 1 2 3 4 5 6 7 8 9
0 1 2 3 4 5 6 7 8 9
0 1 2 3 4 5 6 7 8 9

**Test Of Written English (TWE) Answer Sheet**

| TEST CENTER | TEST BOOK SERIAL NUMBER | TEST DATE |
|---|---|---|

**Begin your essay here. If you need more space, use the other side.**

**TOPIC**

Reprinted by permission.

SAMPLE

ADDITIONAL SPACE IS AVAILABLE ON THE REVERSE SIDE.

DO NOT WRITE BELOW THIS LINE. FOR ETS USE ONLY.

NO ◯ OFF ◯

1 2 3 4 5 6     1 2 3 4 5 6     1 2 3 4 5 6

1

2

ORS

0 1 2 3 4 5 6 7 8 9     0 1 2 3 4 5 6 7 8 9     0 1 2 3 4 5 6 7 8 9
0 1 2 3 4 5 6 7 8 9     0 1 2 3 4 5 6 7 8 9     0 1 2 3 4 5 6 7 8 9
0 1 2 3 4 5 6 7 8 9     0 1 2 3 4 5 6 7 8 9     0 1 2 3 4 5 6 7 8 9

DO NOT WRITE IN THIS AREA.

9

**Continuation of essay**

**NOTE**

This example of a TWE answer sheet is for practice use only. Do not send it to the TWE office. It cannot be scored, and it will not be returned to you.

I.N. 678580

Reprinted by permission.

TEST OF ENGLISH AS A FOREIGN LANGUAGE

TOEFL ANSWER SHEET   SIDE 1

Use a No. 2 (H.B.) pencil only. Do not use ink. Be sure each mark is dark and completely fills the intended oval. Erase errors or stray marks completely.

**1. NAME:** Copy your name from your admission ticket. Use one box for each letter. First print your family name (surname), then your given name, and then your middle name. Leave one box blank between names. Below each box, fill in the oval that contains the same letter.

**2. REGISTRATION NUMBER**
Start here

**3. INSTITUTION AND DEPARTMENT CODES:** Give the code numbers of the institutions and departments to which you want your official score report sent. Be sure to fill in the corresponding oval below each box.

INSTITUTION CODE | DEPT. CODE | INSTITUTION CODE | DEPT. CODE | INSTITUTION CODE | DEPT. CODE

**4. DO YOU PLAN TO STUDY FOR A DEGREE IN THE U.S.A. OR CANADA?**
○ YES   ○ NO

**5. REASON FOR TAKING TOEFL (FILL IN ONLY ONE OVAL.)**
1. To enter a college or university as an undergraduate student.
2. To enter a college or university as a graduate student.
3. To enter a school other than a college or university.
4. To become licensed to practice my profession in the U.S.A. or Canada.
5. English to the company for which I work or expect to work.
6. Other than the above (please specify).

**6. NUMBER OF TIMES YOU HAVE TAKEN TOEFL BEFORE TODAY**
○ NONE   ○ THREE
○ ONE    ○ FOUR OR MORE
○ TWO

**7. TEST CENTER (Print.)**
CENTER NUMBER
CITY
COUNTRY

**8. PLEASE PRINT YOUR NAME AND MAILING ADDRESS**
FAMILY NAME (SURNAME)   GIVEN NAME   MIDDLE NAME
STREET ADDRESS OR P.O. BOX NO.
CITY   STATE OR PROVINCE
POSTAL OR ZIP CODE   COUNTRY

**9. SIGNATURE AND DATE:** Copy the statement below; use handwriting.
"I hereby agree to the conditions set forth in the Bulletin of Information and affirm that I am the person whose name and address are given on this answer sheet."

SIGNED: _____
(WRITE YOUR NAME IN PENCIL AS IF SIGNING A LEGAL IDENTIFICATION DOCUMENT)

DATE: _____ MO.   DAY   YEAR

SAMPLE

DO NOT MARK IN THIS AREA.

TEST FORM:

575507 • 02362 • TF35M147e

MHCW95065

Reprinted by permission.

195

# SIDE 2

**TEST FORM**

**TEST BOOK SERIAL NUMBER**

| ROOM NUMBER | SEAT NUMBER |
|---|---|

**SEX** ○ Male ○ Female

**DATE OF BIRTH**
MO. / DAY / YEAR

Choose only one answer for each question. Carefully and completely fill in the oval corresponding to the answer you choose so that the letter inside the oval cannot be seen. Completely erase any other marks you may have made.

| CORRECT | WRONG | WRONG | WRONG | WRONG |
|---|---|---|---|---|
| Ⓐ Ⓑ ● Ⓓ | Ⓐ Ⓑ Ⓒ̷ Ⓓ | Ⓐ Ⓑ ⓧ Ⓓ | Ⓐ Ⓑ Ⓒ Ⓓ | Ⓐ Ⓑ ◉ Ⓓ |

**NAME (Print)**

FAMILY NAME (SURNAME)     GIVEN NAME     MIDDLE NAME

**REGISTRATION NUMBER**     **SIGNATURE**

Reprinted by permission.

## SECTION 1

1 Ⓐ Ⓑ Ⓒ Ⓓ
2 Ⓐ Ⓑ Ⓒ Ⓓ
3 Ⓐ Ⓑ Ⓒ Ⓓ
4 Ⓐ Ⓑ Ⓒ Ⓓ
5 Ⓐ Ⓑ Ⓒ Ⓓ
6 Ⓐ Ⓑ Ⓒ Ⓓ
7 Ⓐ Ⓑ Ⓒ Ⓓ
8 Ⓐ Ⓑ Ⓒ Ⓓ
9 Ⓐ Ⓑ Ⓒ Ⓓ
10 Ⓐ Ⓑ Ⓒ Ⓓ
11 Ⓐ Ⓑ Ⓒ Ⓓ
12 Ⓐ Ⓑ Ⓒ Ⓓ
13 Ⓐ Ⓑ Ⓒ Ⓓ
14 Ⓐ Ⓑ Ⓒ Ⓓ
15 Ⓐ Ⓑ Ⓒ Ⓓ
16 Ⓐ Ⓑ Ⓒ Ⓓ
17 Ⓐ Ⓑ Ⓒ Ⓓ
18 Ⓐ Ⓑ Ⓒ Ⓓ
19 Ⓐ Ⓑ Ⓒ Ⓓ
20 Ⓐ Ⓑ Ⓒ Ⓓ
21 Ⓐ Ⓑ Ⓒ Ⓓ
22 Ⓐ Ⓑ Ⓒ Ⓓ
23 Ⓐ Ⓑ Ⓒ Ⓓ
24 Ⓐ Ⓑ Ⓒ Ⓓ
25 Ⓐ Ⓑ Ⓒ Ⓓ
26 Ⓐ Ⓑ Ⓒ Ⓓ
27 Ⓐ Ⓑ Ⓒ Ⓓ
28 Ⓐ Ⓑ Ⓒ Ⓓ
29 Ⓐ Ⓑ Ⓒ Ⓓ
30 Ⓐ Ⓑ Ⓒ Ⓓ
31 Ⓐ Ⓑ Ⓒ Ⓓ
32 Ⓐ Ⓑ Ⓒ Ⓓ
33 Ⓐ Ⓑ Ⓒ Ⓓ
34 Ⓐ Ⓑ Ⓒ Ⓓ
35 Ⓐ Ⓑ Ⓒ Ⓓ
36 Ⓐ Ⓑ Ⓒ Ⓓ
37 Ⓐ Ⓑ Ⓒ Ⓓ
38 Ⓐ Ⓑ Ⓒ Ⓓ
39 Ⓐ Ⓑ Ⓒ Ⓓ
40 Ⓐ Ⓑ Ⓒ Ⓓ
41 Ⓐ Ⓑ Ⓒ Ⓓ
42 Ⓐ Ⓑ Ⓒ Ⓓ
43 Ⓐ Ⓑ Ⓒ Ⓓ
44 Ⓐ Ⓑ Ⓒ Ⓓ
45 Ⓐ Ⓑ Ⓒ Ⓓ
46 Ⓐ Ⓑ Ⓒ Ⓓ
47 Ⓐ Ⓑ Ⓒ Ⓓ
48 Ⓐ Ⓑ Ⓒ Ⓓ
49 Ⓐ Ⓑ Ⓒ Ⓓ
50 Ⓐ Ⓑ Ⓒ Ⓓ

## SECTION 2

1 Ⓐ Ⓑ Ⓒ Ⓓ
2 Ⓐ Ⓑ Ⓒ Ⓓ
3 Ⓐ Ⓑ Ⓒ Ⓓ
4 Ⓐ Ⓑ Ⓒ Ⓓ
5 Ⓐ Ⓑ Ⓒ Ⓓ
6 Ⓐ Ⓑ Ⓒ Ⓓ
7 Ⓐ Ⓑ Ⓒ Ⓓ
8 Ⓐ Ⓑ Ⓒ Ⓓ
9 Ⓐ Ⓑ Ⓒ Ⓓ
10 Ⓐ Ⓑ Ⓒ Ⓓ
11 Ⓐ Ⓑ Ⓒ Ⓓ
12 Ⓐ Ⓑ Ⓒ Ⓓ
13 Ⓐ Ⓑ Ⓒ Ⓓ
14 Ⓐ Ⓑ Ⓒ Ⓓ
15 Ⓐ Ⓑ Ⓒ Ⓓ
16 Ⓐ Ⓑ Ⓒ Ⓓ
17 Ⓐ Ⓑ Ⓒ Ⓓ
18 Ⓐ Ⓑ Ⓒ Ⓓ
19 Ⓐ Ⓑ Ⓒ Ⓓ
20 Ⓐ Ⓑ Ⓒ Ⓓ
21 Ⓐ Ⓑ Ⓒ Ⓓ
22 Ⓐ Ⓑ Ⓒ Ⓓ
23 Ⓐ Ⓑ Ⓒ Ⓓ
24 Ⓐ Ⓑ Ⓒ Ⓓ
25 Ⓐ Ⓑ Ⓒ Ⓓ
26 Ⓐ Ⓑ Ⓒ Ⓓ
27 Ⓐ Ⓑ Ⓒ Ⓓ
28 Ⓐ Ⓑ Ⓒ Ⓓ
29 Ⓐ Ⓑ Ⓒ Ⓓ
30 Ⓐ Ⓑ Ⓒ Ⓓ
31 Ⓐ Ⓑ Ⓒ Ⓓ
32 Ⓐ Ⓑ Ⓒ Ⓓ
33 Ⓐ Ⓑ Ⓒ Ⓓ
34 Ⓐ Ⓑ Ⓒ Ⓓ
35 Ⓐ Ⓑ Ⓒ Ⓓ
36 Ⓐ Ⓑ Ⓒ Ⓓ
37 Ⓐ Ⓑ Ⓒ Ⓓ
38 Ⓐ Ⓑ Ⓒ Ⓓ
39 Ⓐ Ⓑ Ⓒ Ⓓ
40 Ⓐ Ⓑ Ⓒ Ⓓ

## SECTION 3

1 Ⓐ Ⓑ Ⓒ Ⓓ     31 Ⓐ Ⓑ Ⓒ Ⓓ
2 Ⓐ Ⓑ Ⓒ Ⓓ     32 Ⓐ Ⓑ Ⓒ Ⓓ
3 Ⓐ Ⓑ Ⓒ Ⓓ     33 Ⓐ Ⓑ Ⓒ Ⓓ
4 Ⓐ Ⓑ Ⓒ Ⓓ     34 Ⓐ Ⓑ Ⓒ Ⓓ
5 Ⓐ Ⓑ Ⓒ Ⓓ     35 Ⓐ Ⓑ Ⓒ Ⓓ
6 Ⓐ Ⓑ Ⓒ Ⓓ     36 Ⓐ Ⓑ Ⓒ Ⓓ
7 Ⓐ Ⓑ Ⓒ Ⓓ     37 Ⓐ Ⓑ Ⓒ Ⓓ
8 Ⓐ Ⓑ Ⓒ Ⓓ     38 Ⓐ Ⓑ Ⓒ Ⓓ
9 Ⓐ Ⓑ Ⓒ Ⓓ     39 Ⓐ Ⓑ Ⓒ Ⓓ
10 Ⓐ Ⓑ Ⓒ Ⓓ     40 Ⓐ Ⓑ Ⓒ Ⓓ
11 Ⓐ Ⓑ Ⓒ Ⓓ     41 Ⓐ Ⓑ Ⓒ Ⓓ
12 Ⓐ Ⓑ Ⓒ Ⓓ     42 Ⓐ Ⓑ Ⓒ Ⓓ
13 Ⓐ Ⓑ Ⓒ Ⓓ     43 Ⓐ Ⓑ Ⓒ Ⓓ
14 Ⓐ Ⓑ Ⓒ Ⓓ     44 Ⓐ Ⓑ Ⓒ Ⓓ
15 Ⓐ Ⓑ Ⓒ Ⓓ     45 Ⓐ Ⓑ Ⓒ Ⓓ
16 Ⓐ Ⓑ Ⓒ Ⓓ     46 Ⓐ Ⓑ Ⓒ Ⓓ
17 Ⓐ Ⓑ Ⓒ Ⓓ     47 Ⓐ Ⓑ Ⓒ Ⓓ
18 Ⓐ Ⓑ Ⓒ Ⓓ     48 Ⓐ Ⓑ Ⓒ Ⓓ
19 Ⓐ Ⓑ Ⓒ Ⓓ     49 Ⓐ Ⓑ Ⓒ Ⓓ
20 Ⓐ Ⓑ Ⓒ Ⓓ     50 Ⓐ Ⓑ Ⓒ Ⓓ
21 Ⓐ Ⓑ Ⓒ Ⓓ
22 Ⓐ Ⓑ Ⓒ Ⓓ
23 Ⓐ Ⓑ Ⓒ Ⓓ
24 Ⓐ Ⓑ Ⓒ Ⓓ
25 Ⓐ Ⓑ Ⓒ Ⓓ
26 Ⓐ Ⓑ Ⓒ Ⓓ
27 Ⓐ Ⓑ Ⓒ Ⓓ
28 Ⓐ Ⓑ Ⓒ Ⓓ
29 Ⓐ Ⓑ Ⓒ Ⓓ
30 Ⓐ Ⓑ Ⓒ Ⓓ

SAMPLE

### IF YOU DO NOT WANT THIS ANSWER SHEET TO BE SCORED

If you want to cancel your scores from this administration, complete A and B below. The scores will not be sent to you or your designated recipients, and they will be removed from your permanent record.

**To cancel your scores from this test administration, you must:**

A. fill in both ovals here     and   B. sign your name below

○ — ○

**ONCE A SCORE IS CANCELLED, IT CANNOT BE REPORTED AT ANY TIME.**

| 1R | 2R | 3R | TCS | FOR ETS USE ONLY | F |
|---|---|---|---|---|---|
| 1CS | 2CS | 3CS | | | |

**Test Of Written English (TWE) Answer Sheet**

2. REGISTRATION NUMBER
Start here

| TEST CENTER | TEST BOOK SERIAL NUMBER | TEST DATE |
|---|---|---|

Begin your essay here. If you need more space, use the other side.

**TOPIC**

Reprinted by permission.

ADDITIONAL SPACE IS AVAILABLE ON THE REVERSE SIDE.

DO NOT WRITE BELOW THIS LINE. FOR ETS USE ONLY.

NO ☐   OFF ☐

9

**Continuation of essay**

Reprinted by permission.